ARCHER & ARMSTRONG

THE
MICHELANGELO
CODE

FRED VAN LENTE | CLAYTON HENRY | MATT MILLA

CONTENTS

Writer: Fred Van Lente
Artist: Clayton Henry with Pere Pérez
Colorist: Matt Milla
Letterer: Dave Lanphear
Cover Artist: Jason Pearson
Variant Cover Artist: Juan Doe
Assistant Editor: Josh Johns
Executive Editor: Warren Simons

Archer & Armstrong #1 Variant Cover
Archer & Armstrong #1 Variant Cover
Archer & Armstrong #1 Pullbox Exclusive
Archer & Armstrong #1 Second Printing Cover
Archer & Armstrong #2 Variant Cover
Archer & Armstrong #3 Variant Cover
Archer & Armstrong #4 Variant Cover
Archer & Armstrong #1 Cover Pencils

Collection Cover Art: Mico Suayan

VALIANT.

Peter Cuneo
Chairman

Dinesh Shamdasani
CEO and Chief Creative Officer

Gavin Cuneo
CFO and Head of Strategic Development

Fred Pierce
Publisher

Warren Simons
VP Executive Editor

Walter Black
VP Operations

Hunter Gorinson
Marketing and Communications Manager

Atom! Freeman
Sales Manager

Travis Escarfullery
Production and Design Manager

Rian Hughes/Device
Trade Dress and Book Design

Jody LeHeup
Associate Editor

Josh Johns
Assistant Editor

Peter Stern
Operations Coordinator

Ivan Cohen
Collection Editor

Russell Brown
President, Consumer Products,
Promotions & Ad Sales

Archer & Armstrong®: The Michelangelo Code.
Published by Valiant Entertainment, LLC. Office of Publication:
424 West 33rd Street, New York, NY 10001. Compilation copyright
©2013 Valiant Entertainment, Inc. All rights reserved. Contains
materials originally published in single magazine form as *Archer
& Armstrong®* #1-4. Copyright ©2012 Valiant Entertainment, Inc.
All rights reserved. All characters, their distinctive likenesses
and related indicia featured in this publication are trademarks
of Valiant Entertainment, Inc. The stories, characters, and
incidents featured in this publication are entirely fictional. Valiant
Entertainment does not read or accept unsolicited submissions of
ideas, stories, or artwork. Printed in the U.S.A. First Printing.
ISBN: 9780979640988.

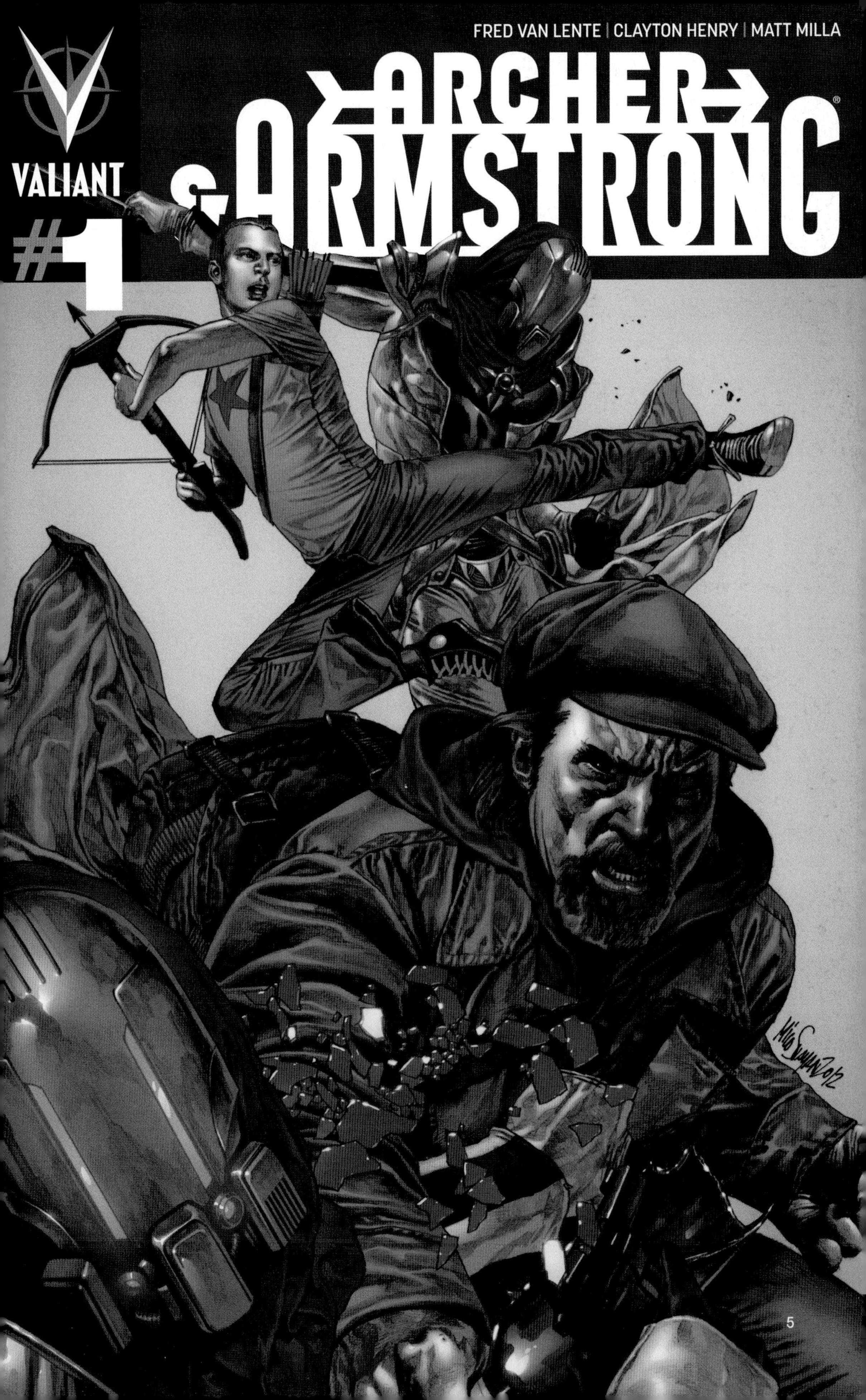
VALIANT
#1
FRED VAN LENTE | CLAYTON HENRY | MATT MILLA
ARCHER & ARMSTRONG®

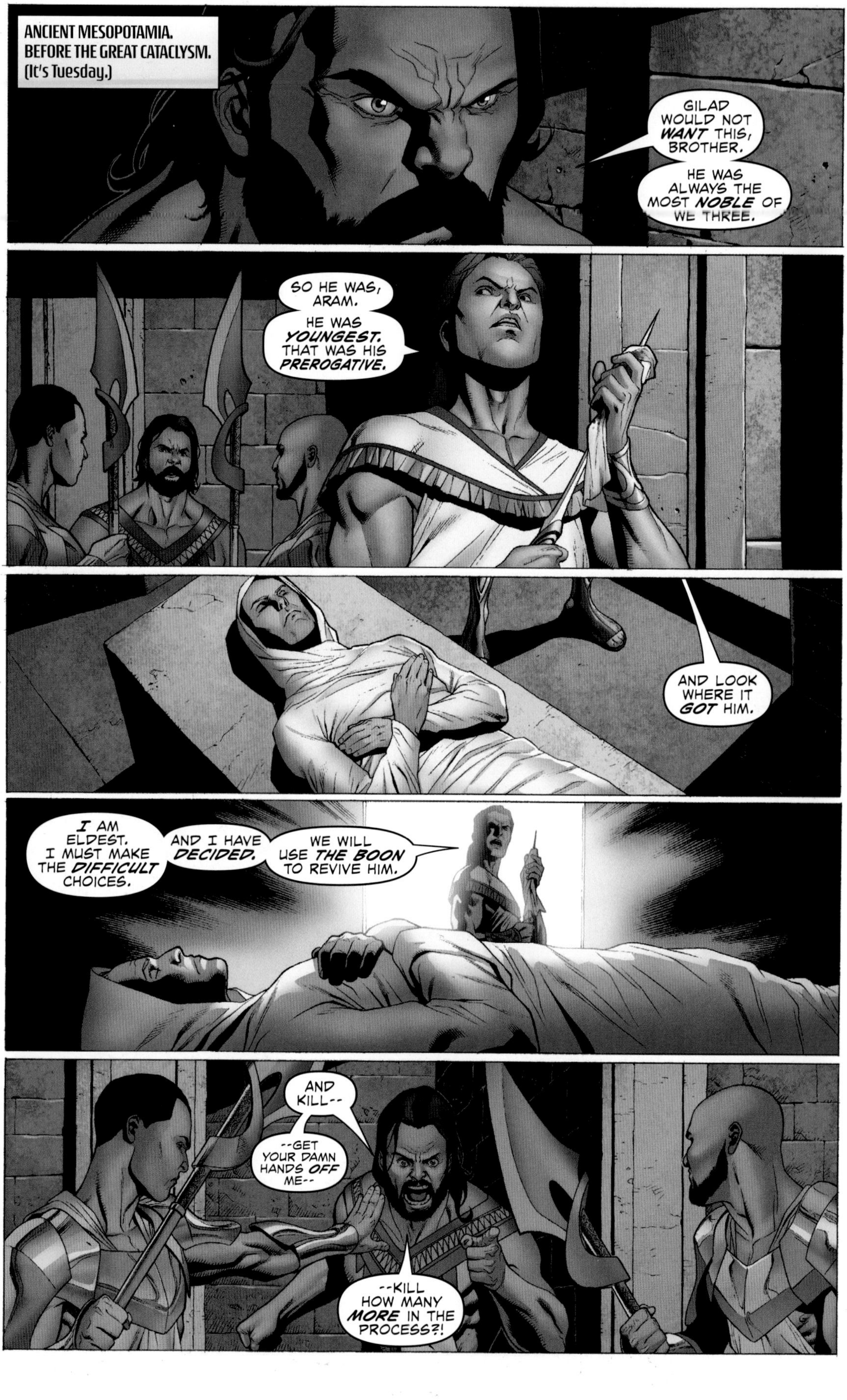
ANCIENT MESOPOTAMIA.
BEFORE THE GREAT CATACLYSM.
(It's Tuesday.)
GILAD WOULD NOT WANT THIS, BROTHER.
HE WAS ALWAYS THE MOST NOBLE OF WE THREE.
SO HE WAS, ARAM.
HE WAS YOUNGEST. THAT WAS HIS PREROGATIVE.
AND LOOK WHERE IT GOT HIM.
I AM ELDEST. I MUST MAKE THE DIFFICULT CHOICES.
AND I HAVE DECIDED.
WE WILL USE THE BOON TO REVIVE HIM.
AND KILL--
--GET YOUR DAMN HANDS OFF ME--
--KILL HOW MANY MORE IN THE PROCESS?!

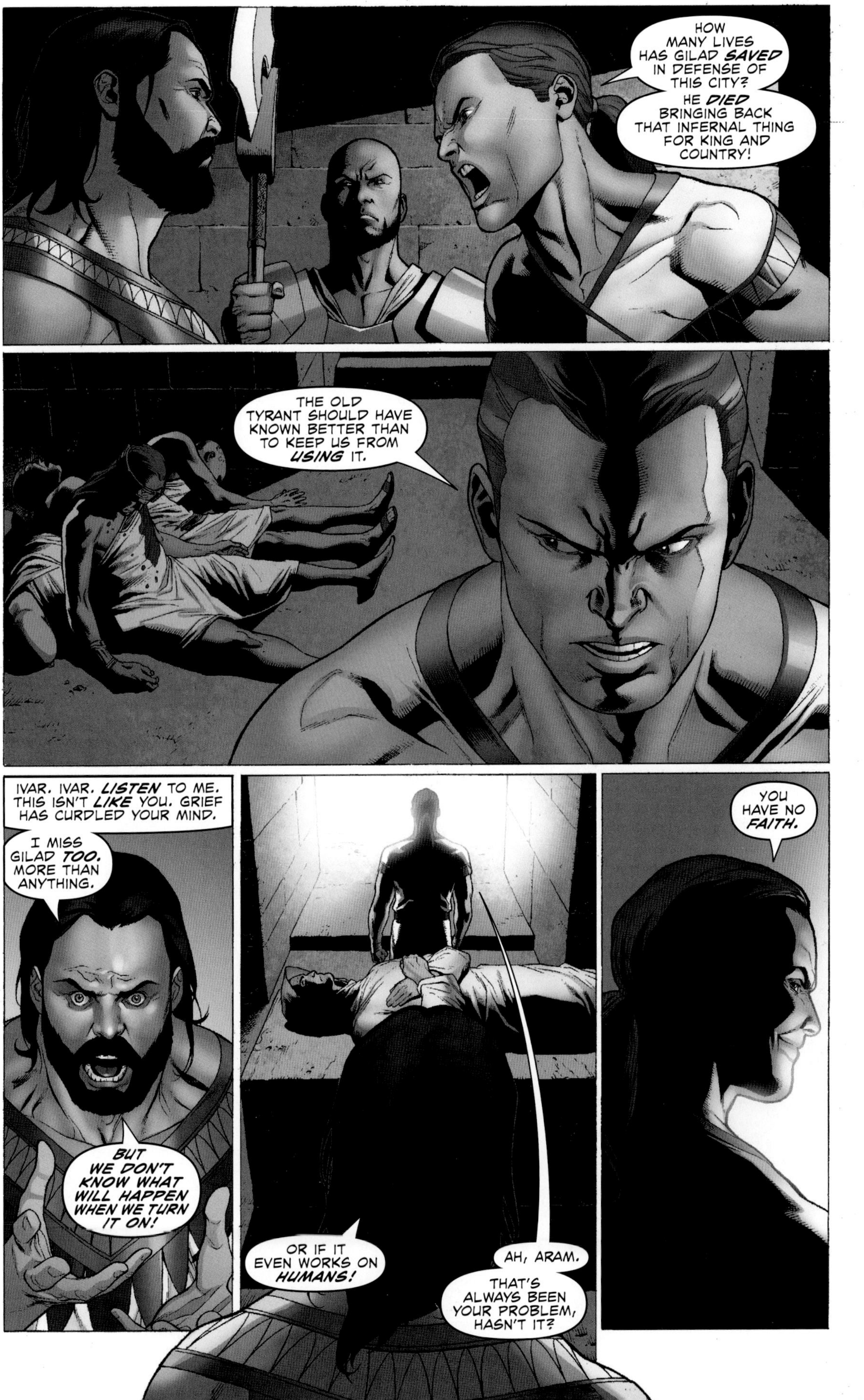
HOW MANY LIVES HAS GILAD SAVED IN DEFENSE OF THIS CITY?
HE DIED BRINGING BACK THAT INFERNAL THING FOR KING AND COUNTRY!
THE OLD TYRANT SHOULD HAVE KNOWN BETTER THAN TO KEEP US FROM USING IT.
IVAR. IVAR. LISTEN TO ME. THIS ISN'T LIKE YOU. GRIEF HAS CURDLED YOUR MIND.
I MISS GILAD TOO. MORE THAN ANYTHING.
BUT WE DON'T KNOW WHAT WILL HAPPEN WHEN WE TURN IT ON!
OR IF IT EVEN WORKS ON HUMANS!
AH, ARAM.
THAT'S ALWAYS BEEN YOUR PROBLEM, HASN'T IT?
YOU HAVE NO FAITH.

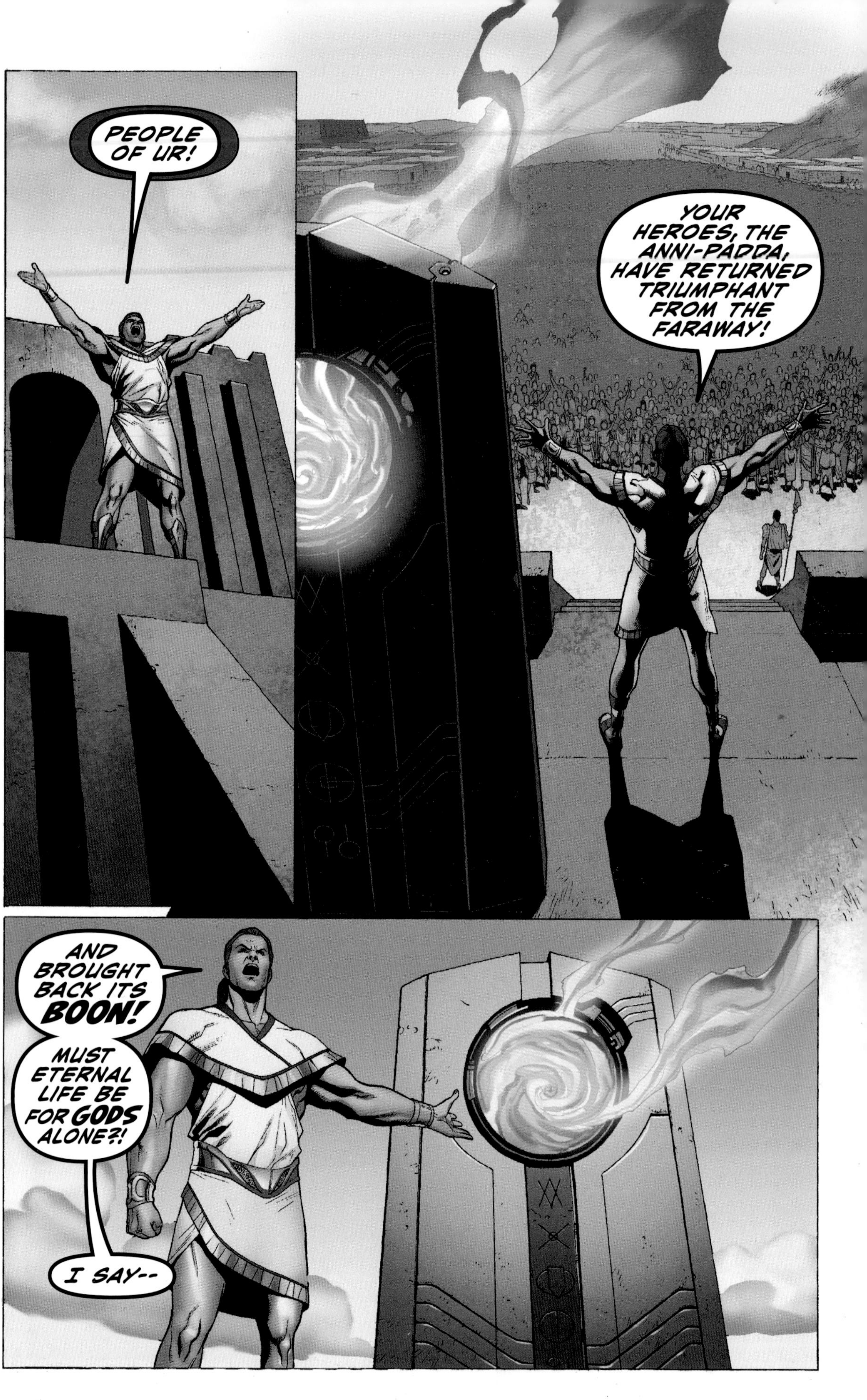
PEOPLE OF UR!
YOUR HEROES, THE ANNI-PADDA, HAVE RETURNED TRIUMPHANT FROM THE FARAWAY!
AND BROUGHT BACK ITS **BOON!**
MUST ETERNAL LIFE BE FOR **GODS** ALONE?!
I SAY--

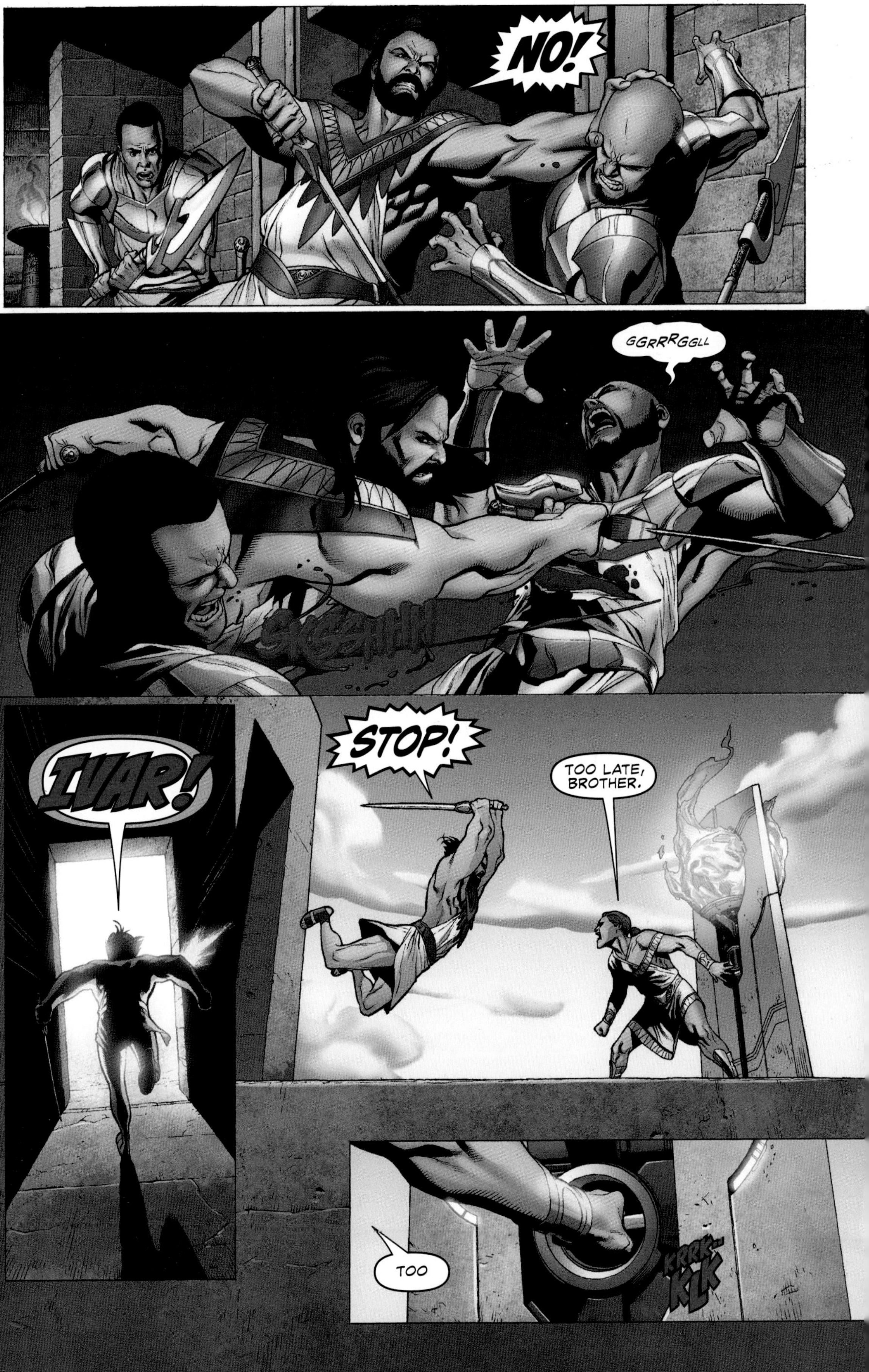
NO!
GGRRRGGLL
SKSSHHH!
IVAR!
STOP!
TOO LATE, BROTHER.
TOO
KRRK... KLK

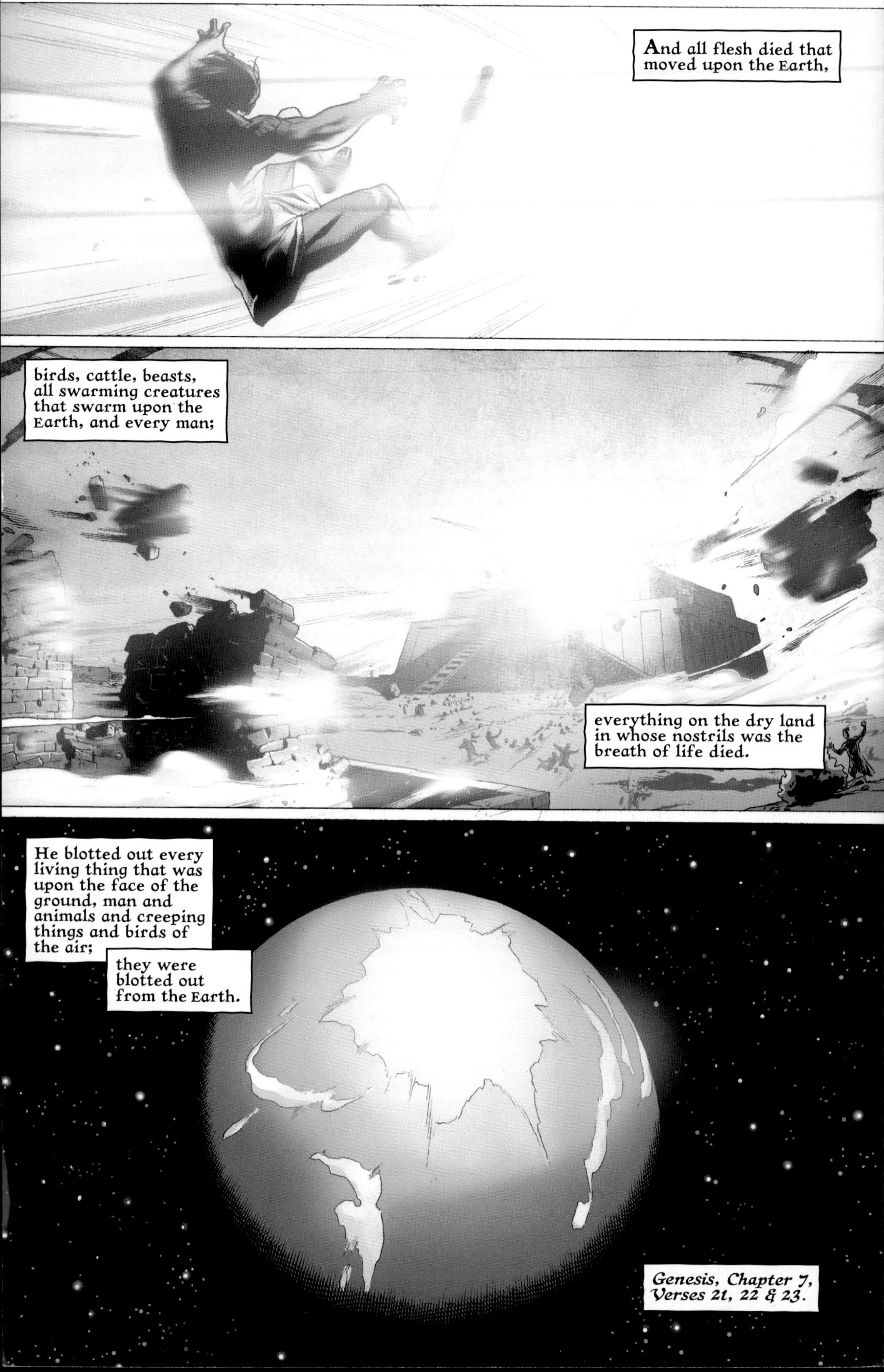
And all flesh died that moved upon the Earth,
birds, cattle, beasts, all swarming creatures that swarm upon the Earth, and every man;
everything on the dry land in whose nostrils was the breath of life died.
He blotted out every living thing that was upon the face of the ground, man and animals and creeping things and birds of the air;
they were blotted out from the Earth.
Genesis, Chapter 7, Verses 21, 22 & 23.

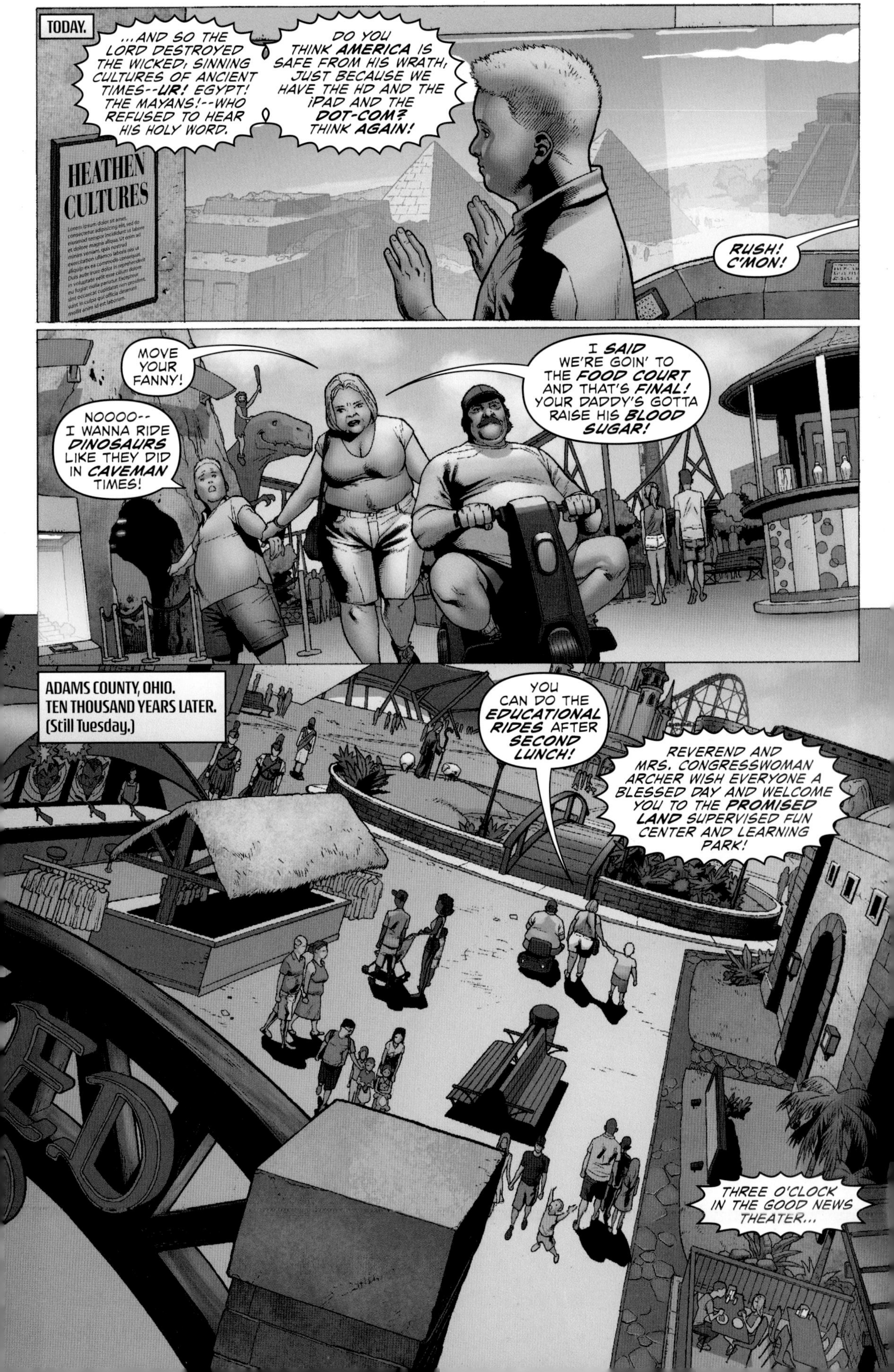

TODAY.
...AND SO THE LORD DESTROYED THE WICKED, SINNING CULTURES OF ANCIENT TIMES--UR! EGYPT! THE MAYANS!--WHO REFUSED TO HEAR HIS HOLY WORD.
DO YOU THINK AMERICA IS SAFE FROM HIS WRATH, JUST BECAUSE WE HAVE THE HD AND THE iPAD AND THE DOT-COM? THINK AGAIN!
HEATHEN CULTURES
RUSH! C'MON!
MOVE YOUR FANNY!
I SAID WE'RE GOIN' TO THE FOOD COURT AND THAT'S FINAL! YOUR DADDY'S GOTTA RAISE HIS BLOOD SUGAR!
NOOOO-- I WANNA RIDE DINOSAURS LIKE THEY DID IN CAVEMAN TIMES!
ADAMS COUNTY, OHIO. TEN THOUSAND YEARS LATER. (Still Tuesday.)
YOU CAN DO THE EDUCATIONAL RIDES AFTER SECOND LUNCH!
REVEREND AND MRS. CONGRESSWOMAN ARCHER WISH EVERYONE A BLESSED DAY AND WELCOME YOU TO THE PROMISED LAND SUPERVISED FUN CENTER AND LEARNING PARK!
THREE O'CLOCK IN THE GOOD NEWS THEATER...

...DARWIN THE CHIMP STARS IN *JUNK SCIENCE FOLLIES...*

YOU READY, SON?

I AM, FATHER.

GOOD.

THIS IS YOUR FINAL TEST.

RRRAAAAHHH

CHANK

RRRAAAAHHH

CHANK

RRRAAAAHHH

YOU'RE GOING DOWN, OBADIAH! THE HOLY MISSION'S GONNA BE MINE!

I WISH IT *COULD,* JEAN-PAUL.

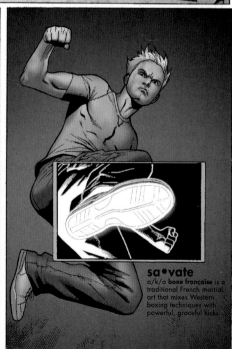

sa•vate
a/k/a **boxe française** is a traditional French martial art that mixes Western boxing techniques with powerful, graceful kicks

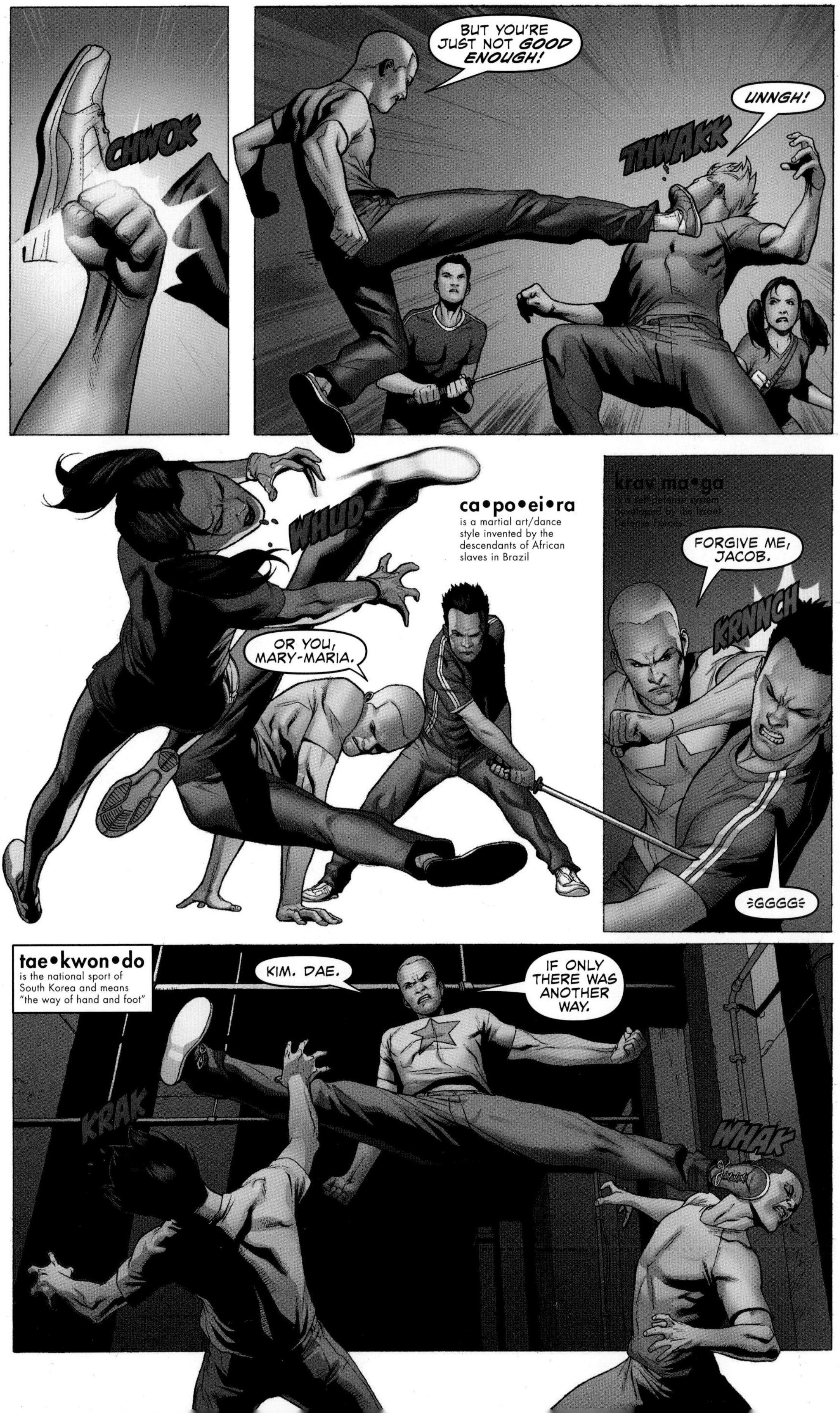
CHWOK
BUT YOU'RE JUST NOT GOOD ENOUGH!
THWAKK
UNNGH!
WHUD
ca•po•ei•ra
is a martial art/dance style invented by the descendants of African slaves in Brazil
OR YOU, MARY-MARIA.
krav ma•ga
is a self-defense system developed by the Israel Defense Forces.
FORGIVE ME, JACOB.
KRNNCH
GGGG
tae•kwon•do
is the national sport of South Korea and means "the way of hand and foot"
KIM. DAE.
IF ONLY THERE WAS ANOTHER WAY.
KRAK
WHAK

I...I AM OVERCOME.
OUR DARLING BOY.
YOU WERE BORN SPECIAL. WE ALWAYS KNEW THAT.
EVER SINCE YOU WERE LITTLE, IF YOU SAW SOMETHING, YOU COULD DO IT.
WE BELIEVED IN OUR HEART OF HEARTS YOU WERE CHOSEN TO COMPLETE THE SACRED PLAN OF OUR ORDER, THE DOMINION...
...AND NOW YOU HAVE PROVEN IT.
TELL ME WHAT THE MISSION IS, FATHER. I WANT THAT MORE THAN ANYTHING.
"THE MAN OF SIN IS REVEALED, THE SON OF PERDITION--
"--WHO OPPOSES AND EXALTS HIMSELF ABOVE ALL THAT IS CALLED GOD OR THAT IS WORSHIPED."
SO IT IS WRITTEN.
THE DOMINION TEACHES THAT EARTH CANNOT BECOME PARADISE--
--UNTIL HE WHO IS NOT TO BE NAMED IS DESTROYED.
YOU WILL SMITE HIM WITH THE SWORD OF THE RIGHTEOUS, OBADIAH.
WHERE IS HE, FATHER? TELL ME!
OUR AGENTS HAVE FOUND HIM ON THAT FESTERING ISLE OF CORRUPTION AND CRIMINALITY.
NEW YORK?
I AM AFRAID SO, MY BOY.
AND YOU WILL TRACK HIM WITH THIS.

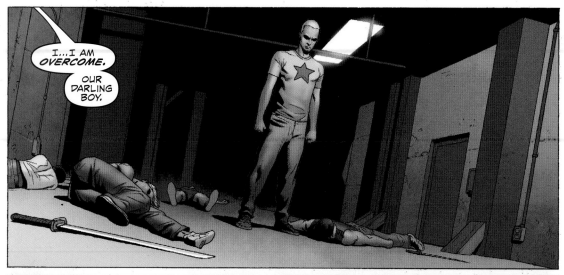

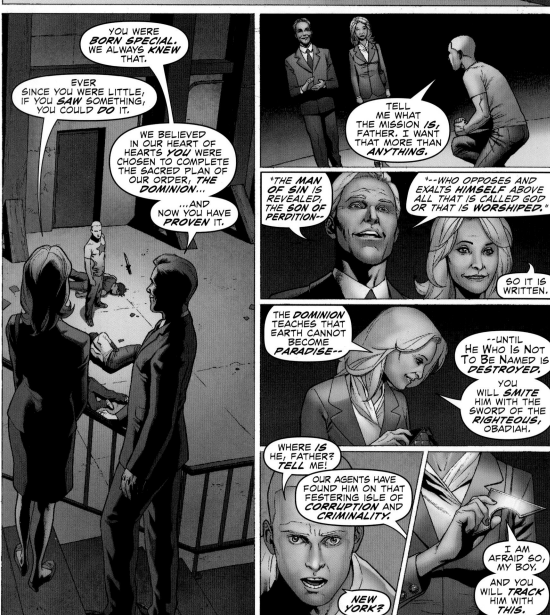

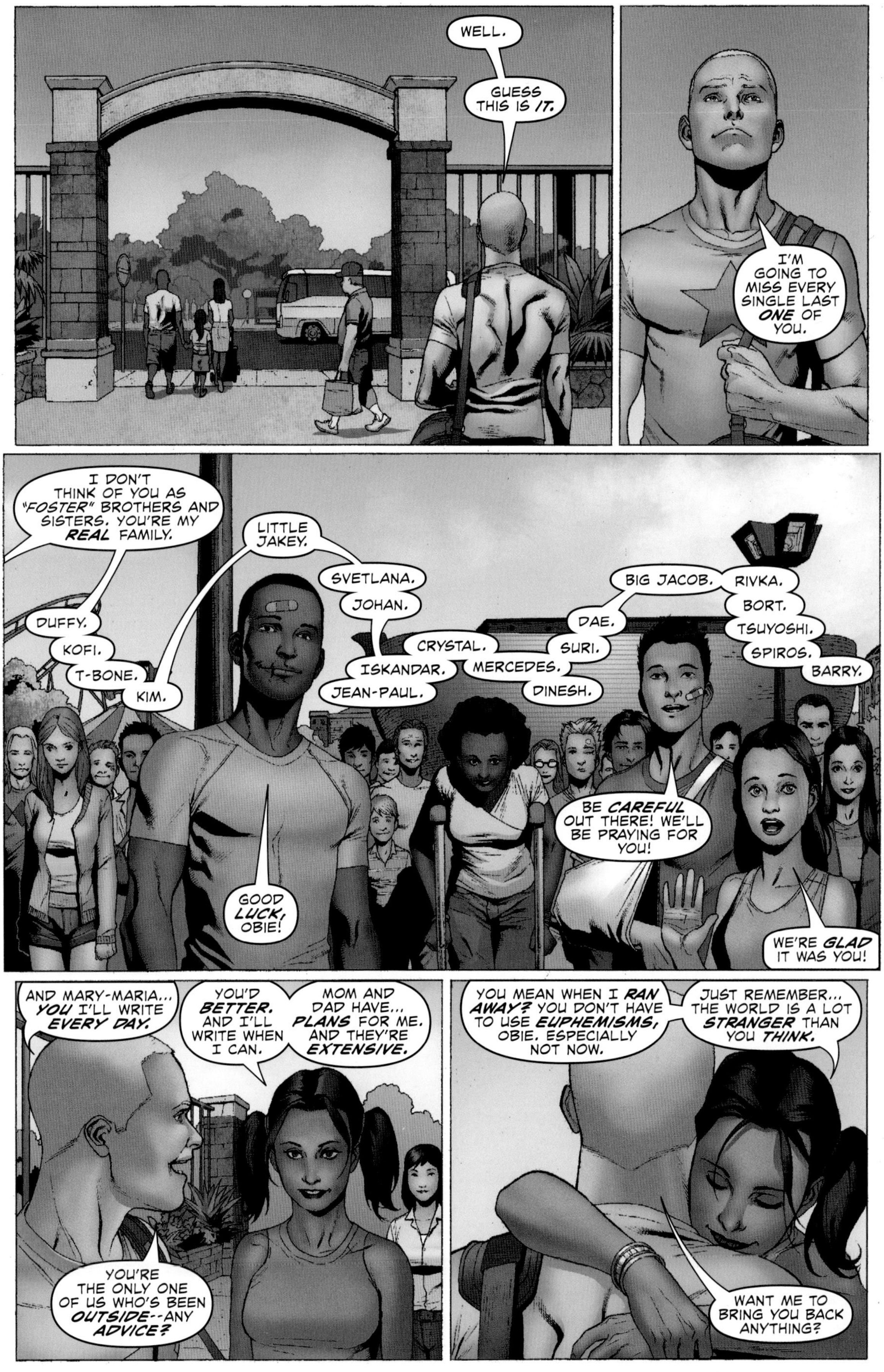
WELL.
GUESS THIS IS *IT.*
I'M GOING TO MISS EVERY SINGLE LAST *ONE* OF YOU.
I DON'T THINK OF YOU AS *"FOSTER"* BROTHERS AND SISTERS. YOU'RE MY *REAL* FAMILY.
DUFFY.
KOFI.
T-BONE.
KIM.
LITTLE JAKEY.
SVETLANA.
JOHAN.
CRYSTAL.
ISKANDAR.
JEAN-PAUL.
MERCEDES.
DINESH.
SURI.
DAE.
BIG JACOB.
RIVKA.
BORT.
TSUYOSHI.
SPIROS.
BARRY.
GOOD *LUCK,* OBIE!
BE *CAREFUL* OUT THERE! WE'LL BE PRAYING FOR YOU!
WE'RE *GLAD* IT WAS YOU!
AND MARY-MARIA... *YOU* I'LL WRITE *EVERY DAY.*
YOU'D *BETTER.* AND I'LL WRITE WHEN I CAN.
MOM AND DAD HAVE... *PLANS* FOR ME. AND THEY'RE *EXTENSIVE.*
YOU'RE THE ONLY ONE OF US WHO'S BEEN *OUTSIDE*--ANY *ADVICE?*
YOU MEAN WHEN I *RAN AWAY?* YOU DON'T HAVE TO USE *EUPHEMISMS,* OBIE. ESPECIALLY NOT NOW.
JUST REMEMBER... THE WORLD IS A LOT *STRANGER* THAN YOU *THINK.*
WANT ME TO BRING YOU BACK ANYTHING?

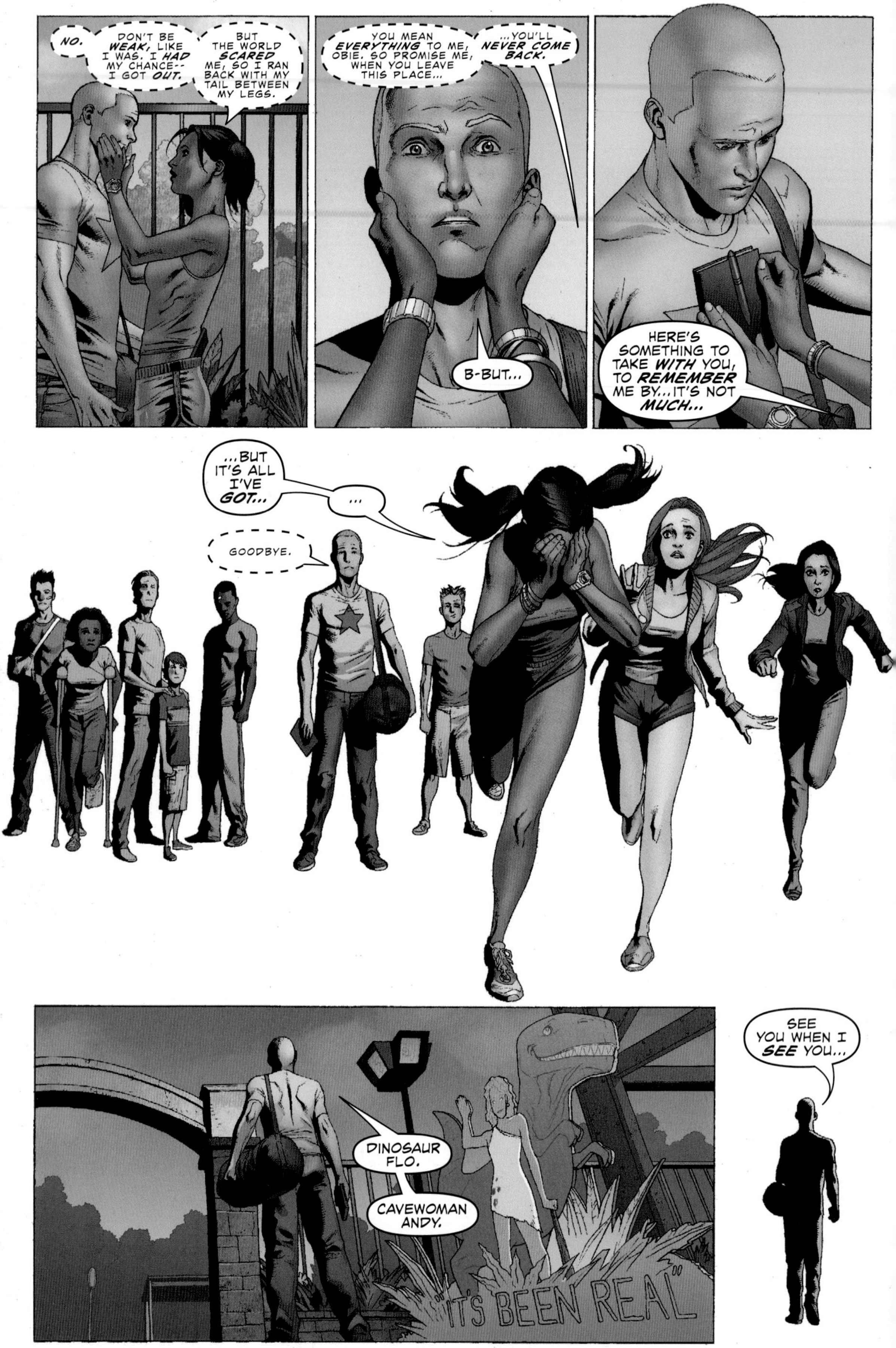
NO.
DON'T BE WEAK, LIKE I WAS. I HAD MY CHANCE-- I GOT OUT.
BUT THE WORLD SCARED ME, SO I RAN BACK WITH MY TAIL BETWEEN MY LEGS.
YOU MEAN EVERYTHING TO ME, OBIE. SO PROMISE ME, WHEN YOU LEAVE THIS PLACE...
...YOU'LL NEVER COME BACK.
B-BUT...
HERE'S SOMETHING TO TAKE WITH YOU, TO REMEMBER ME BY...IT'S NOT MUCH...
...BUT IT'S ALL I'VE GOT...
...
GOODBYE.
DINOSAUR FLO.
CAVEWOMAN ANDY.
"IT'S BEEN REAL"
SEE YOU WHEN I SEE YOU...

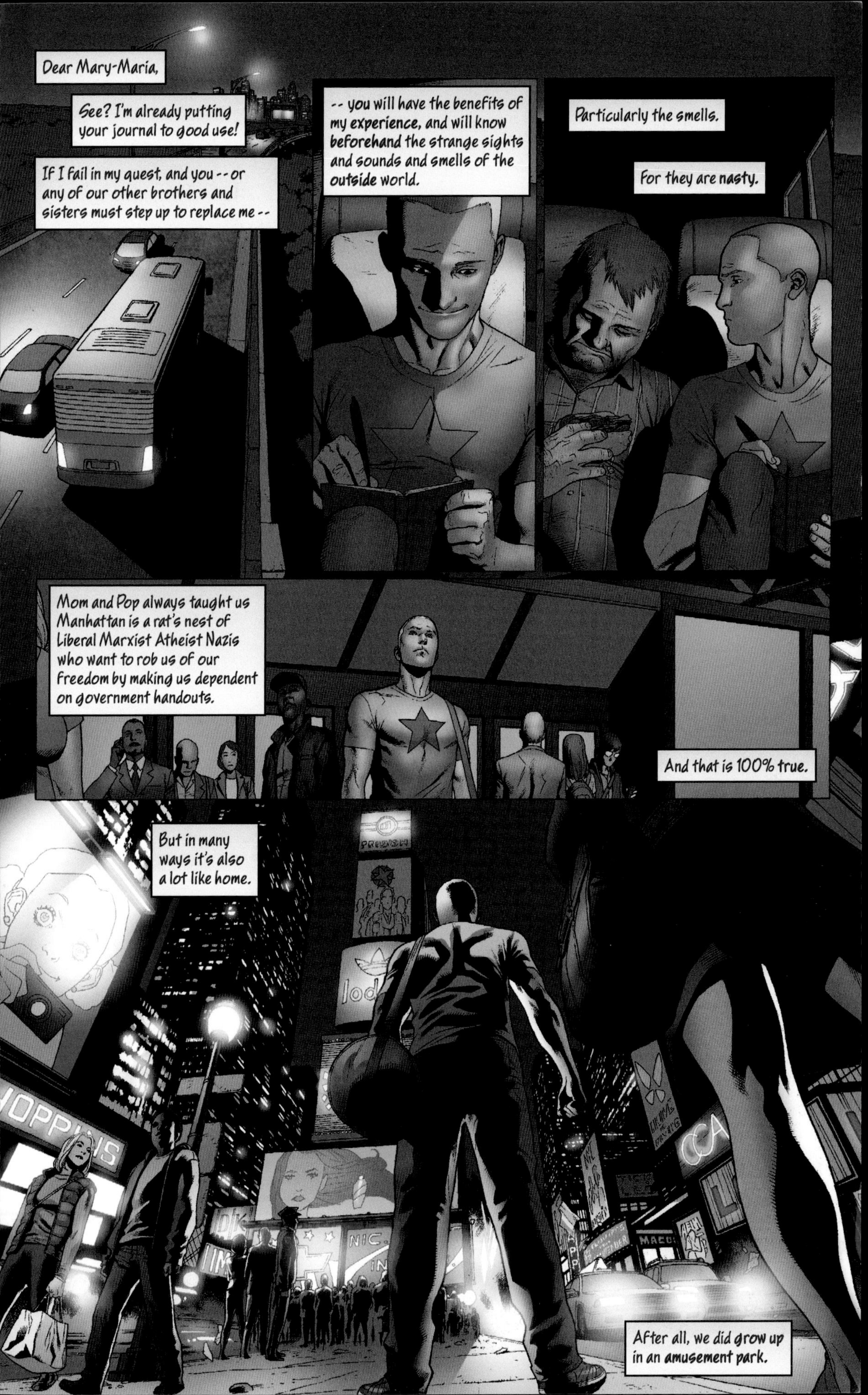
Dear Mary-Maria,
See? I'm already putting your journal to good use!
If I fail in my quest, and you -- or any of our other brothers and sisters must step up to replace me --
-- you will have the benefits of my experience, and will know beforehand the strange sights and sounds and smells of the outside world.
Particularly the smells.
For they are nasty.
Mom and Pop always taught us Manhattan is a rat's nest of Liberal Marxist Atheist Nazis who want to rob us of our freedom by making us dependent on government handouts.
And that is 100% true.
But in many ways it's also a lot like home.
After all, we did grow up in an amusement park.

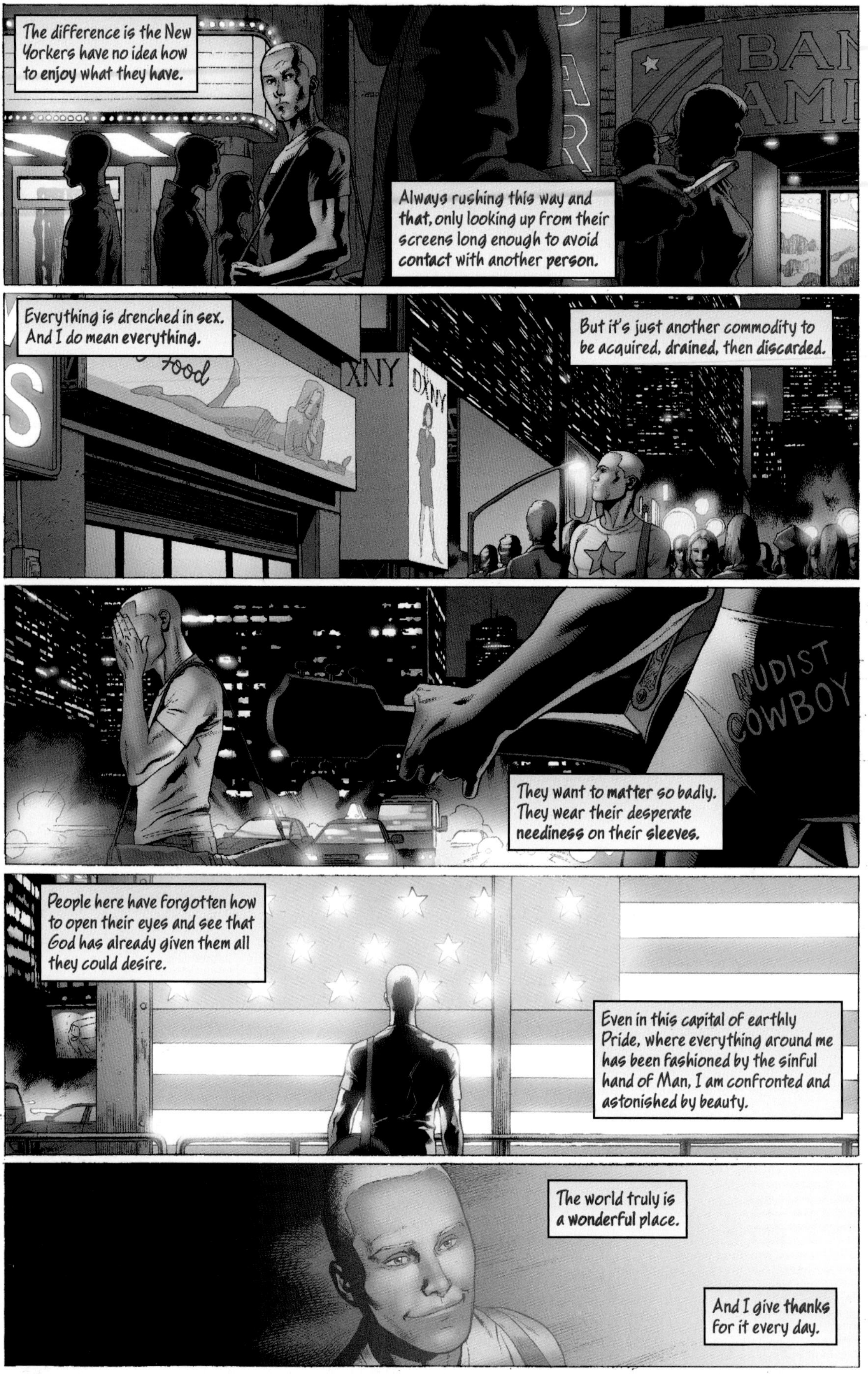
The difference is the New Yorkers have no idea how to enjoy what they have.
Always rushing this way and that, only looking up from their screens long enough to avoid contact with another person.
BAR
Everything is drenched in sex. And I do mean everything.
But it's just another commodity to be acquired, drained, then discarded.
XNY
DXNY
NUDIST COWBOY
They want to matter so badly. They wear their desperate neediness on their sleeves.
People here have forgotten how to open their eyes and see that God has already given them all they could desire.
Even in this capital of earthly Pride, where everything around me has been fashioned by the sinful hand of Man, I am confronted and astonished by beauty.
The world truly is a wonderful place.
And I give thanks for it every day.

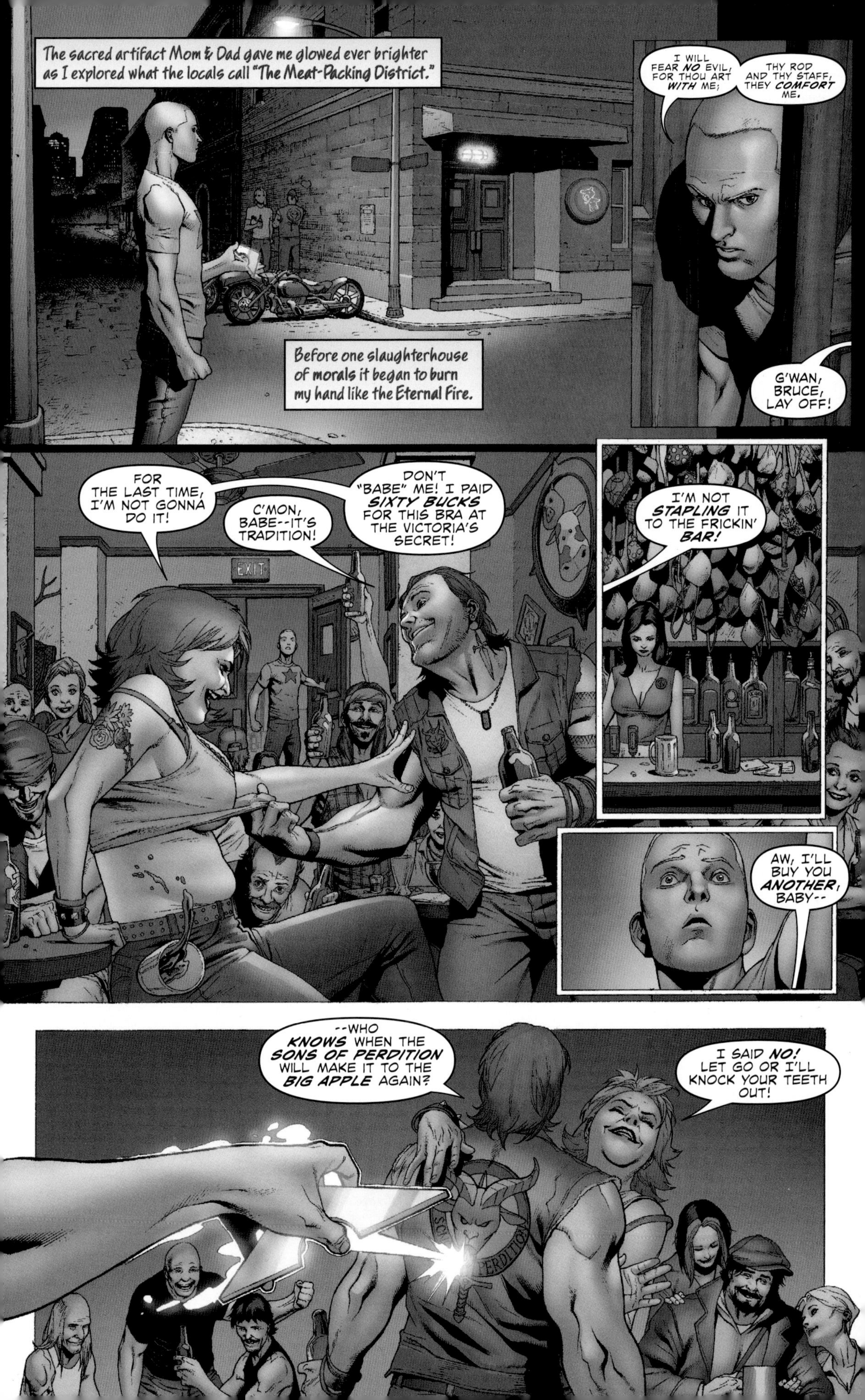
The sacred artifact Mom & Dad gave me glowed ever brighter as I explored what the locals call "The Meat-Packing District."
Before one slaughterhouse of morals it began to burn my hand like the Eternal Fire.
I WILL FEAR NO EVIL, FOR THOU ART WITH ME;
THY ROD AND THY STAFF, THEY COMFORT ME.
G'WAN, BRUCE, LAY OFF!
FOR THE LAST TIME, I'M NOT GONNA DO IT!
C'MON, BABE--IT'S TRADITION!
DON'T "BABE" ME! I PAID SIXTY BUCKS FOR THIS BRA AT THE VICTORIA'S SECRET!
EXIT
I'M NOT STAPLING IT TO THE FRICKIN' BAR!
AW, I'LL BUY YOU ANOTHER, BABY--
--WHO KNOWS WHEN THE SONS OF PERDITION WILL MAKE IT TO THE BIG APPLE AGAIN?
I SAID NO! LET GO OR I'LL KNOCK YOUR TEETH OUT!

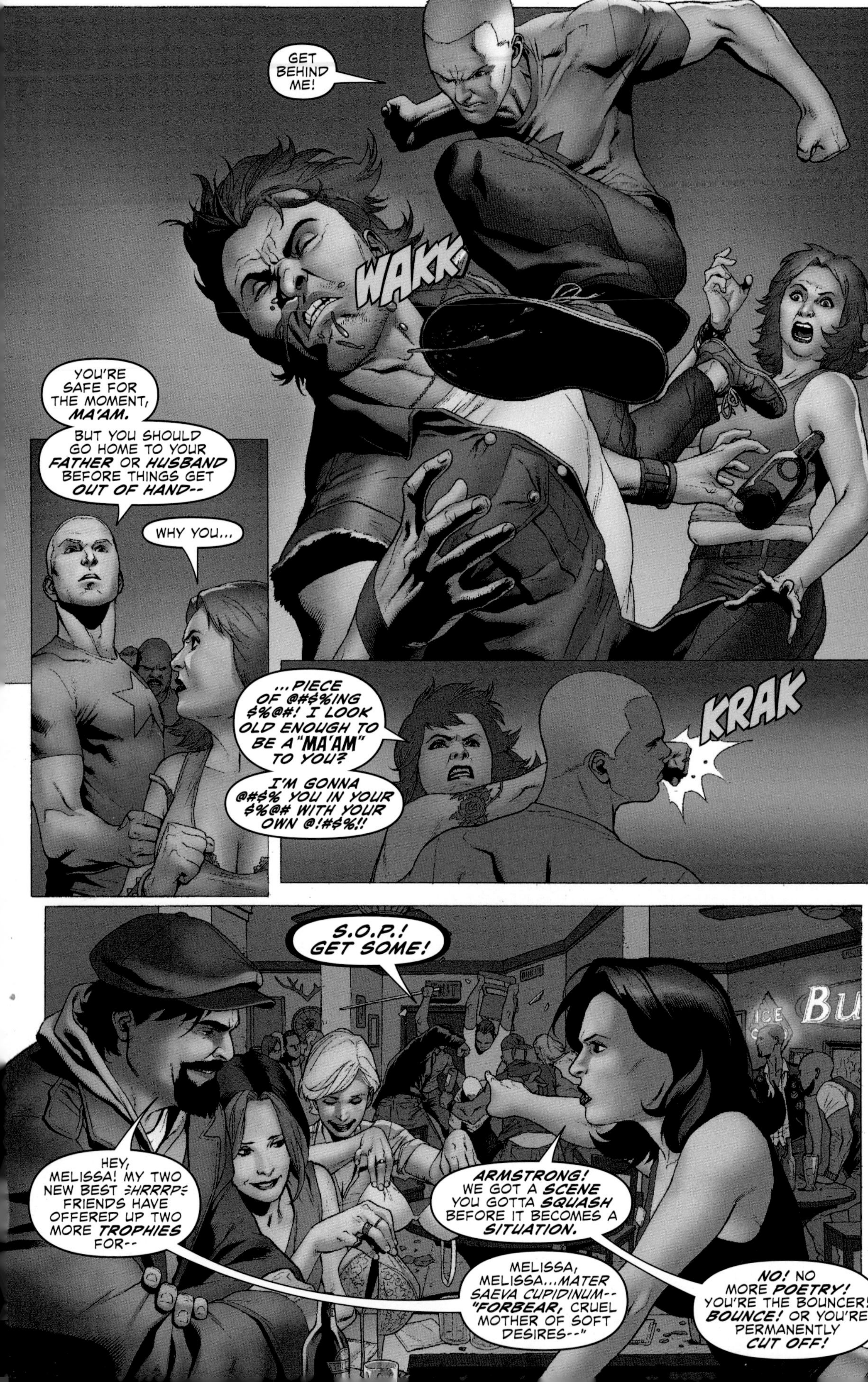

GET BEHIND ME!
WAKK
YOU'RE SAFE FOR THE MOMENT, MA'AM.
BUT YOU SHOULD GO HOME TO YOUR FATHER OR HUSBAND BEFORE THINGS GET OUT OF HAND--
WHY YOU...
...PIECE OF @#$%ING $%@#! I LOOK OLD ENOUGH TO BE A "MA'AM" TO YOU?
I'M GONNA @#$% YOU IN YOUR $%@# WITH YOUR OWN @!#$%!!
KRAK
S.O.P.! GET SOME!
ICE
BU
HEY, MELISSA! MY TWO NEW BEST HRRRP FRIENDS HAVE OFFERED UP TWO MORE TROPHIES FOR--
ARMSTRONG! WE GOT A SCENE YOU GOTTA SQUASH BEFORE IT BECOMES A SITUATION.
MELISSA, MELISSA...MATER SAEVA CUPIDINUM--"FORBEAR, CRUEL MOTHER OF SOFT DESIRES--"
NO! NO MORE POETRY! YOU'RE THE BOUNCER! BOUNCE! OR YOU'RE PERMANENTLY CUT OFF!

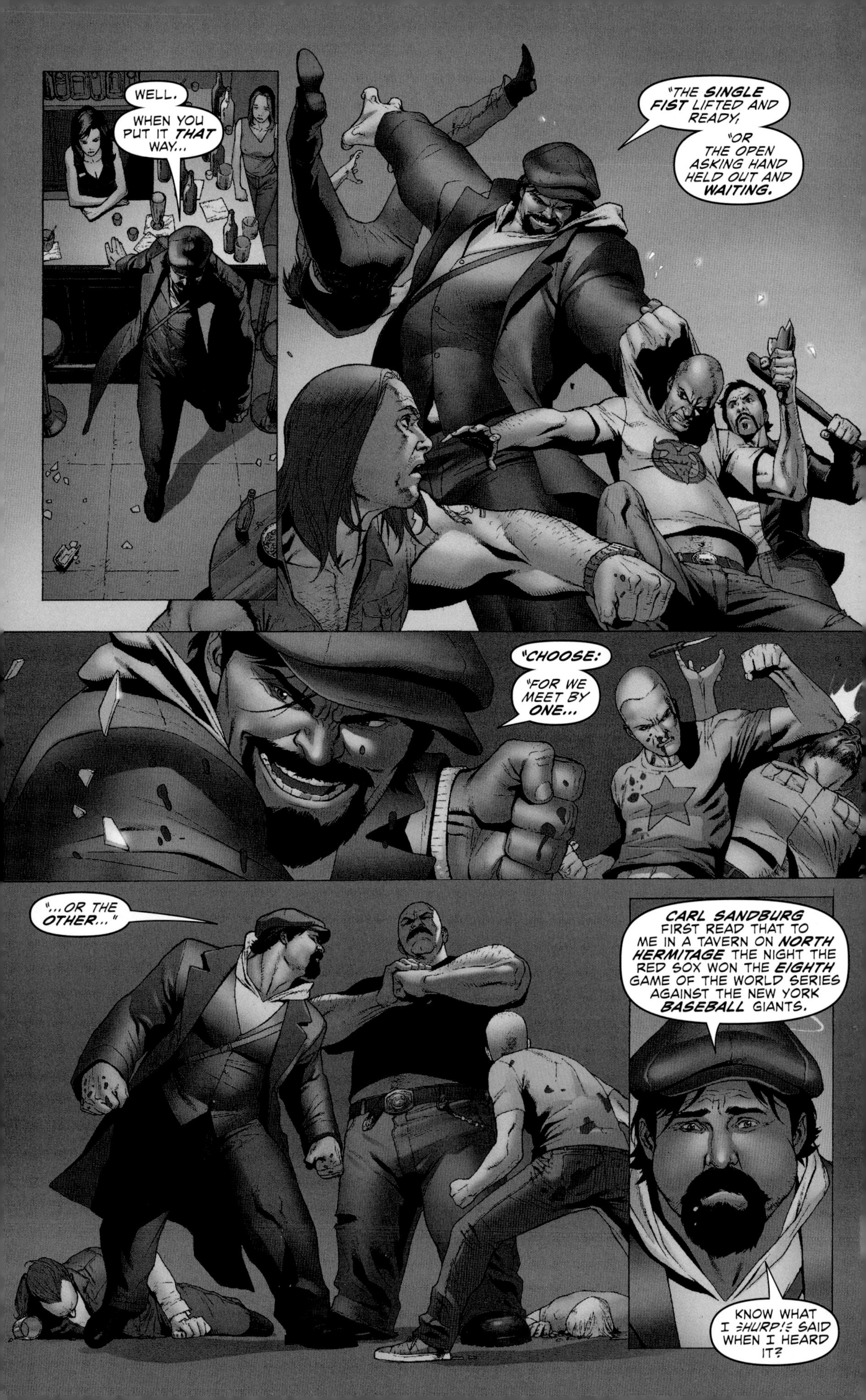
WELL.
WHEN YOU PUT IT THAT WAY...
"THE SINGLE FIST LIFTED AND READY,
"OR THE OPEN ASKING HAND HELD OUT AND WAITING.
"CHOOSE:
"FOR WE MEET BY ONE...
"...OR THE OTHER..."
CARL SANDBURG FIRST READ THAT TO ME IN A TAVERN ON NORTH HERMITAGE THE NIGHT THE RED SOX WON THE EIGHTH GAME OF THE WORLD SERIES AGAINST THE NEW YORK BASEBALL GIANTS.
KNOW WHAT I =HURP!= SAID WHEN I HEARD IT?

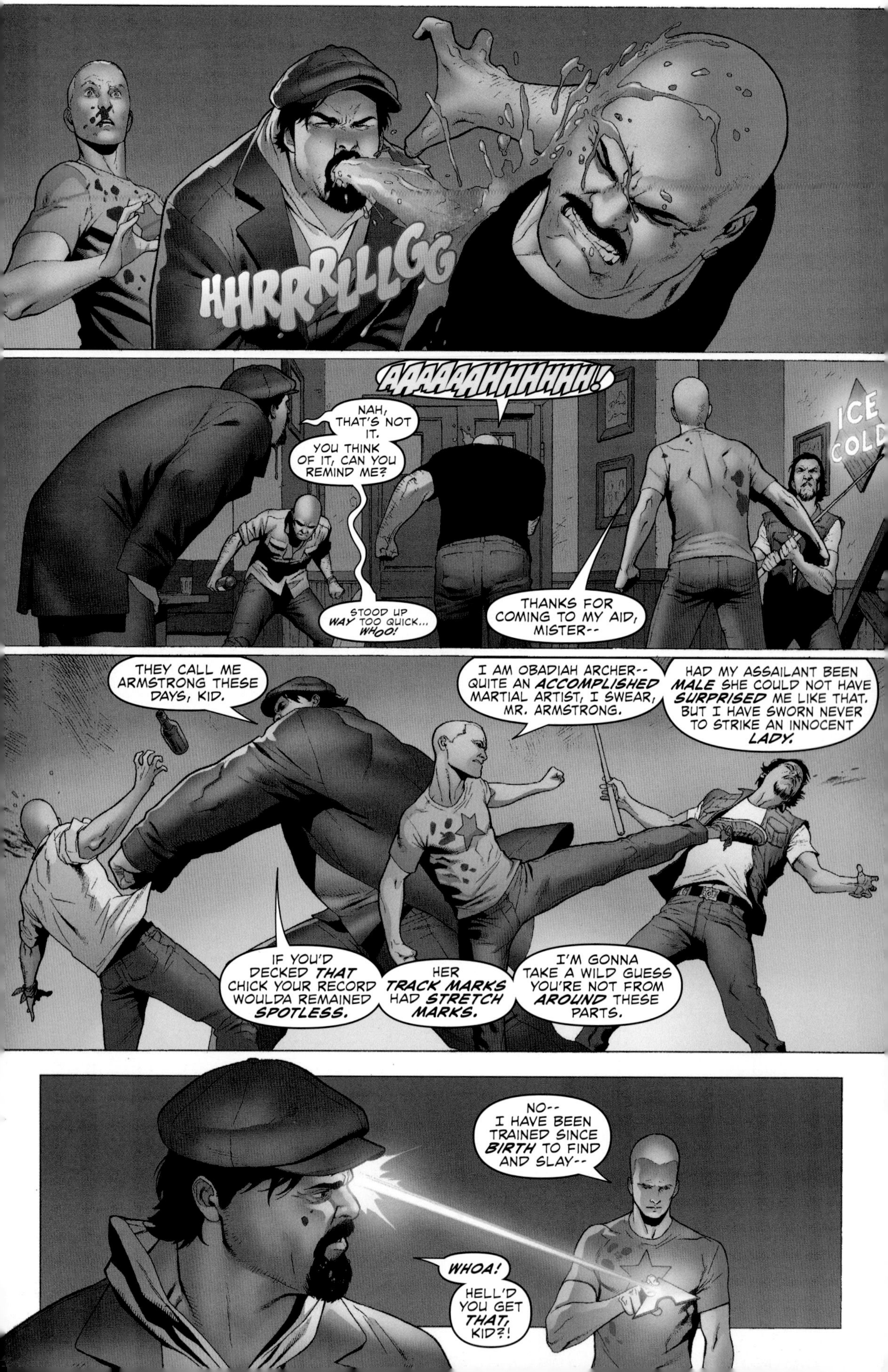
HHRRRLLLGG
AAAAAAHHHHHH!
NAH, THAT'S NOT IT. YOU THINK OF IT, CAN YOU REMIND ME?
STOOD UP WAY TOO QUICK... WHOO!
THANKS FOR COMING TO MY AID, MISTER--
THEY CALL ME ARMSTRONG THESE DAYS, KID.
I AM OBADIAH ARCHER-- QUITE AN ACCOMPLISHED MARTIAL ARTIST, I SWEAR, MR. ARMSTRONG.
HAD MY ASSAILANT BEEN MALE SHE COULD NOT HAVE SURPRISED ME LIKE THAT. BUT I HAVE SWORN NEVER TO STRIKE AN INNOCENT LADY.
IF YOU'D DECKED THAT CHICK YOUR RECORD WOULDA REMAINED SPOTLESS.
HER TRACK MARKS HAD STRETCH MARKS.
I'M GONNA TAKE A WILD GUESS YOU'RE NOT FROM AROUND THESE PARTS.
NO-- I HAVE BEEN TRAINED SINCE BIRTH TO FIND AND SLAY--
WHOA!
HELL'D YOU GET THAT, KID?!
ICE COLD

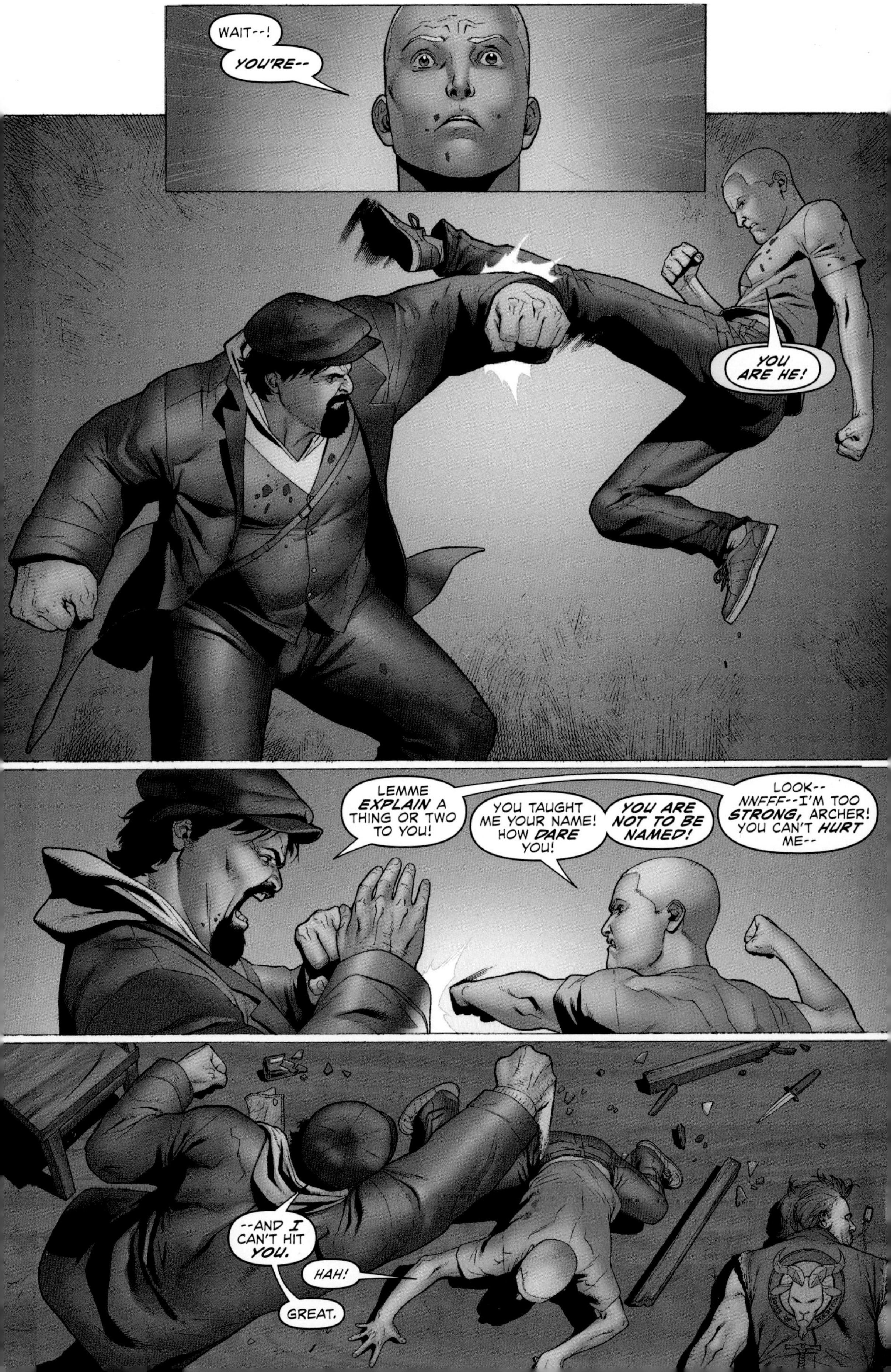
WAIT--!
YOU'RE--
YOU ARE HE!
LEMME EXPLAIN A THING OR TWO TO YOU!
YOU TAUGHT ME YOUR NAME! HOW DARE YOU!
YOU ARE NOT TO BE NAMED!
LOOK-- NNFFF--I'M TOO STRONG, ARCHER! YOU CAN'T HURT ME--
--AND I CAN'T HIT YOU.
HAH!
GREAT.

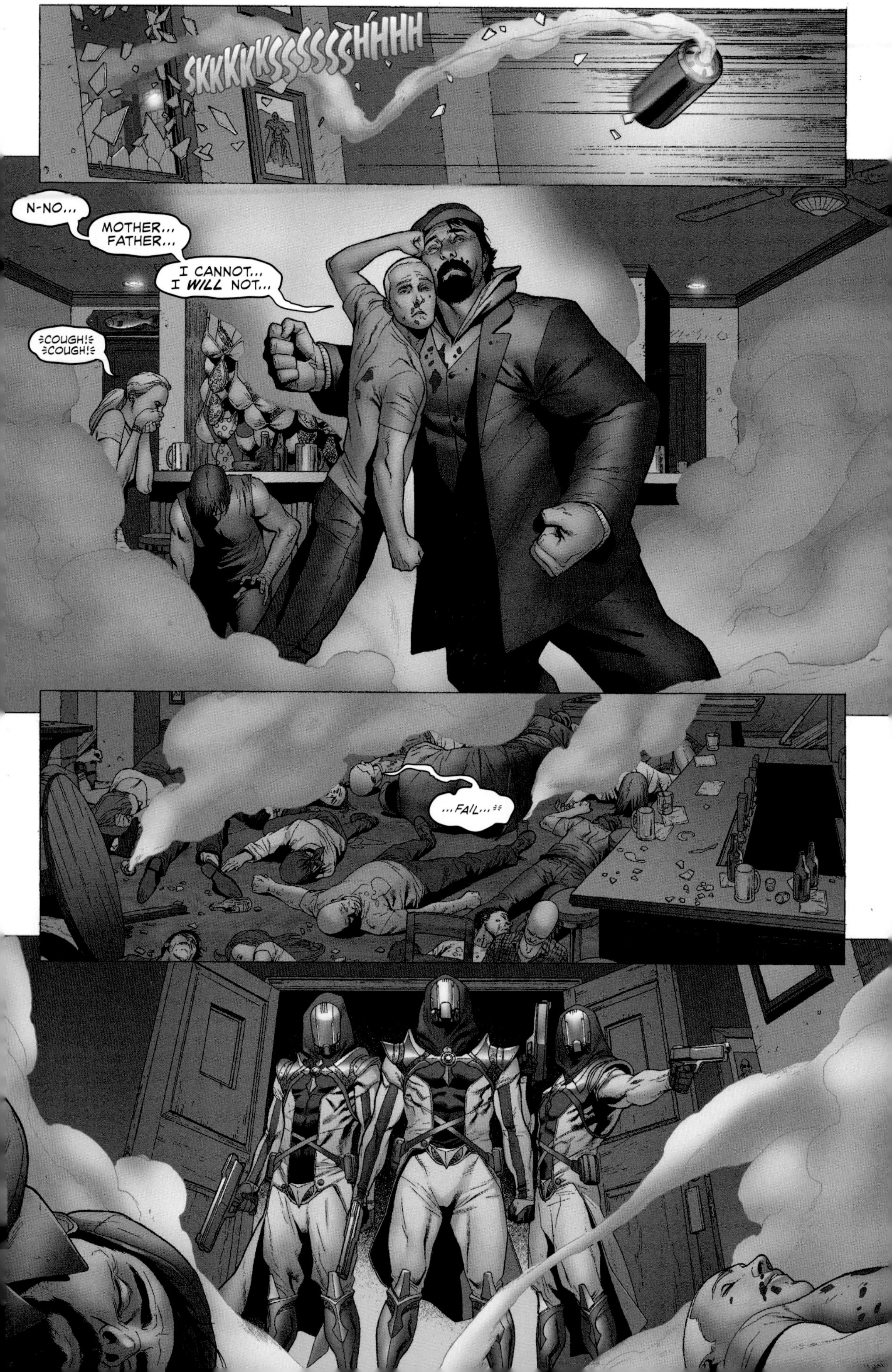
SKKKKSSSSSSSHHHH
N-NO...
MOTHER... FATHER...
I CANNOT... I WILL NOT...
COUGH! COUGH!
...FAIL...

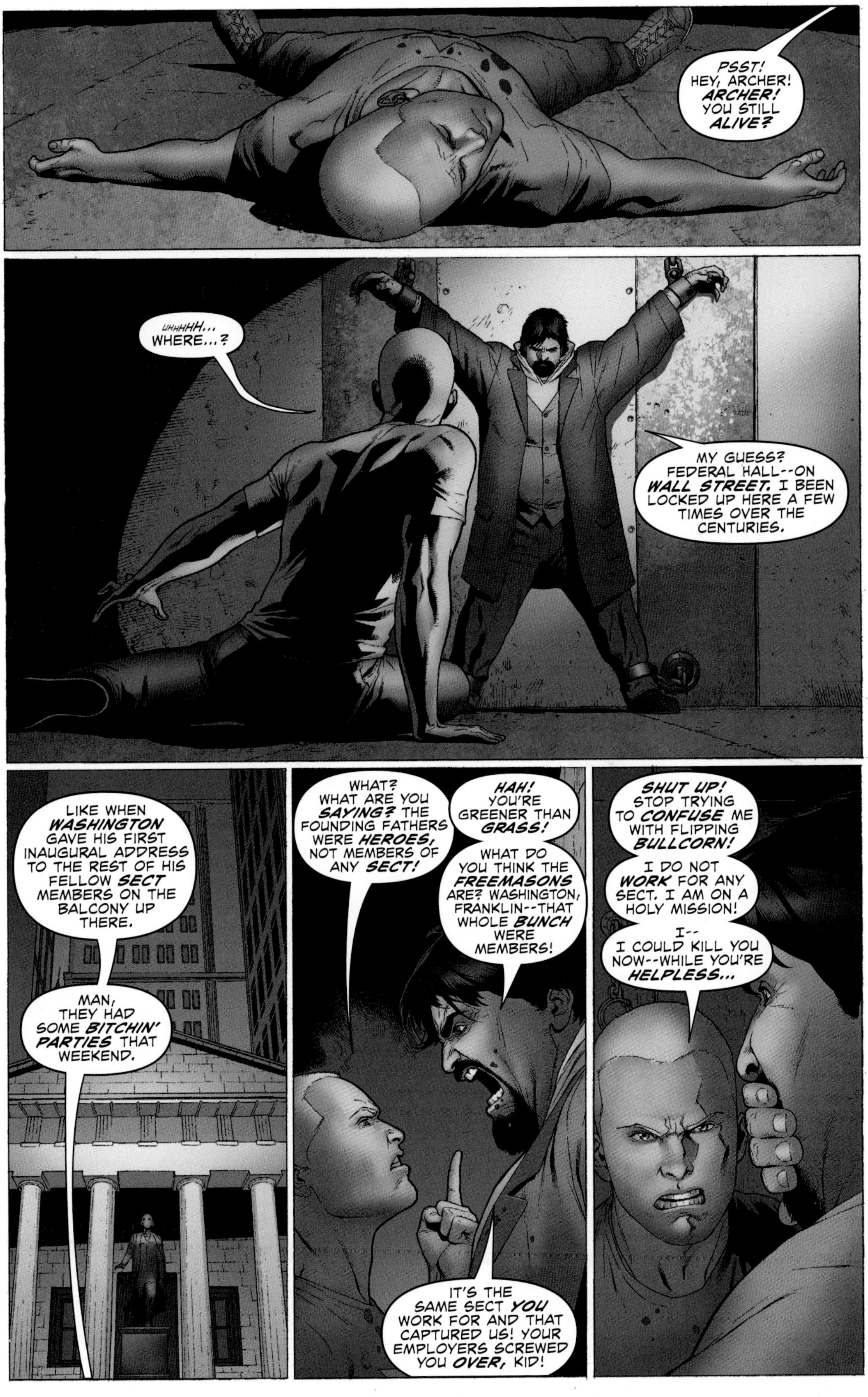
PSST! HEY, ARCHER! ARCHER! YOU STILL ALIVE?
UHHHHH... WHERE...?
MY GUESS? FEDERAL HALL--ON WALL STREET. I BEEN LOCKED UP HERE A FEW TIMES OVER THE CENTURIES.
LIKE WHEN WASHINGTON GAVE HIS FIRST INAUGURAL ADDRESS TO THE REST OF HIS FELLOW SECT MEMBERS ON THE BALCONY UP THERE.
MAN, THEY HAD SOME BITCHIN' PARTIES THAT WEEKEND.
WHAT? WHAT ARE YOU SAYING? THE FOUNDING FATHERS WERE HEROES, NOT MEMBERS OF ANY SECT!
HAH! YOU'RE GREENER THAN GRASS!
WHAT DO YOU THINK THE FREEMASONS ARE? WASHINGTON, FRANKLIN--THAT WHOLE BUNCH WERE MEMBERS!
IT'S THE SAME SECT YOU WORK FOR AND THAT CAPTURED US! YOUR EMPLOYERS SCREWED YOU OVER, KID!
SHUT UP! STOP TRYING TO CONFUSE ME WITH FLIPPING BULLCORN!
I DO NOT WORK FOR ANY SECT. I AM ON A HOLY MISSION!
I-- I COULD KILL YOU NOW--WHILE YOU'RE HELPLESS...

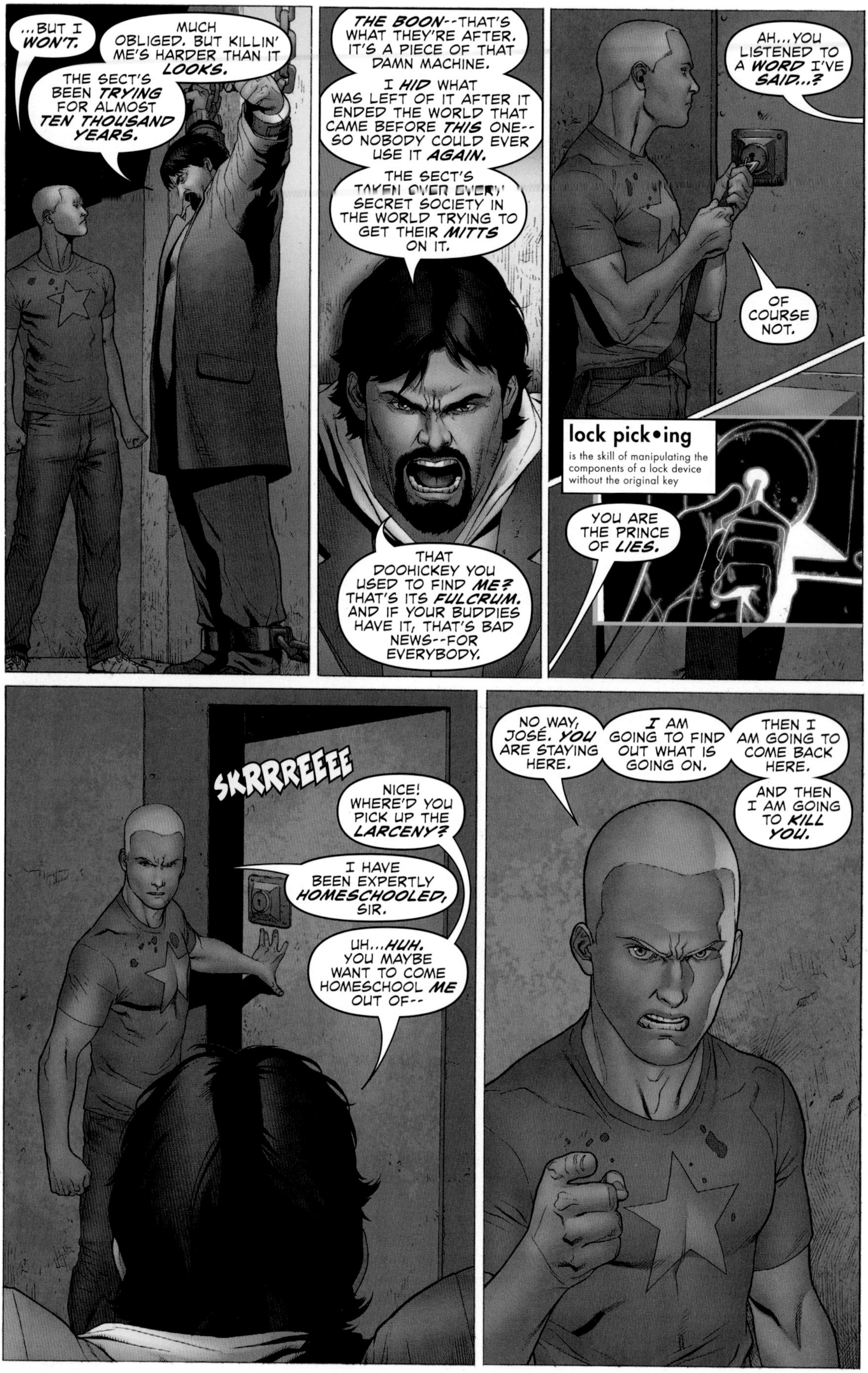
...BUT I WON'T.
MUCH OBLIGED. BUT KILLIN' ME'S HARDER THAN IT LOOKS.
THE SECT'S BEEN TRYING FOR ALMOST TEN THOUSAND YEARS.
THE BOON--THAT'S WHAT THEY'RE AFTER. IT'S A PIECE OF THAT DAMN MACHINE.
I HID WHAT WAS LEFT OF IT AFTER IT ENDED THE WORLD THAT CAME BEFORE THIS ONE--SO NOBODY COULD EVER USE IT AGAIN.
THE SECT'S TAKEN OVER EVERY SECRET SOCIETY IN THE WORLD TRYING TO GET THEIR MITTS ON IT.
THAT DOOHICKEY YOU USED TO FIND ME? THAT'S ITS FULCRUM. AND IF YOUR BUDDIES HAVE IT, THAT'S BAD NEWS--FOR EVERYBODY.
AH...YOU LISTENED TO A WORD I'VE SAID...?
OF COURSE NOT.
lock pick•ing
is the skill of manipulating the components of a lock device without the original key
YOU ARE THE PRINCE OF LIES.
SKRRREEEE
NICE! WHERE'D YOU PICK UP THE LARCENY?
I HAVE BEEN EXPERTLY HOMESCHOOLED, SIR.
UH...HUH. YOU MAYBE WANT TO COME HOMESCHOOL ME OUT OF--
NO WAY, JOSÉ. YOU ARE STAYING HERE.
I AM GOING TO FIND OUT WHAT IS GOING ON.
THEN I AM GOING TO COME BACK HERE.
AND THEN I AM GOING TO KILL YOU.

YOU'RE MAKING A *BIG MISTAKE,* ARCHER! THE WORLD IS A LOT *STRANGER* THAN YOU THINK!

YOU NEED A GUY LIKE *ME,* WHO'S BEEN *AROUND,* TO SHOW YOU THE *ROPES!*

ARCHER!!

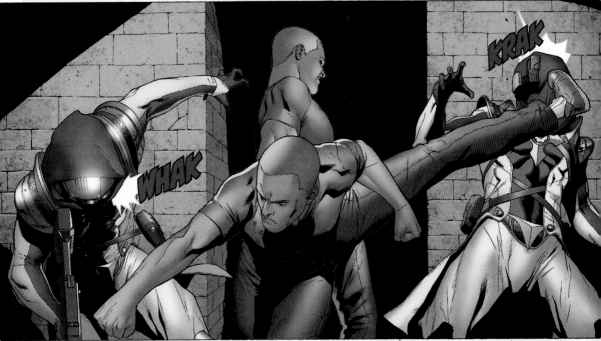

WHAK

KRAK

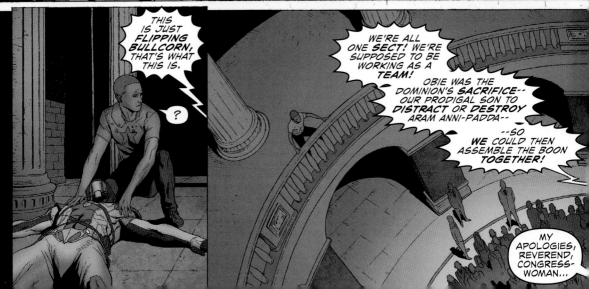

THIS IS JUST FLIPPING *BULLCORN,* THAT'S WHAT THIS IS.

?

WE'RE ALL ONE *SECT!* WE'RE SUPPOSED TO BE WORKING AS A *TEAM!*

OBIE WAS THE DOMINION'S *SACRIFICE*-- OUR *PRODIGAL SON* TO *DISTRACT* OR *DESTROY* ARAM ANNI-PADDA--

--SO WE COULD THEN ASSEMBLE THE BOON *TOGETHER!*

MY APOLOGIES, REVEREND, CONGRESS-WOMAN...

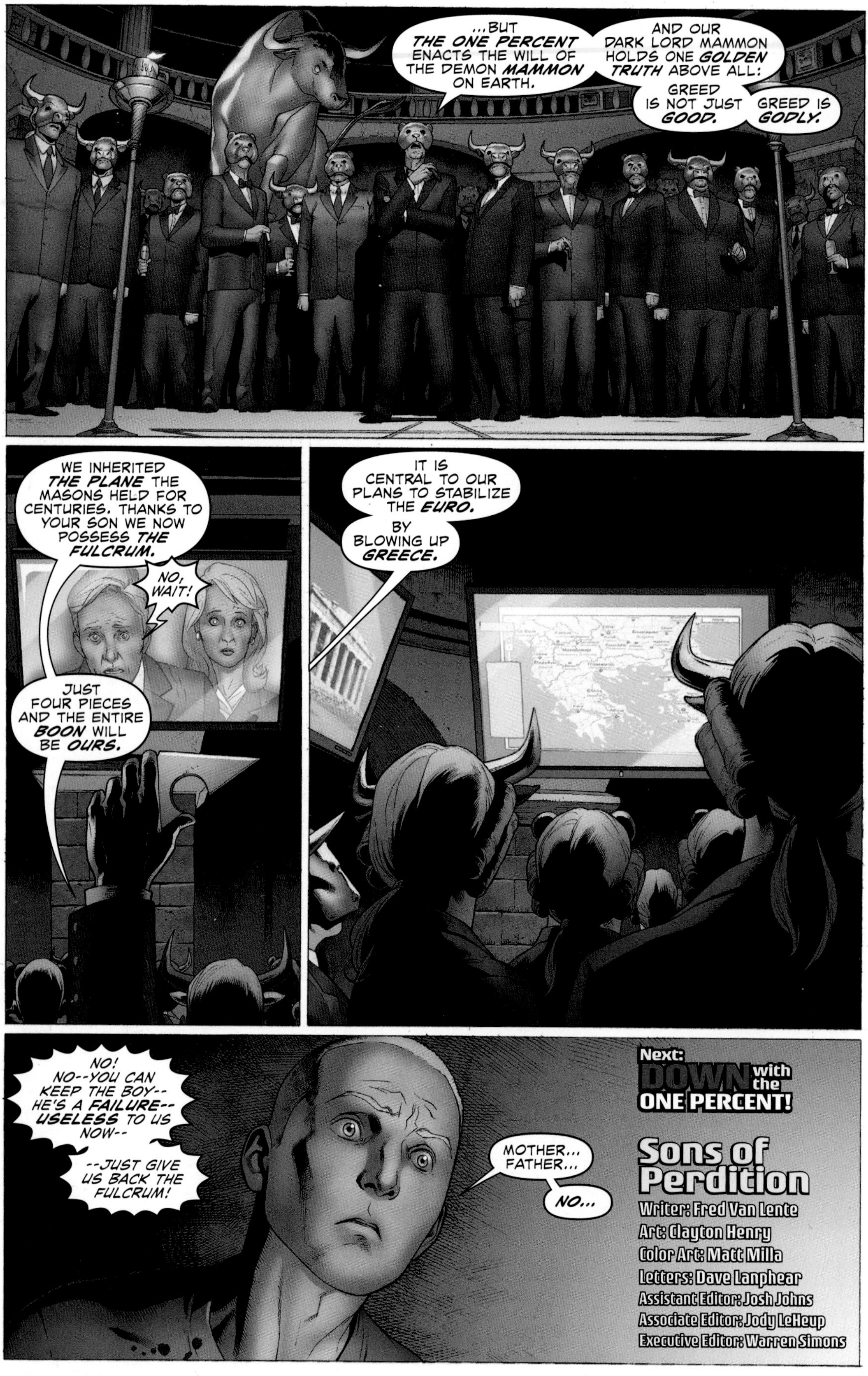
...BUT THE ONE PERCENT ENACTS THE WILL OF THE DEMON MAMMON ON EARTH.
AND OUR DARK LORD MAMMON HOLDS ONE GOLDEN TRUTH ABOVE ALL:
GREED IS NOT JUST GOOD.
GREED IS GODLY.
WE INHERITED THE PLANE THE MASONS HELD FOR CENTURIES. THANKS TO YOUR SON WE NOW POSSESS THE FULCRUM.
NO, WAIT!
JUST FOUR PIECES AND THE ENTIRE BOON WILL BE OURS.
IT IS CENTRAL TO OUR PLANS TO STABILIZE THE EURO.
BY BLOWING UP GREECE.
NO! NO--YOU CAN KEEP THE BOY--HE'S A FAILURE--USELESS TO US NOW--
--JUST GIVE US BACK THE FULCRUM!
MOTHER... FATHER...
NO...
Next: DOWN with the ONE PERCENT!
Sons of Perdition
Writer: Fred Van Lente
Art: Clayton Henry
Color Art: Matt Milla
Letters: Dave Lanphear
Assistant Editor: Josh Johns
Associate Editor: Jody LeHeup
Executive Editor: Warren Simons

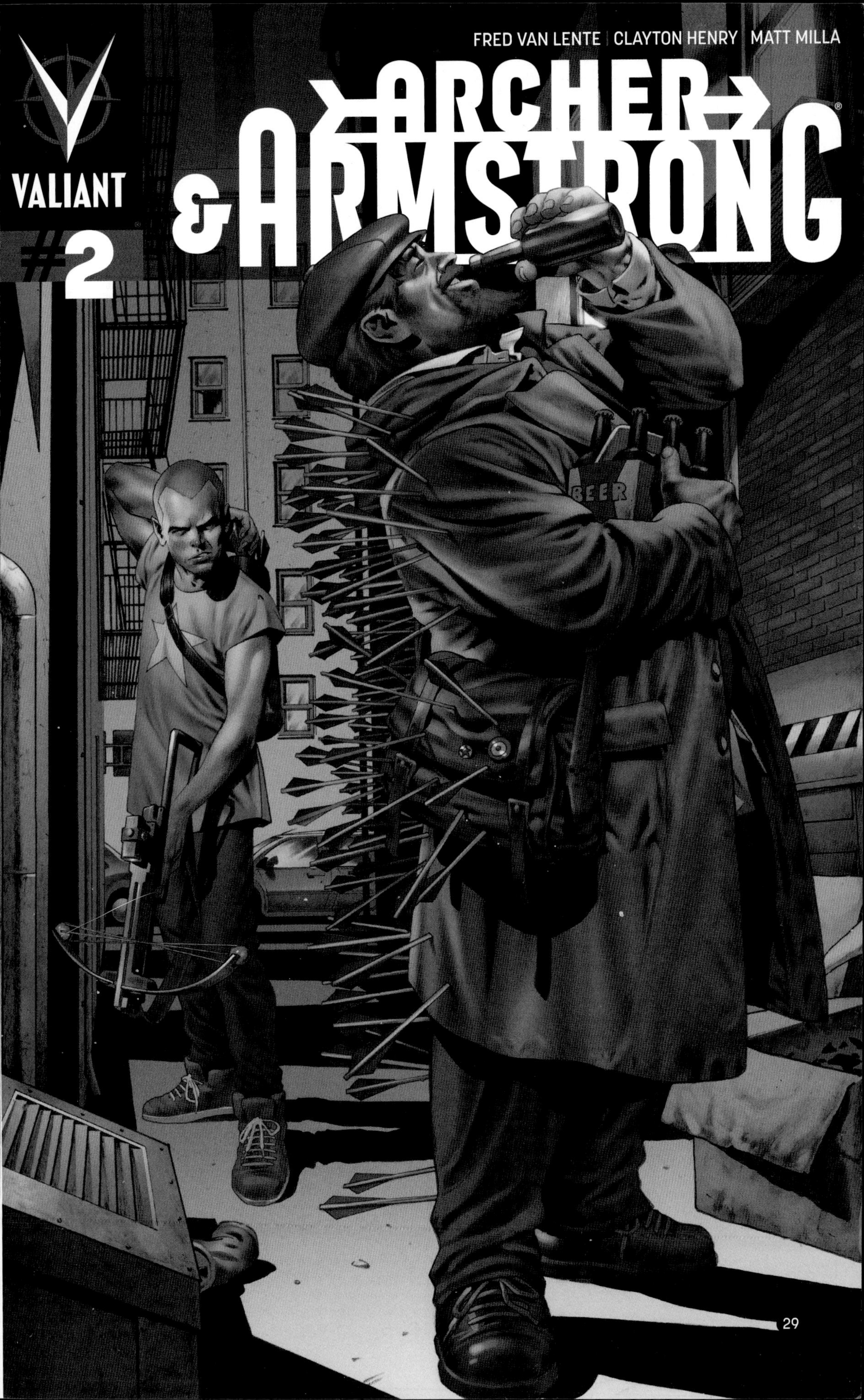
VALIANT
#2
FRED VAN LENTE | CLAYTON HENRY | MATT MILLA
ARCHER & ARMSTRONG
BEER

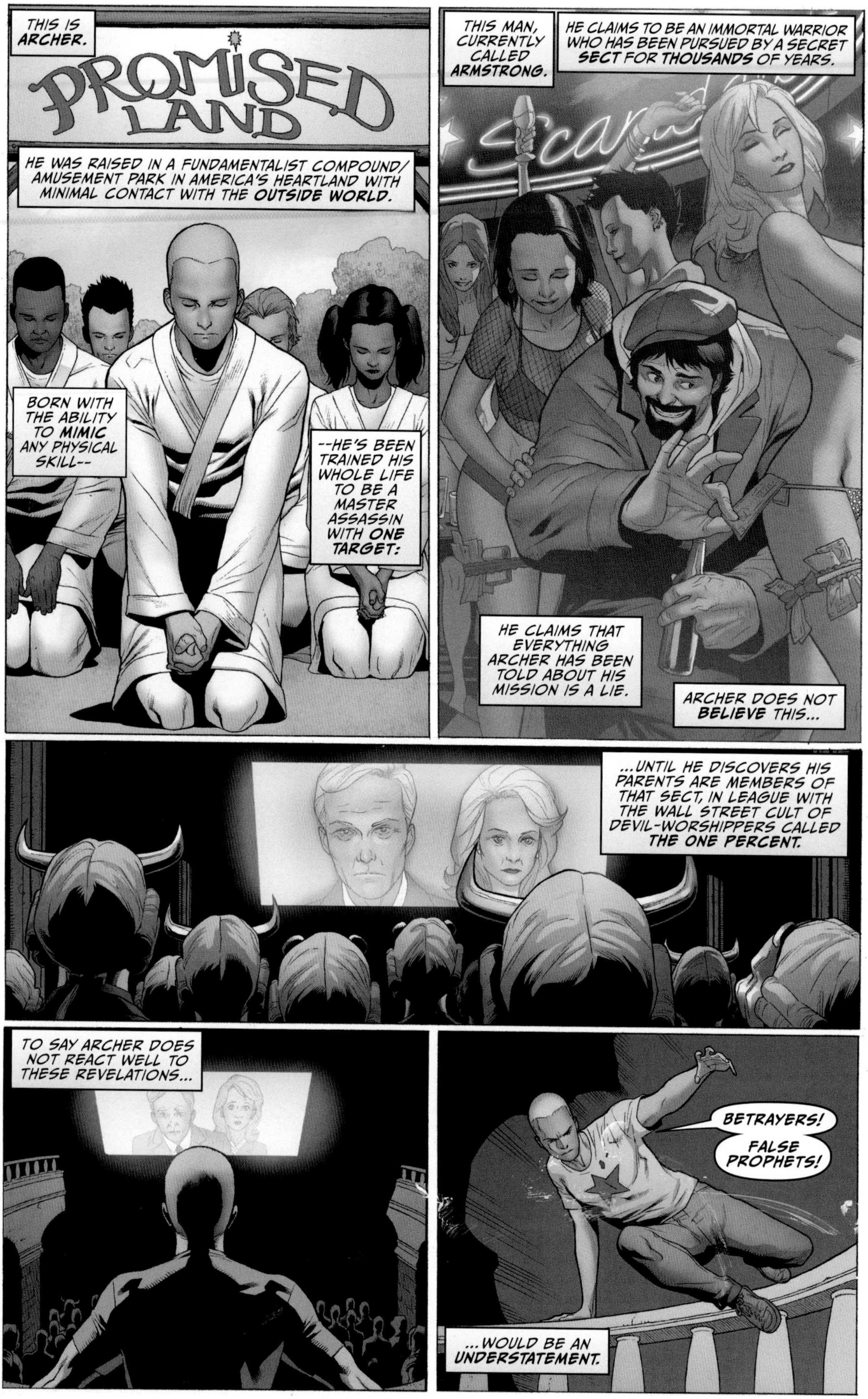
THIS IS ARCHER.
PROMISED LAND
HE WAS RAISED IN A FUNDAMENTALIST COMPOUND/ AMUSEMENT PARK IN AMERICA'S HEARTLAND WITH MINIMAL CONTACT WITH THE OUTSIDE WORLD.
BORN WITH THE ABILITY TO MIMIC ANY PHYSICAL SKILL--
--HE'S BEEN TRAINED HIS WHOLE LIFE TO BE A MASTER ASSASSIN WITH ONE TARGET:
THIS MAN, CURRENTLY CALLED ARMSTRONG.
HE CLAIMS TO BE AN IMMORTAL WARRIOR WHO HAS BEEN PURSUED BY A SECRET SECT FOR THOUSANDS OF YEARS.
HE CLAIMS THAT EVERYTHING ARCHER HAS BEEN TOLD ABOUT HIS MISSION IS A LIE.
ARCHER DOES NOT BELIEVE THIS...
...UNTIL HE DISCOVERS HIS PARENTS ARE MEMBERS OF THAT SECT, IN LEAGUE WITH THE WALL STREET CULT OF DEVIL-WORSHIPPERS CALLED THE ONE PERCENT.
TO SAY ARCHER DOES NOT REACT WELL TO THESE REVELATIONS...
BETRAYERS!
FALSE PROPHETS!
...WOULD BE AN UNDERSTATEMENT.

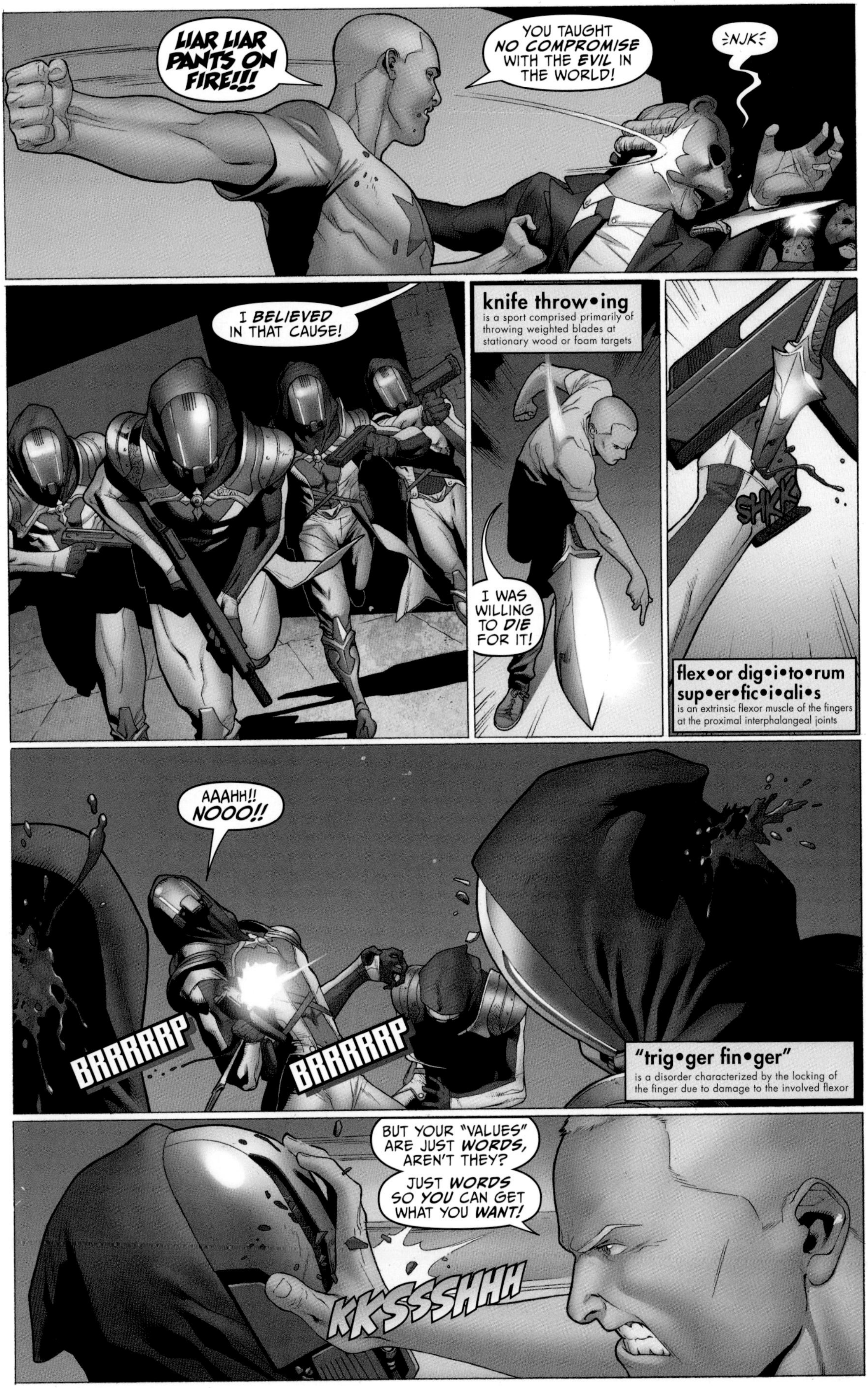

LIAR LIAR PANTS ON FIRE!!!
YOU TAUGHT NO COMPROMISE WITH THE EVIL IN THE WORLD!
NJK
I BELIEVED IN THAT CAUSE!
knife throw•ing
is a sport comprised primarily of throwing weighted blades at stationary wood or foam targets
I WAS WILLING TO DIE FOR IT!
SHKK
flex•or dig•i•to•rum sup•er•fic•i•ali•s
is an extrinsic flexor muscle of the fingers at the proximal interphalangeal joints
AAAHH!! NOOO!!
BRRRRRP
BRRRRRP
"trig•ger fin•ger"
is a disorder characterized by the locking of the finger due to damage to the involved flexor
BUT YOUR "VALUES" ARE JUST WORDS, AREN'T THEY?
JUST WORDS SO YOU CAN GET WHAT YOU WANT!
KKSSSHHH

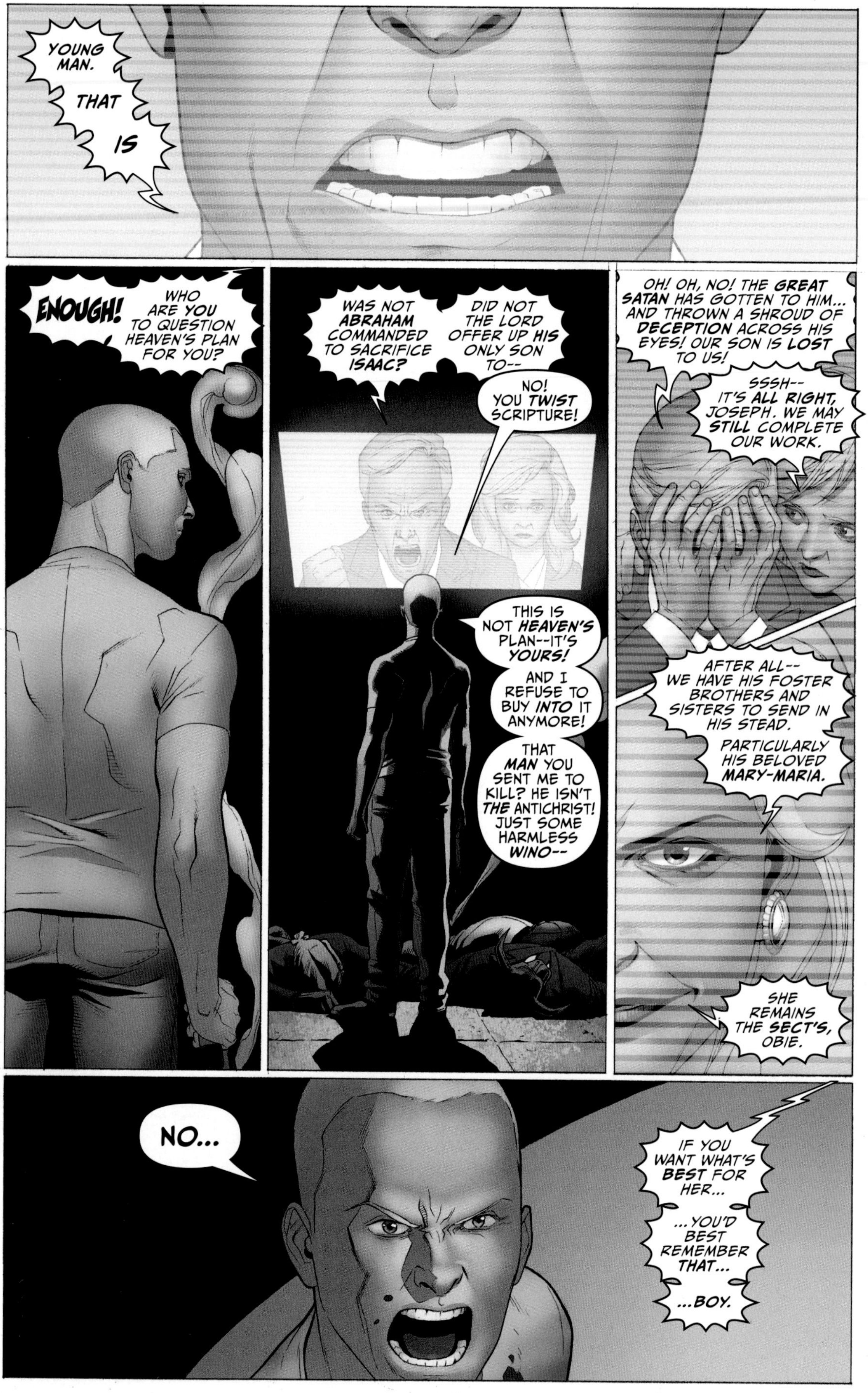
YOUNG MAN.
THAT
IS
ENOUGH!
WHO ARE YOU TO QUESTION HEAVEN'S PLAN FOR YOU?
WAS NOT ABRAHAM COMMANDED TO SACRIFICE ISAAC?
DID NOT THE LORD OFFER UP HIS ONLY SON TO--
NO! YOU TWIST SCRIPTURE!
THIS IS NOT HEAVEN'S PLAN--IT'S YOURS!
AND I REFUSE TO BUY INTO IT ANYMORE!
THAT MAN YOU SENT ME TO KILL? HE ISN'T THE ANTICHRIST! JUST SOME HARMLESS WINO--
OH! OH, NO! THE GREAT SATAN HAS GOTTEN TO HIM... AND THROWN A SHROUD OF DECEPTION ACROSS HIS EYES! OUR SON IS LOST TO US!
SSSH-- IT'S ALL RIGHT, JOSEPH. WE MAY STILL COMPLETE OUR WORK.
AFTER ALL-- WE HAVE HIS FOSTER BROTHERS AND SISTERS TO SEND IN HIS STEAD.
PARTICULARLY HIS BELOVED MARY-MARIA.
SHE REMAINS THE SECT'S, OBIE.
NO...
IF YOU WANT WHAT'S BEST FOR HER...
...YOU'D BEST REMEMBER THAT...
...BOY.

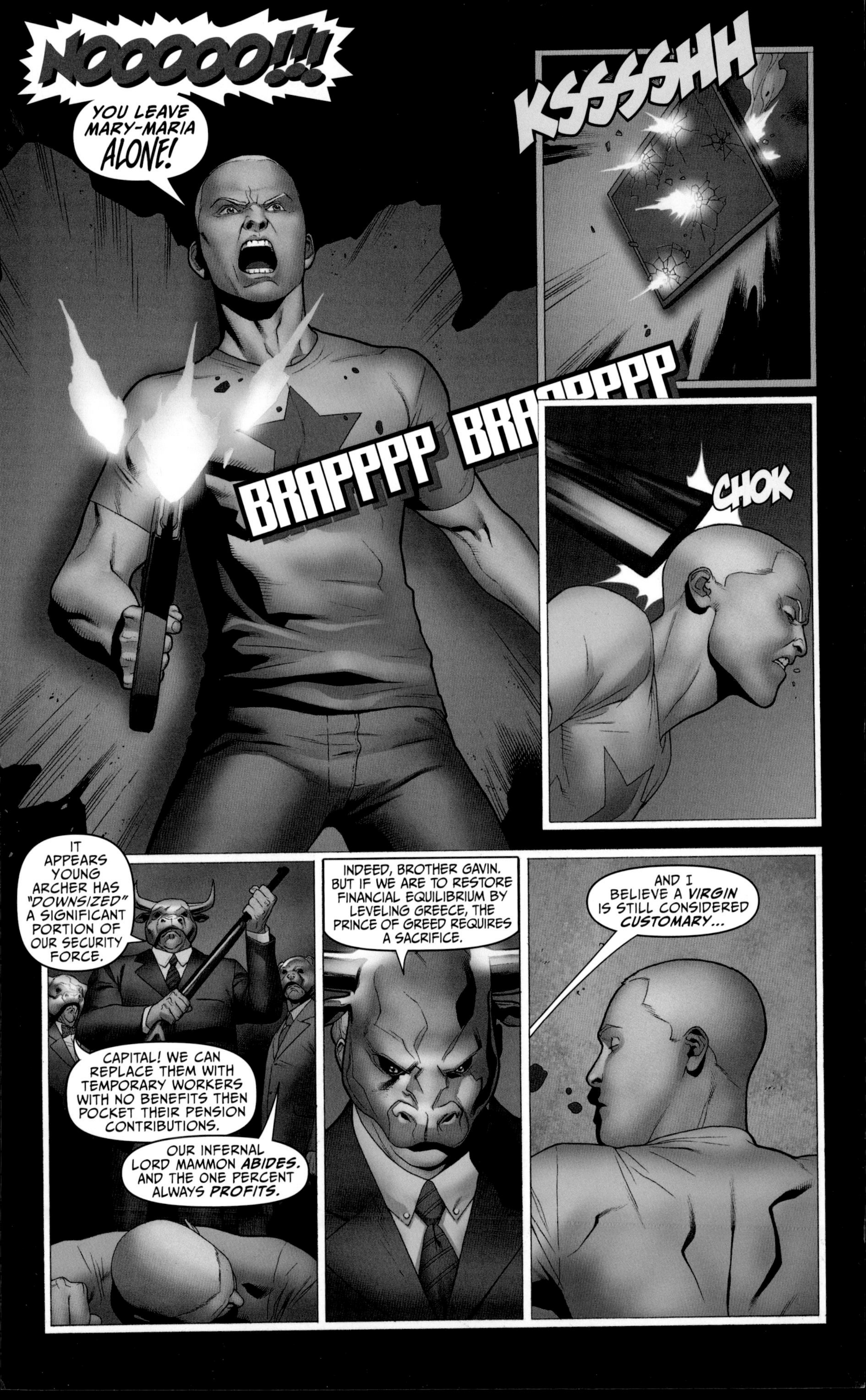
NOOOOO!!!
YOU LEAVE MARY-MARIA ALONE!
KSSSSHH
BRAPPPP BRAPPPPP
CHOK
IT APPEARS YOUNG ARCHER HAS "DOWNSIZED" A SIGNIFICANT PORTION OF OUR SECURITY FORCE.
CAPITAL! WE CAN REPLACE THEM WITH TEMPORARY WORKERS WITH NO BENEFITS THEN POCKET THEIR PENSION CONTRIBUTIONS.
OUR INFERNAL LORD MAMMON ABIDES. AND THE ONE PERCENT ALWAYS PROFITS.
INDEED, BROTHER GAVIN. BUT IF WE ARE TO RESTORE FINANCIAL EQUILIBRIUM BY LEVELING GREECE, THE PRINCE OF GREED REQUIRES A SACRIFICE.
AND I BELIEVE A VIRGIN IS STILL CONSIDERED CUSTOMARY...

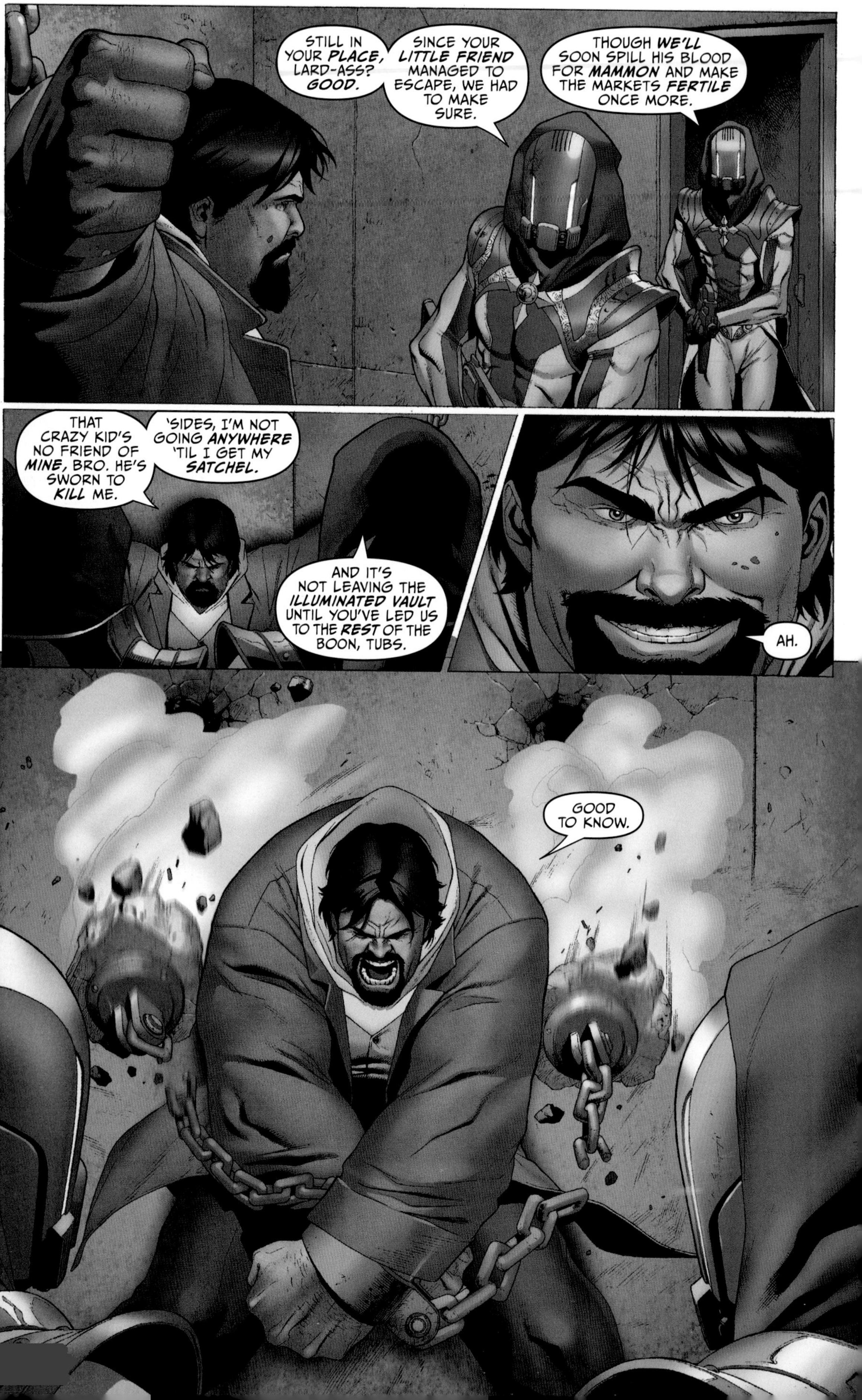
STILL IN YOUR PLACE, LARD-ASS? GOOD.
SINCE YOUR LITTLE FRIEND MANAGED TO ESCAPE, WE HAD TO MAKE SURE.
THOUGH WE'LL SOON SPILL HIS BLOOD FOR MAMMON AND MAKE THE MARKETS FERTILE ONCE MORE.
THAT CRAZY KID'S NO FRIEND OF MINE, BRO. HE'S SWORN TO KILL ME.
'SIDES, I'M NOT GOING ANYWHERE 'TIL I GET MY SATCHEL.
AND IT'S NOT LEAVING THE ILLUMINATED VAULT UNTIL YOU'VE LED US TO THE REST OF THE BOON, TUBS.
AH.
GOOD TO KNOW.

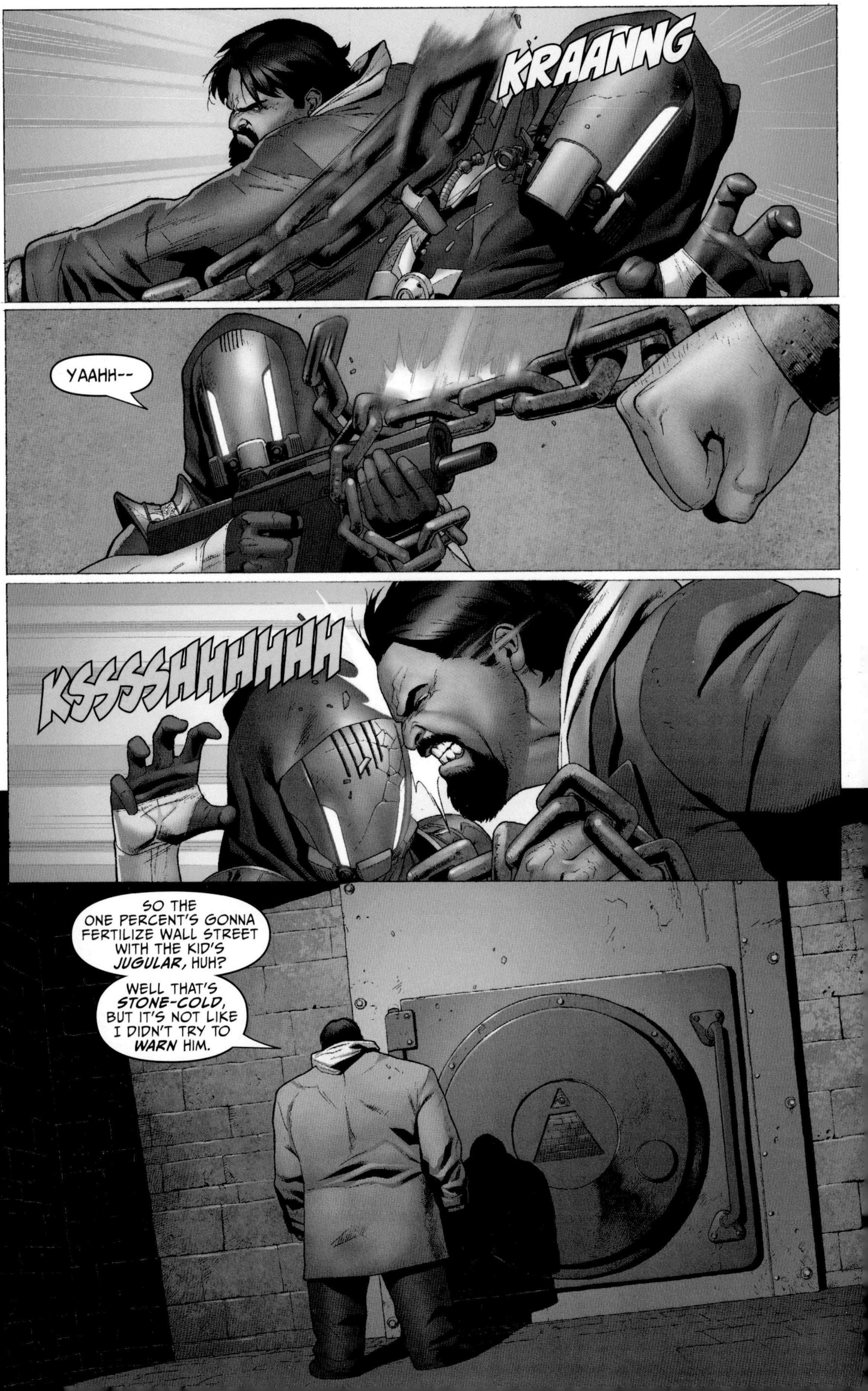
KRAANNG
YAAHH--
KSSSHHHHHH
SO THE ONE PERCENT'S GONNA FERTILIZE WALL STREET WITH THE KID'S JUGULAR, HUH?
WELL THAT'S STONE-COLD, BUT IT'S NOT LIKE I DIDN'T TRY TO WARN HIM.

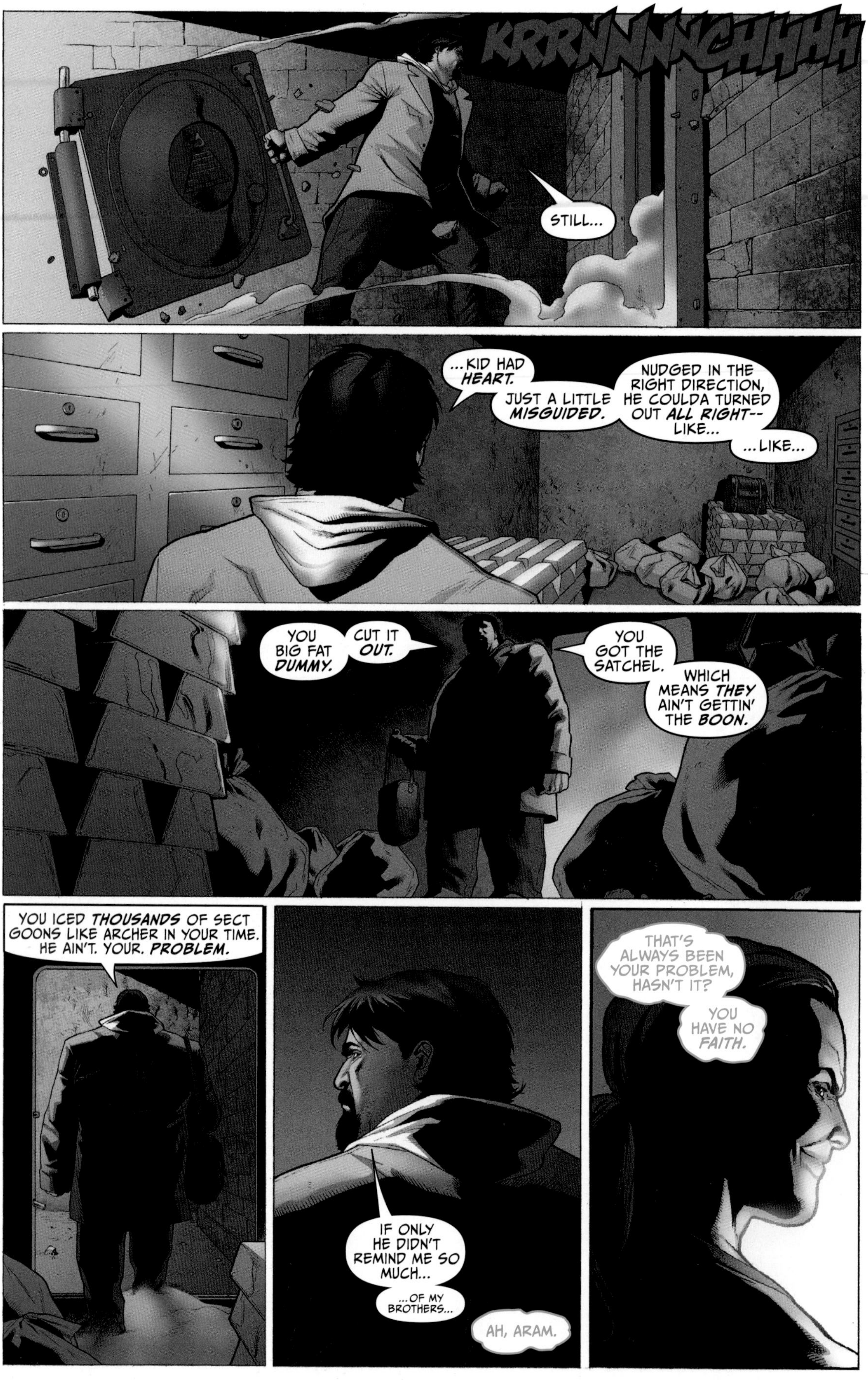
KRRNNNNCHHHH
STILL...
...KID HAD HEART.
JUST A LITTLE MISGUIDED.
NUDGED IN THE RIGHT DIRECTION, HE COULDA TURNED OUT ALL RIGHT-- LIKE...
...LIKE...
YOU BIG FAT DUMMY.
CUT IT OUT.
YOU GOT THE SATCHEL.
WHICH MEANS THEY AIN'T GETTIN' THE BOON.
YOU ICED THOUSANDS OF SECT GOONS LIKE ARCHER IN YOUR TIME. HE AIN'T. YOUR. PROBLEM.
IF ONLY HE DIDN'T REMIND ME SO MUCH...
...OF MY BROTHERS...
AH, ARAM.
THAT'S ALWAYS BEEN YOUR PROBLEM, HASN'T IT?
YOU HAVE NO FAITH.

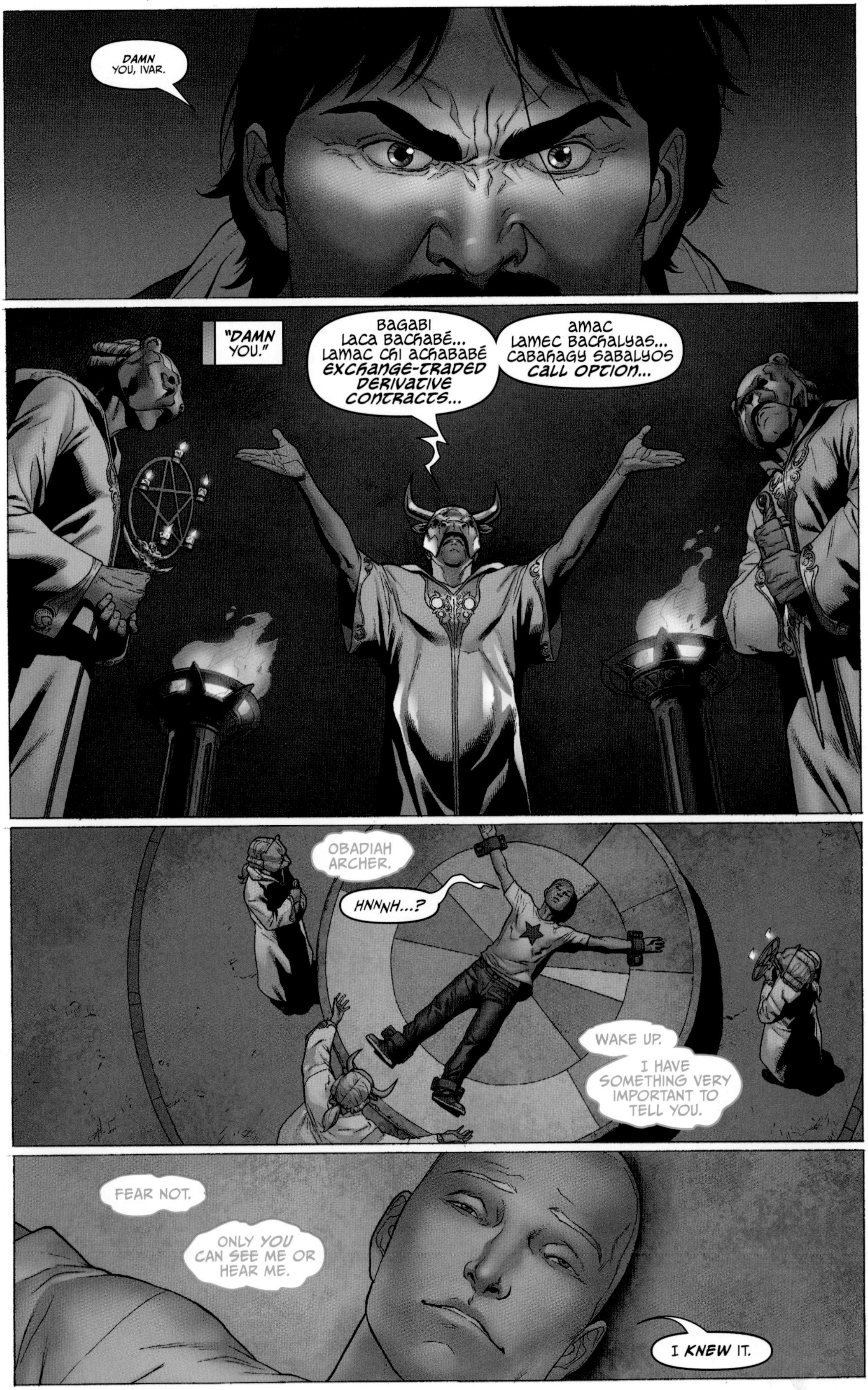
DAMN YOU, IVAR.
"DAMN YOU."
BAGABI LACA BACHABÉ... LAMAC CHI ACHABABÉ EXCHANGE-TRADED DERIVATIVE CONTRACTS...
AMAC LAMEC BACHALYAS... CABAHAGY SABALYOS CALL OPTION...
OBADIAH ARCHER.
HNNNH...?
WAKE UP.
I HAVE SOMETHING VERY IMPORTANT TO TELL YOU.
FEAR NOT.
ONLY YOU CAN SEE ME OR HEAR ME.
I KNEW IT.

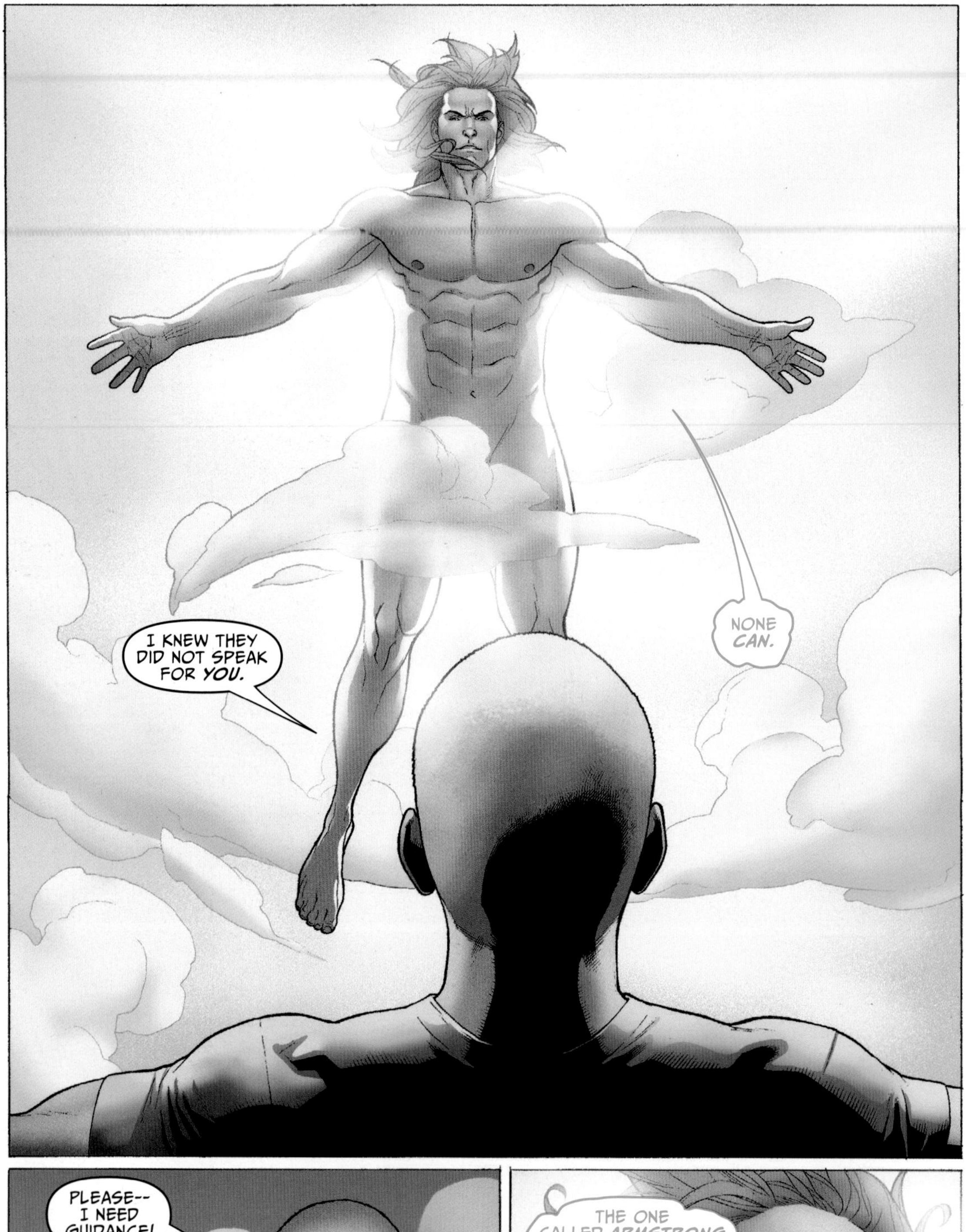
I KNEW THEY DID NOT SPEAK FOR YOU.
NONE CAN.

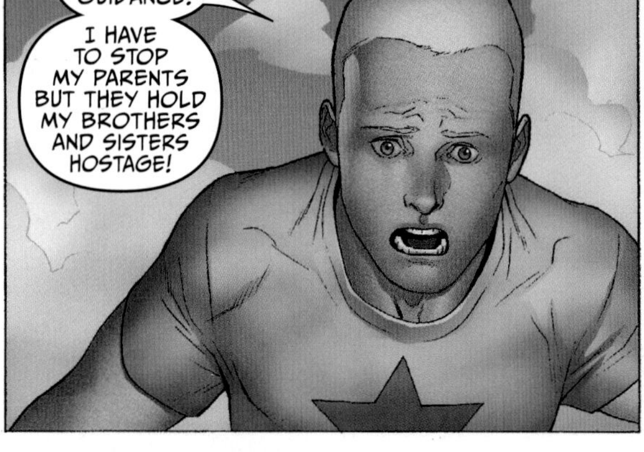
PLEASE-- I NEED GUIDANCE!
I HAVE TO STOP MY PARENTS BUT THEY HOLD MY BROTHERS AND SISTERS HOSTAGE!

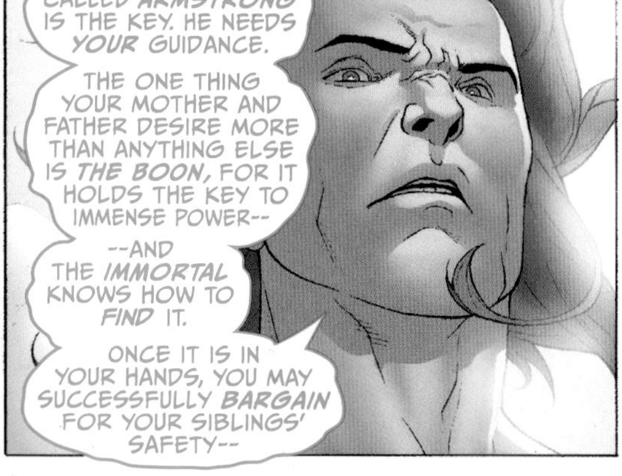
THE ONE CALLED ARMSTRONG IS THE KEY. HE NEEDS YOUR GUIDANCE.
THE ONE THING YOUR MOTHER AND FATHER DESIRE MORE THAN ANYTHING ELSE IS THE BOON, FOR IT HOLDS THE KEY TO IMMENSE POWER--
--AND THE IMMORTAL KNOWS HOW TO FIND IT.
ONCE IT IS IN YOUR HANDS, YOU MAY SUCCESSFULLY BARGAIN FOR YOUR SIBLINGS' SAFETY--

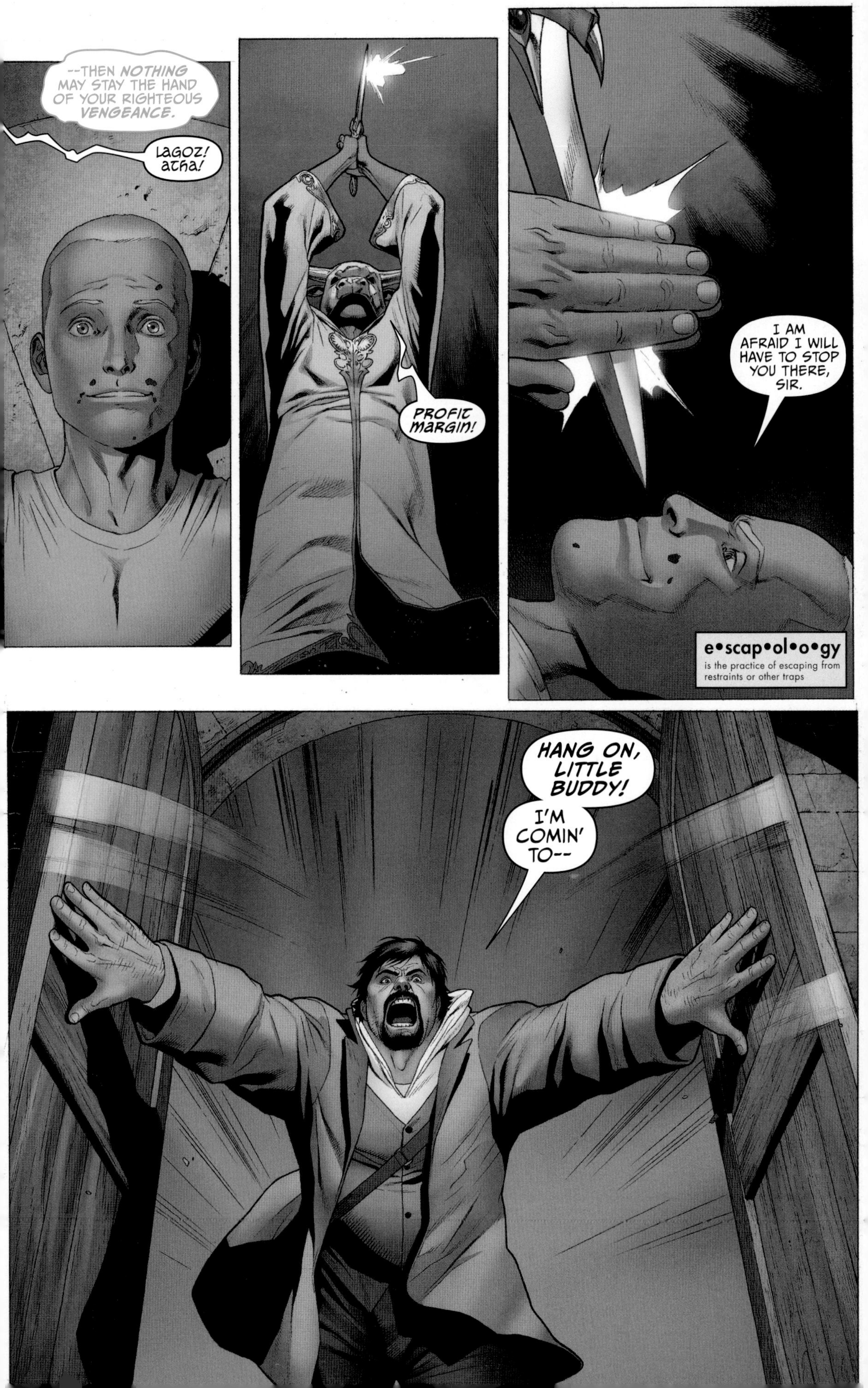

--THEN NOTHING MAY STAY THE HAND OF YOUR RIGHTEOUS VENGEANCE.
LAGOZ! ATHA!
PROFIT MARGIN!
I AM AFRAID I WILL HAVE TO STOP YOU THERE, SIR.
e•scap•ol•o•gy
is the practice of escaping from restraints or other traps
HANG ON, LITTLE BUDDY!
I'M COMIN' TO--

...UH...

...NEVER MIND...

MR. ARMSTRONG! I AM OVERJOYED TO SEE YOU UNHARMED!

WHY, YOU DON'T WANT THE *COMPETITION?*

LISTEN, IF YOU'RE STILL ON YOUR *"KILLIN' ALLEGED ANTICHRISTS"* KICK I'M GONNA TAKE MY BALL AND *GO HOME*--

OH, NO-- NO NOT AT ALL! IN FACT I DEEPLY *REGRET* MY EARLIER HOMICIDAL OVERTURES.

UH...*REALLY?* WHAT CHANGED YOUR *TUNE?* (NOT THAT I'M *COMPLAINING...*)

YOU...YOU WERE *RIGHT*, SIR. MY PARENTS *WERE* IN LEAGUE WITH THOSE WHO TRIED TO SACRIFICE ME.

THE BOON *MUST* BE KEPT OUT OF THEIR HANDS. AND ONLY *WE* CAN DO IT!

NOW YOU'RE TALKIN'!

AND NO BETTER PLACE TO START THAN RIGHT *HERE*--RIGHT *NOW!*

IS ANOTHER PART OF THE BOON *NEARBY?*

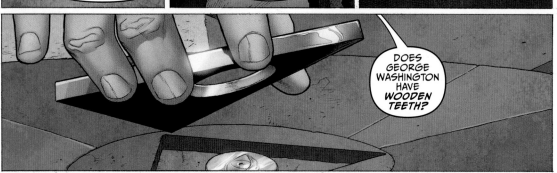

DOES GEORGE WASHINGTON HAVE *WOODEN TEETH?*

THE **SIX** MAIN PIECES I HID AROUND THE WORLD-- THE FULCRUM. THE TORQUE. THE WEDGE. THE AXEL. THE SPHERE.

AND EVEN THE BOON'S INDIVIDUAL PARTS DRAW HUMANS TO 'EM, LIKE MOTHS TO **FLAME.** WHOLE RELIGIONS AND CULTS AND SECRET SOCIETIES SPRUNG UP AROUND 'EM.

THIS LITTLE GUY, **THE INCLINED PLANE,** BECAME THE "EYE OF PROVIDENCE" OF THE FREEMASONS AND THE ILLUMINATI--

--AND THE BACK O' THE **SINGLES** I STICK IN MY FAVORITE GIRL **GERI'S** G-STRING EVERY TUESDAY AT THE SCANDALS GENTLEMEN CLUB'S **BODY SUSHI NIGHT!**

EW. THAT DOES NOT SOUND SANITARY, SIR.

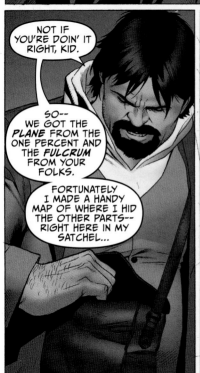

NOT IF YOU'RE DOIN' IT RIGHT, KID.

SO-- WE GOT THE **PLANE** FROM THE ONE PERCENT AND THE **FULCRUM** FROM YOUR FOLKS.

FORTUNATELY I MADE A HANDY MAP OF WHERE I HID THE OTHER PARTS-- RIGHT HERE IN MY SATCHEL...

...EXCEPT, **UH,** I SCRAWLED MOST O' THESE NOTES A FEW SHEETS TO THE **WIND...** A LOTTA **IN JOKES** AND MEN'S ROOM HUMOR...

LIKE... "MIKEY KEEPS THE **TORQUE** IN **CHAINS...**" HMMM...

DO YOU... DO YOU HAVE ANY IDEA WHAT THAT MEANS?

NONE WHATSOEVER! HARD ENOUGH TO REMEMBER 10,000 YEARS OF LIFE WHEN YOU SPENT MOST OF THAT TIME DRUNKER THAN A **KENNEDY** ON **ST. PATRICK'S DAY.**

BUT I KNOW WHO **WILL** KNOW.

LET'S SCOUR THIS DUMP FOR KEYS TO THE ONE PERCENT'S **PRIVATE JET,** KIDDO...

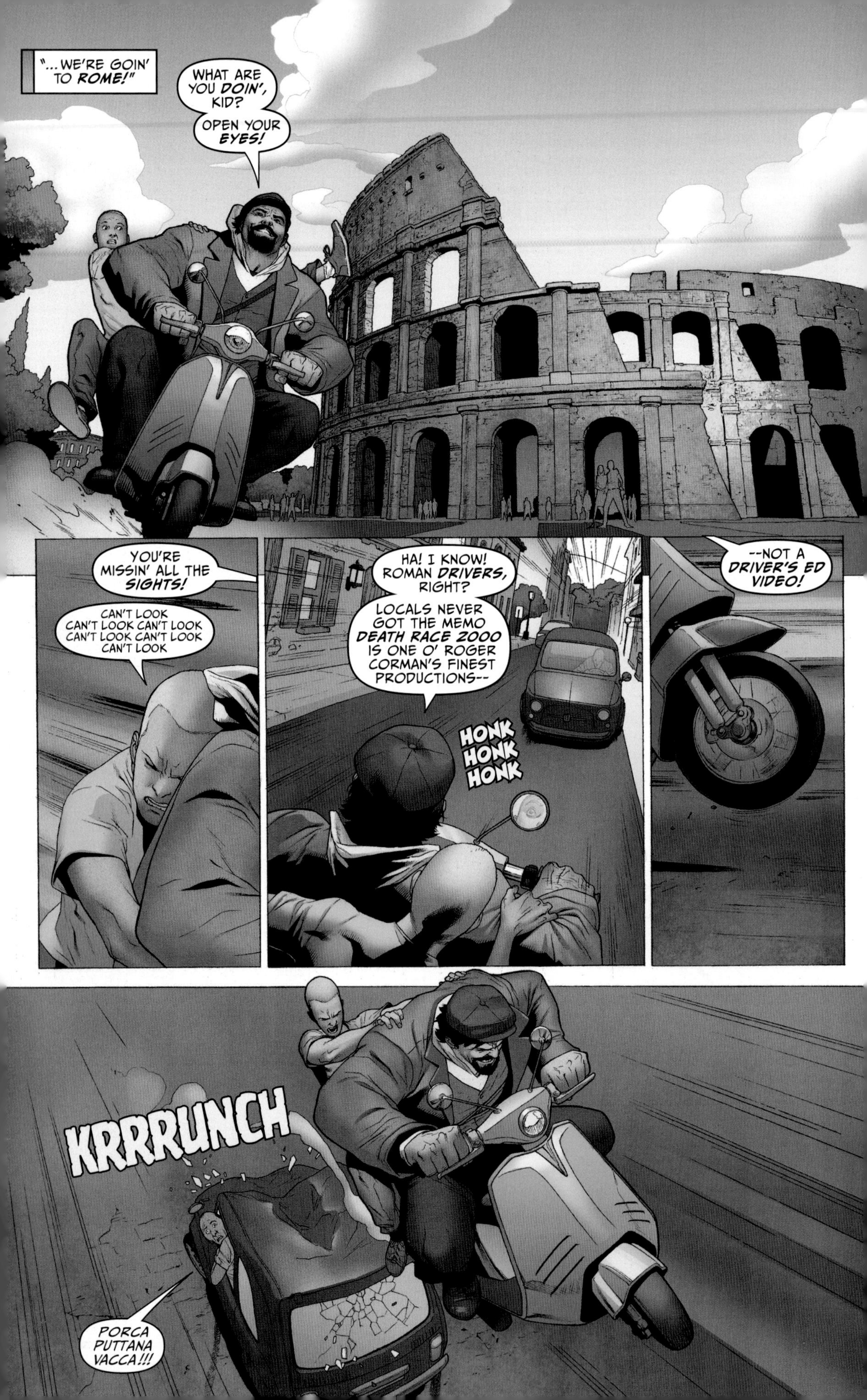
"...WE'RE GOIN' TO ROME!"
WHAT ARE YOU DOIN', KID?
OPEN YOUR EYES!
YOU'RE MISSIN' ALL THE SIGHTS!
CAN'T LOOK CAN'T LOOK CAN'T LOOK CAN'T LOOK CAN'T LOOK CAN'T LOOK
HA! I KNOW! ROMAN DRIVERS, RIGHT?
LOCALS NEVER GOT THE MEMO DEATH RACE 2000 IS ONE O' ROGER CORMAN'S FINEST PRODUCTIONS--
HONK HONK HONK
--NOT A DRIVER'S ED VIDEO!
KRRRUNCH
PORCA PUTTANA VACCA!!!

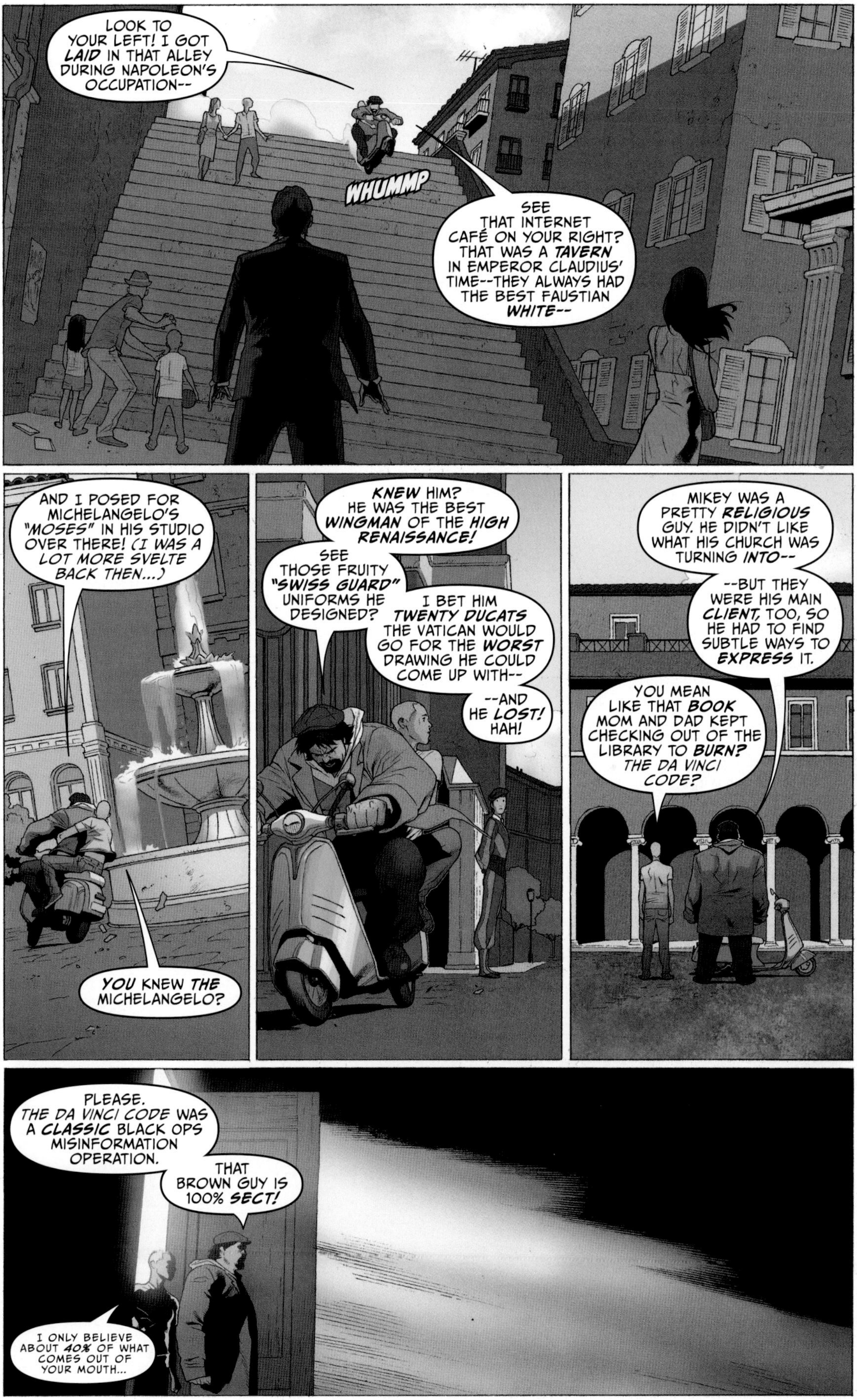
LOOK TO YOUR LEFT! I GOT LAID IN THAT ALLEY DURING NAPOLEON'S OCCUPATION--
WHUMMP
SEE THAT INTERNET CAFÉ ON YOUR RIGHT? THAT WAS A TAVERN IN EMPEROR CLAUDIUS' TIME--THEY ALWAYS HAD THE BEST FAUSTIAN WHITE--
AND I POSED FOR MICHELANGELO'S "MOSES" IN HIS STUDIO OVER THERE! (I WAS A LOT MORE SVELTE BACK THEN...)
YOU KNEW THE MICHELANGELO?
KNEW HIM? HE WAS THE BEST WINGMAN OF THE HIGH RENAISSANCE!
SEE THOSE FRUITY "SWISS GUARD" UNIFORMS HE DESIGNED?
I BET HIM TWENTY DUCATS THE VATICAN WOULD GO FOR THE WORST DRAWING HE COULD COME UP WITH--
--AND HE LOST! HAH!
MIKEY WAS A PRETTY RELIGIOUS GUY. HE DIDN'T LIKE WHAT HIS CHURCH WAS TURNING INTO--
--BUT THEY WERE HIS MAIN CLIENT, TOO, SO HE HAD TO FIND SUBTLE WAYS TO EXPRESS IT.
YOU MEAN LIKE THAT BOOK MOM AND DAD KEPT CHECKING OUT OF THE LIBRARY TO BURN? THE DA VINCI CODE?
PLEASE. THE DA VINCI CODE WAS A CLASSIC BLACK OPS MISINFORMATION OPERATION.
THAT BROWN GUY IS 100% SECT!
I ONLY BELIEVE ABOUT 40% OF WHAT COMES OUT OF YOUR MOUTH...

AAAAAGH!

BWHOOOOM!

TOMMY! IT'S ME!

THE ENTIRE *SECT* IS ON HIGH-ALERT AFTER YOUR ESCAPE FROM NEW YORK! IT IS *DANGEROUS* HERE! COME STA?

ARMSTRONG! I THOUGHT YOU WOULD COME *ALONE!*

ANNH... ONLY A *FLESH WOUND*, TO COIN A PHRASE...

MY YOUNG ASSOCIATE IS OBADIAH ARCHER-- HE'S EX-SECT, JUST LIKE YOU.

ARCHER, THIS IS MY GO-TO-GAL IN ROME, THE VATICAN LIBRARY'S VERY OWN *ART EXPERT*, SISTER THOMAS AQUINAS.

PLEASURE TO MEET YOU, MA'AM.

AND A *BIGGER* PLEASURE TO SEE MR. ARMSTRONG ASSOCIATES WITH *SOME* PEOPLE OF *STRONG MORAL CHARACTER.*

OH-- OUR FRIEND MET ME *LONG* BEFORE I TOOK MY VOWS, YOUNG MAN.

HE HELPED MY RESISTANCE FIGHTERS AGAINST MUSSOLINI IN THE HILLS OF ROMAGNA!

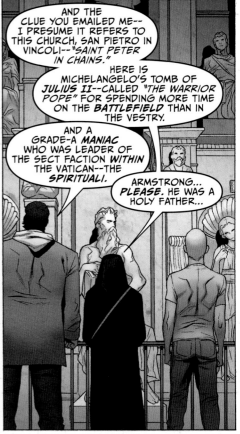

AND THE CLUE YOU EMAILED ME-- I PRESUME IT REFERS TO THIS CHURCH, SAN PIETRO IN VINCOLI--*"SAINT PETER IN CHAINS."*

HERE IS MICHELANGELO'S TOMB OF *JULIUS II*--CALLED *"THE WARRIOR POPE"* FOR SPENDING MORE TIME ON THE *BATTLEFIELD* THAN IN THE VESTRY.

AND A GRADE-A *MANIAC* WHO WAS LEADER OF THE SECT FACTION *WITHIN* THE VATICAN--THE *SPIRITUALI.*

ARMSTRONG... *PLEASE.* HE WAS A HOLY FATHER...

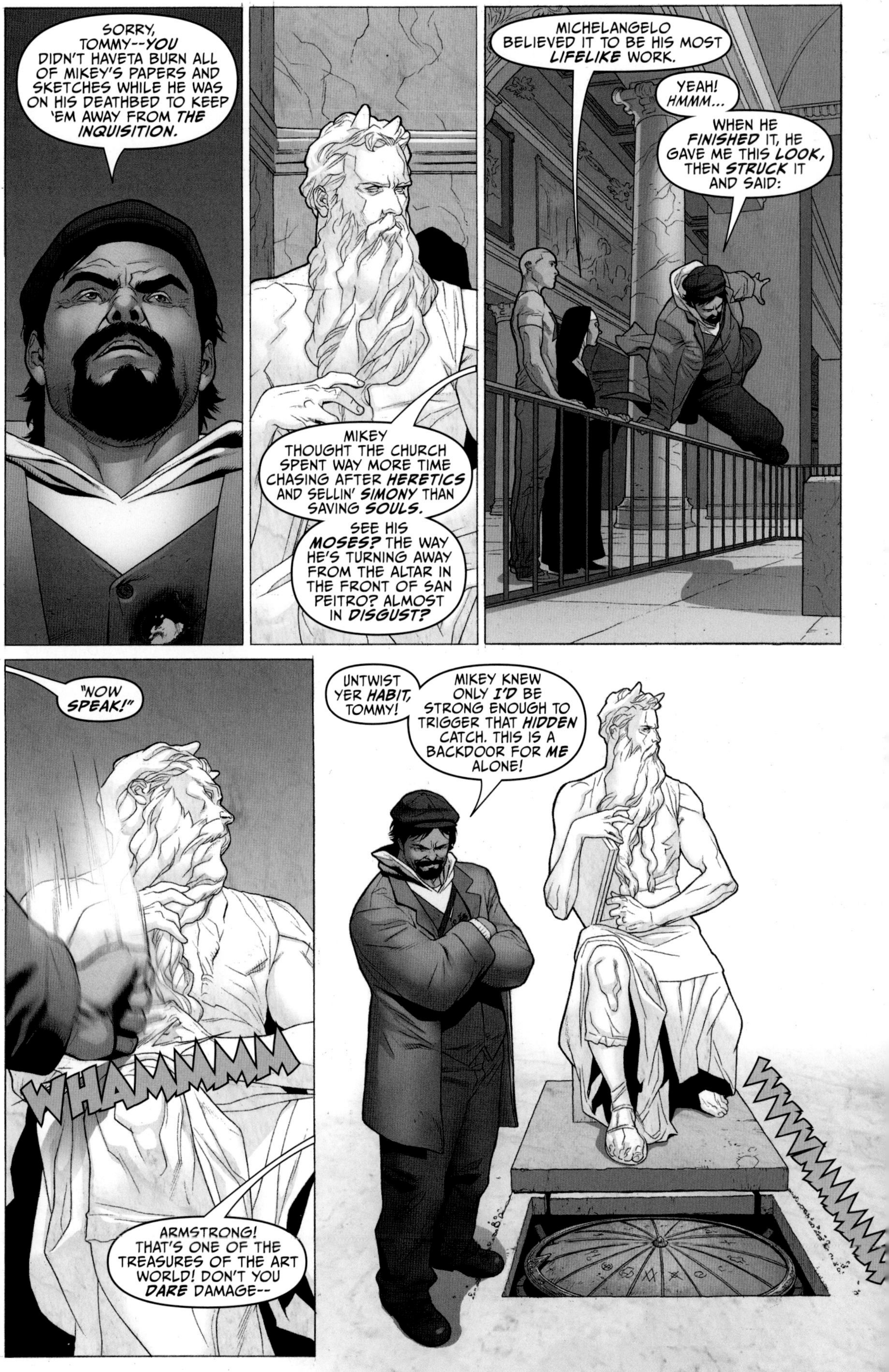

SORRY, TOMMY--YOU DIDN'T HAVETA BURN ALL OF MIKEY'S PAPERS AND SKETCHES WHILE HE WAS ON HIS DEATHBED TO KEEP 'EM AWAY FROM THE INQUISITION.
MIKEY THOUGHT THE CHURCH SPENT WAY MORE TIME CHASING AFTER HERETICS AND SELLIN' SIMONY THAN SAVING SOULS.
SEE HIS MOSES? THE WAY HE'S TURNING AWAY FROM THE ALTAR IN THE FRONT OF SAN PEITRO? ALMOST IN DISGUST?
MICHELANGELO BELIEVED IT TO BE HIS MOST LIFELIKE WORK.
YEAH! HMMM...
WHEN HE FINISHED IT, HE GAVE ME THIS LOOK, THEN STRUCK IT AND SAID:
"NOW SPEAK!"
WHAMMMM
ARMSTRONG! THAT'S ONE OF THE TREASURES OF THE ART WORLD! DON'T YOU DARE DAMAGE--
UNTWIST YER HABIT, TOMMY!
MIKEY KNEW ONLY I'D BE STRONG ENOUGH TO TRIGGER THAT HIDDEN CATCH. THIS IS A BACKDOOR FOR ME ALONE!
WWWMMMMMM

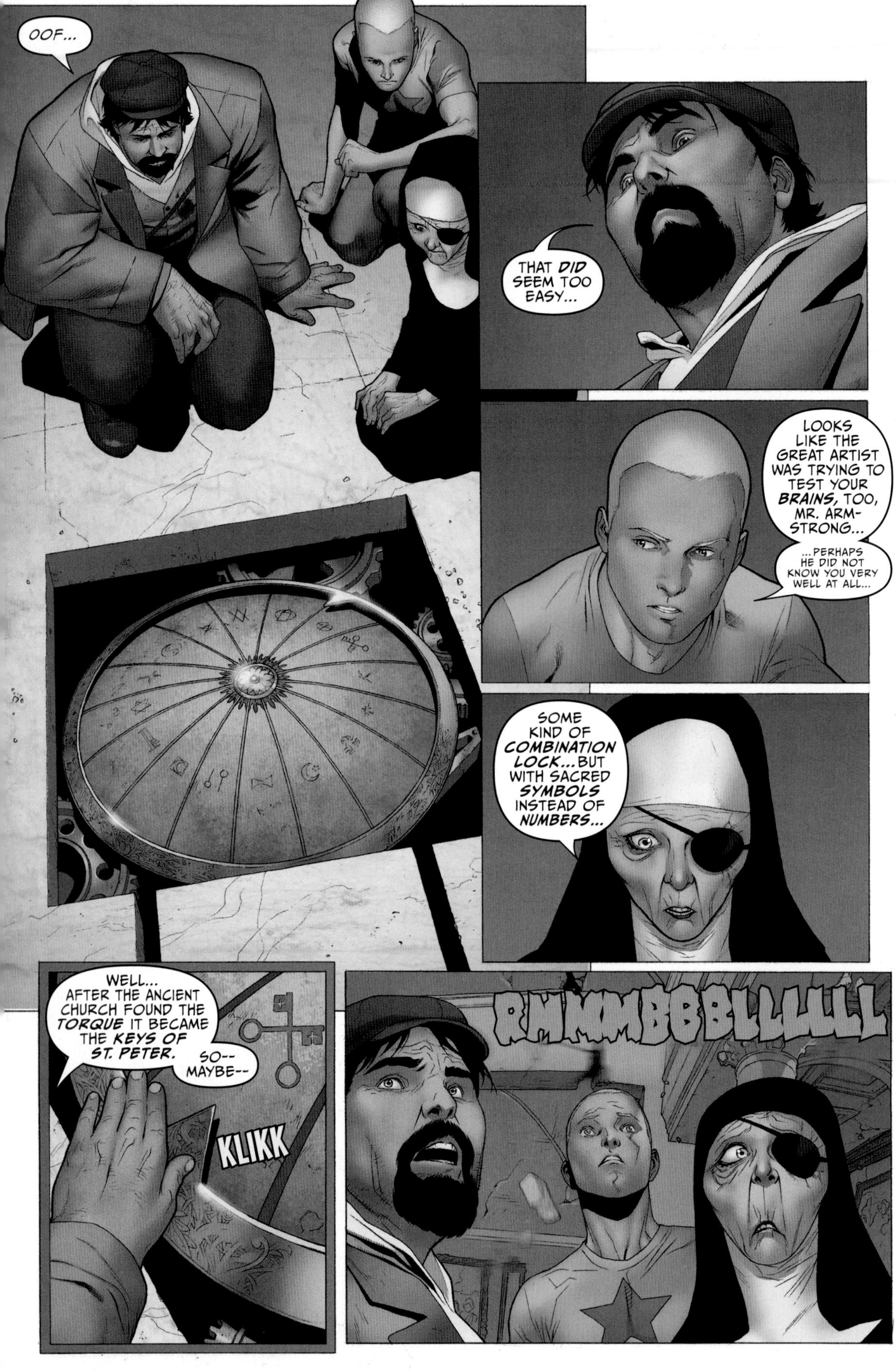
OOF...
THAT DID SEEM TOO EASY...
LOOKS LIKE THE GREAT ARTIST WAS TRYING TO TEST YOUR BRAINS, TOO, MR. ARM-STRONG...
...PERHAPS HE DID NOT KNOW YOU VERY WELL AT ALL...
SOME KIND OF COMBINATION LOCK...BUT WITH SACRED SYMBOLS INSTEAD OF NUMBERS...
WELL... AFTER THE ANCIENT CHURCH FOUND THE TORQUE IT BECAME THE KEYS OF ST. PETER.
SO-- MAYBE--
KLIKK
RHMMBBBLLLLLL

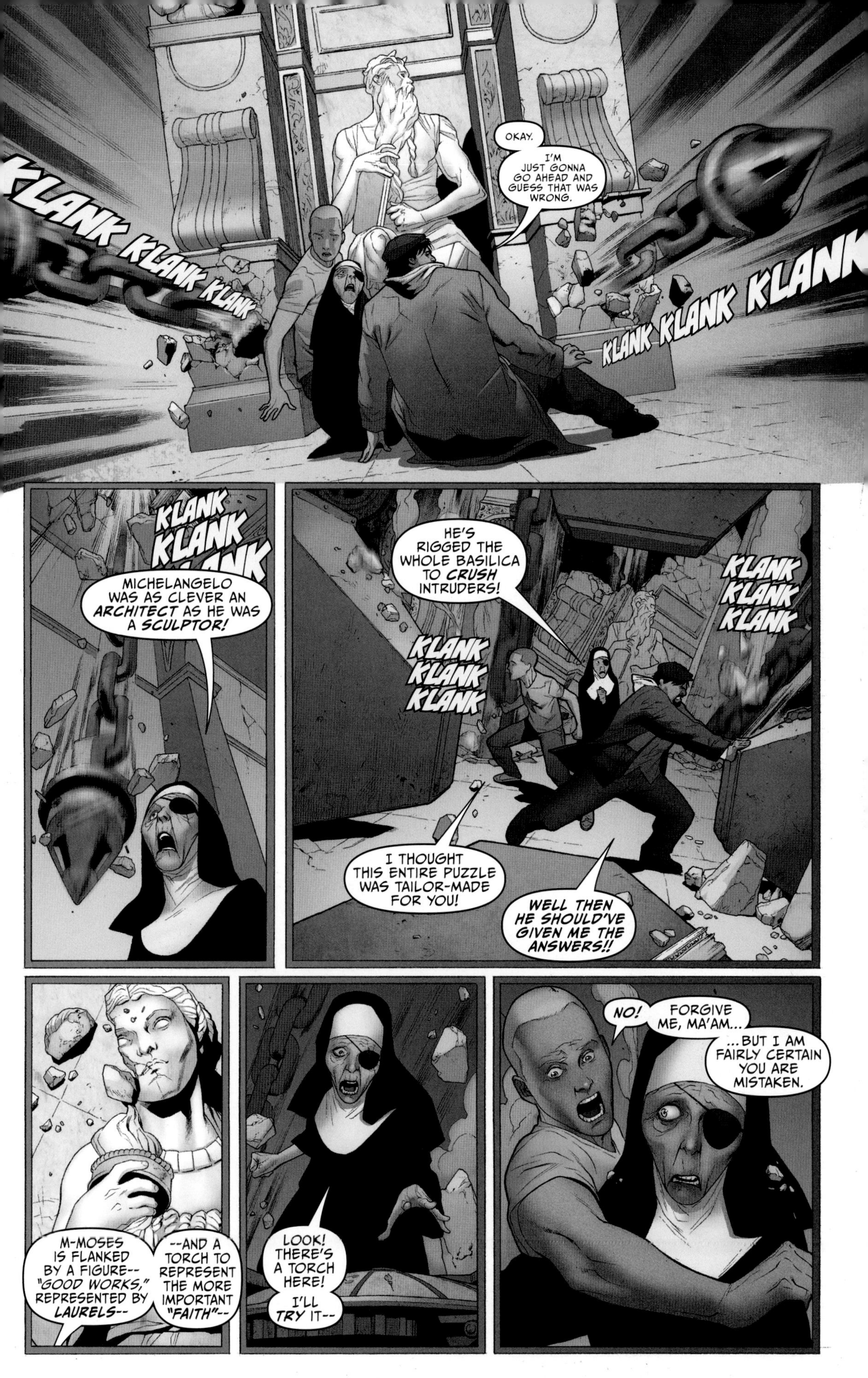
KLANK KLANK KLANK
OKAY.
I'M JUST GONNA GO AHEAD AND GUESS THAT WAS WRONG.
KLANK KLANK KLANK
KLANK KLANK
MICHELANGELO WAS AS CLEVER AN *ARCHITECT* AS HE WAS A *SCULPTOR!*
HE'S RIGGED THE WHOLE BASILICA TO *CRUSH* INTRUDERS!
KLANK KLANK KLANK
KLANK KLANK KLANK
I THOUGHT THIS ENTIRE PUZZLE WAS TAILOR-MADE FOR YOU!
WELL THEN HE SHOULD'VE GIVEN ME THE ANSWERS!!
M-MOSES IS FLANKED BY A FIGURE-- *"GOOD WORKS,"* REPRESENTED BY *LAURELS--*
--AND A TORCH TO REPRESENT THE MORE IMPORTANT *"FAITH"--*
LOOK! THERE'S A TORCH HERE!
I'LL *TRY* IT--
NO!
FORGIVE ME, MA'AM...
...BUT I AM FAIRLY CERTAIN YOU ARE MISTAKEN.

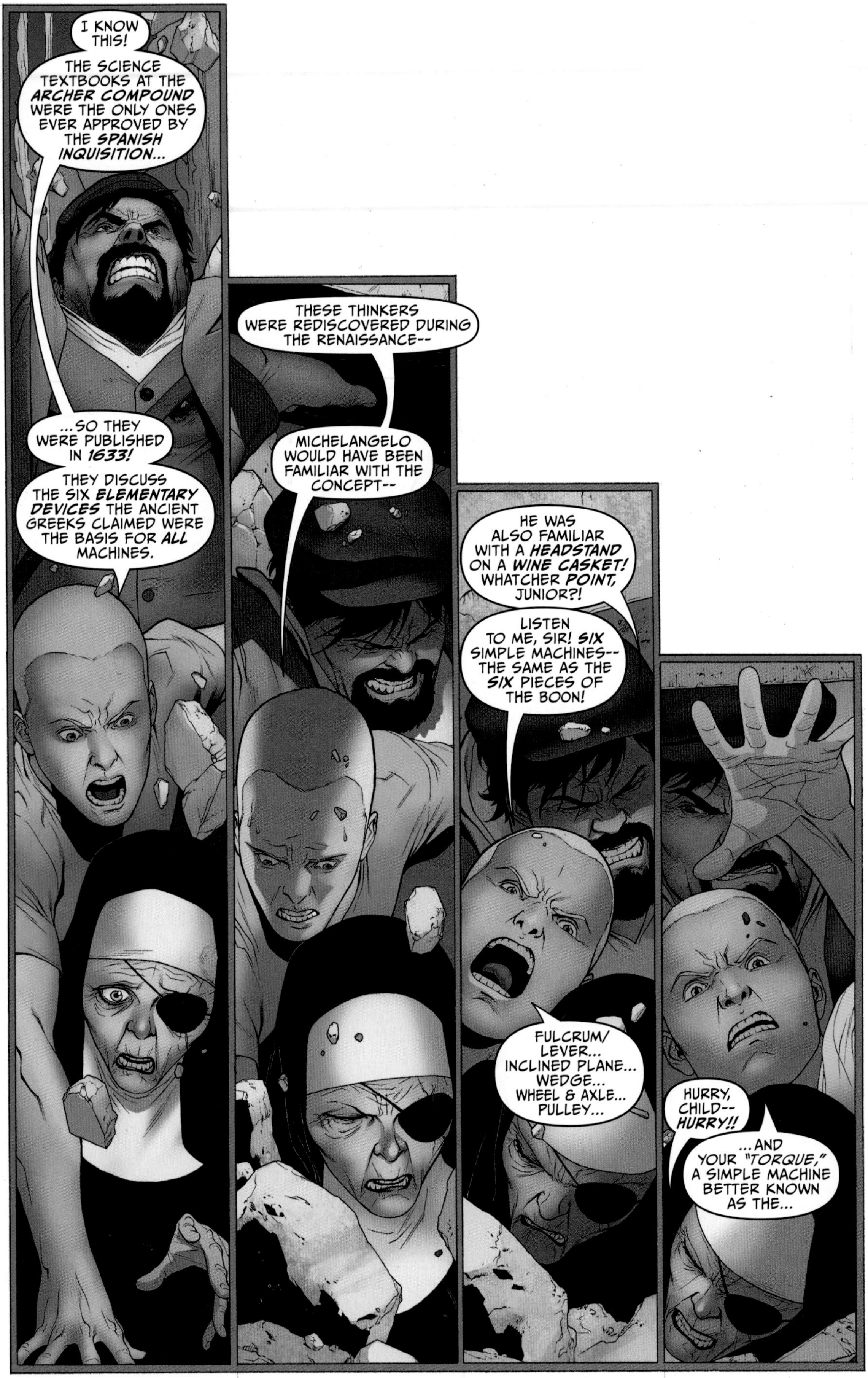
I KNOW THIS!
THE SCIENCE TEXTBOOKS AT THE ARCHER COMPOUND WERE THE ONLY ONES EVER APPROVED BY THE SPANISH INQUISITION...
...SO THEY WERE PUBLISHED IN 1633!
THEY DISCUSS THE SIX ELEMENTARY DEVICES THE ANCIENT GREEKS CLAIMED WERE THE BASIS FOR ALL MACHINES.
THESE THINKERS WERE REDISCOVERED DURING THE RENAISSANCE--
MICHELANGELO WOULD HAVE BEEN FAMILIAR WITH THE CONCEPT--
HE WAS ALSO FAMILIAR WITH A HEADSTAND ON A WINE CASKET! WHATCHER POINT, JUNIOR?!
LISTEN TO ME, SIR! SIX SIMPLE MACHINES-- THE SAME AS THE SIX PIECES OF THE BOON!
FULCRUM/ LEVER... INCLINED PLANE... WEDGE... WHEEL & AXLE... PULLEY...
HURRY, CHILD-- HURRY!!
...AND YOUR "TORQUE," A SIMPLE MACHINE BETTER KNOWN AS THE...

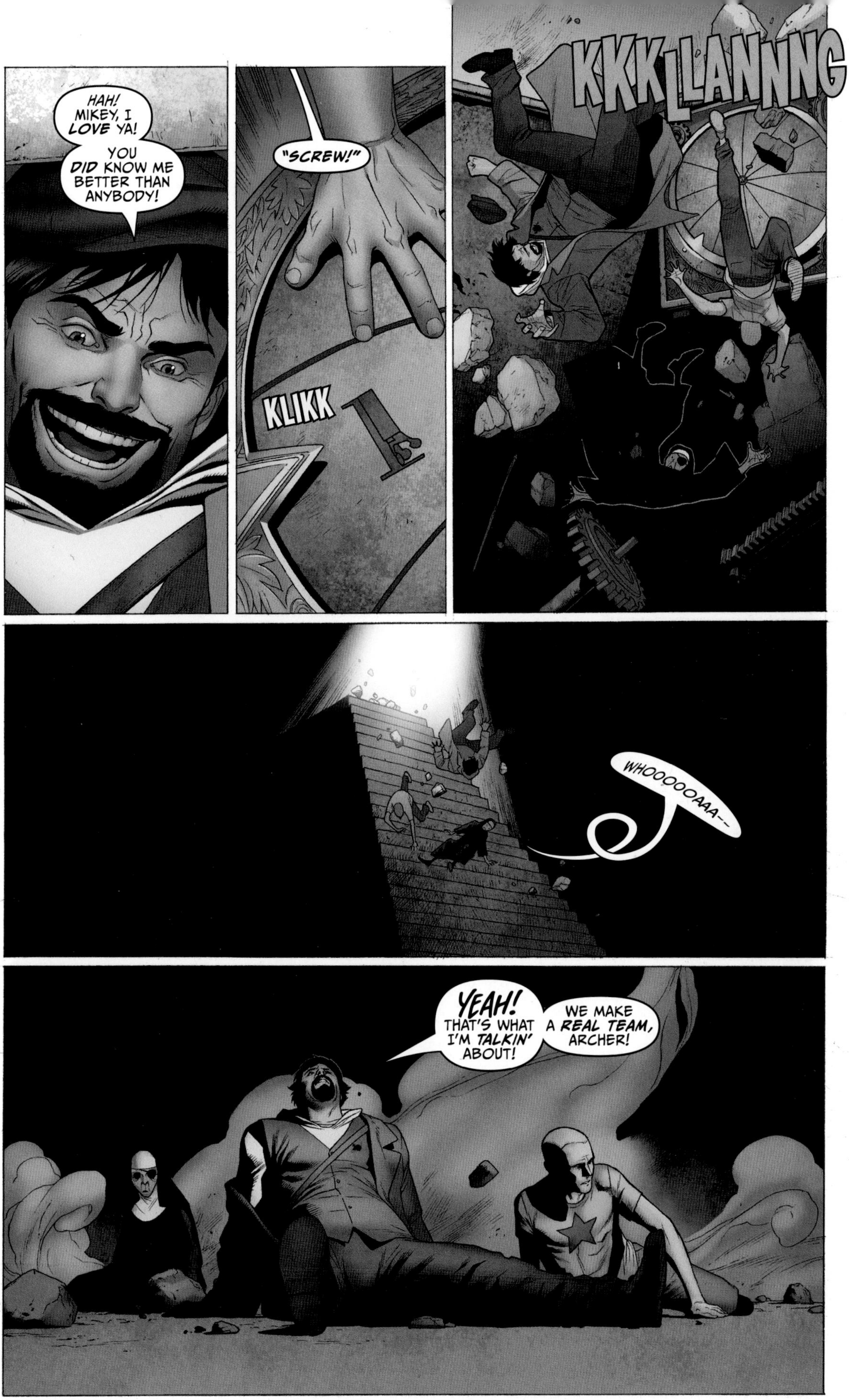
HAH! MIKEY, I LOVE YA!
YOU DID KNOW ME BETTER THAN ANYBODY!
"SCREW!"
KLIKK
KKKLLANNNG
WHOOOOOAAA--
YEAH! THAT'S WHAT I'M TALKIN' ABOUT!
WE MAKE A REAL TEAM, ARCHER!

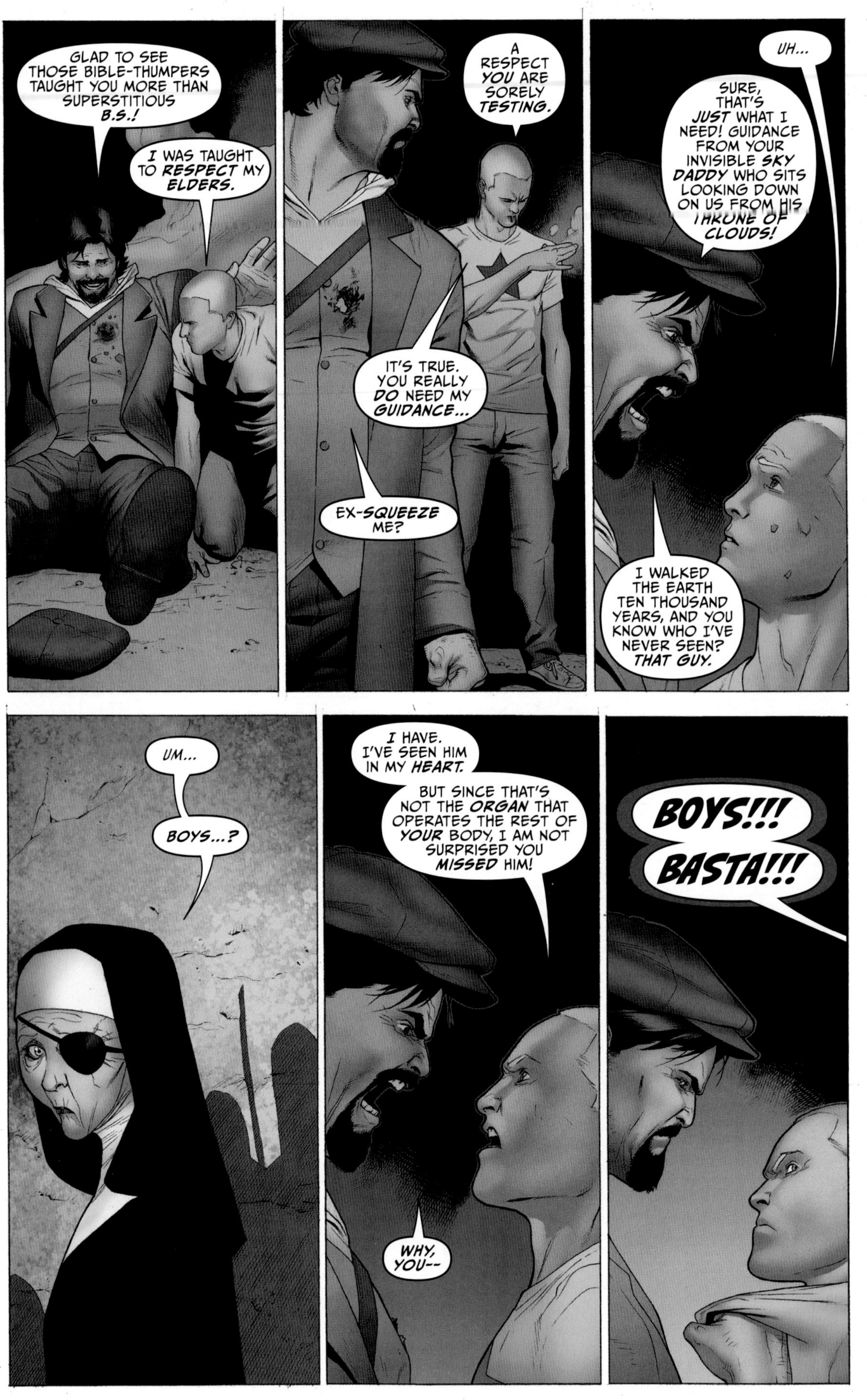
GLAD TO SEE THOSE BIBLE-THUMPERS TAUGHT YOU MORE THAN SUPERSTITIOUS B.S.!
I WAS TAUGHT TO RESPECT MY ELDERS.
A RESPECT YOU ARE SORELY TESTING.
IT'S TRUE. YOU REALLY DO NEED MY GUIDANCE...
EX-SQUEEZE ME?
UH...
SURE, THAT'S JUST WHAT I NEED! GUIDANCE FROM YOUR INVISIBLE SKY DADDY WHO SITS LOOKING DOWN ON US FROM HIS THRONE OF CLOUDS!
I WALKED THE EARTH TEN THOUSAND YEARS, AND YOU KNOW WHO I'VE NEVER SEEN? THAT GUY.
UM...
BOYS...?
I HAVE. I'VE SEEN HIM IN MY HEART.
BUT SINCE THAT'S NOT THE ORGAN THAT OPERATES THE REST OF YOUR BODY, I AM NOT SURPRISED YOU MISSED HIM!
WHY, YOU--
BOYS!!! BASTA!!!

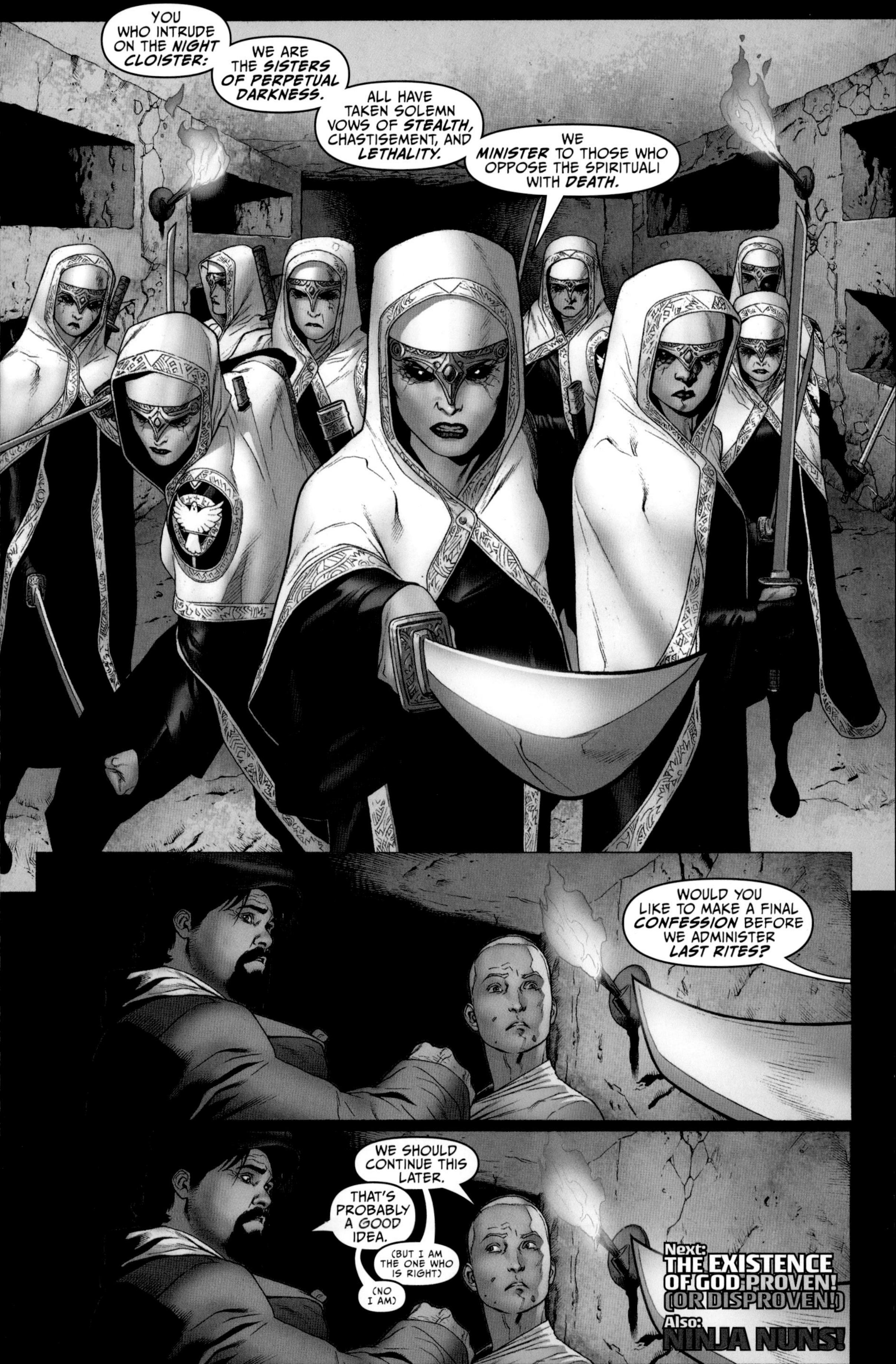
YOU WHO INTRUDE ON THE NIGHT CLOISTER:
WE ARE THE SISTERS OF PERPETUAL DARKNESS.
ALL HAVE TAKEN SOLEMN VOWS OF STEALTH, CHASTISEMENT, AND LETHALITY.
WE MINISTER TO THOSE WHO OPPOSE THE SPIRITUALI WITH DEATH.
WOULD YOU LIKE TO MAKE A FINAL CONFESSION BEFORE WE ADMINISTER LAST RITES?
WE SHOULD CONTINUE THIS LATER.
THAT'S PROBABLY A GOOD IDEA.
(BUT I AM THE ONE WHO IS RIGHT)
(NO I AM)
Next: THE EXISTENCE OF GOD PROVEN! (OR DISPROVEN!)
Also: NINJA NUNS!

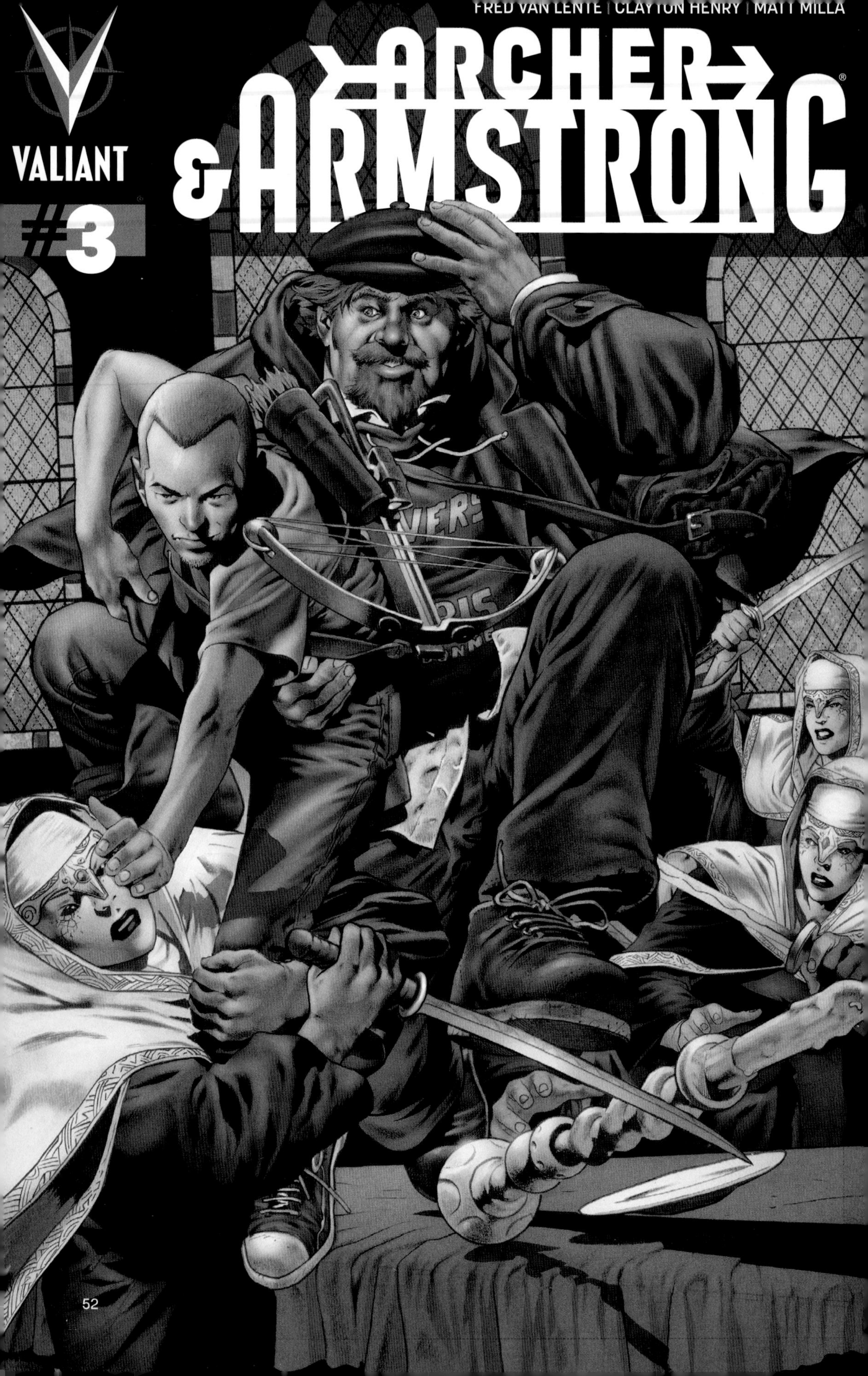
FRED VAN LENTE | CLAYTON HENRY | MATT MILLA
VALIANT
#3
ARCHER
& ARMSTRONG

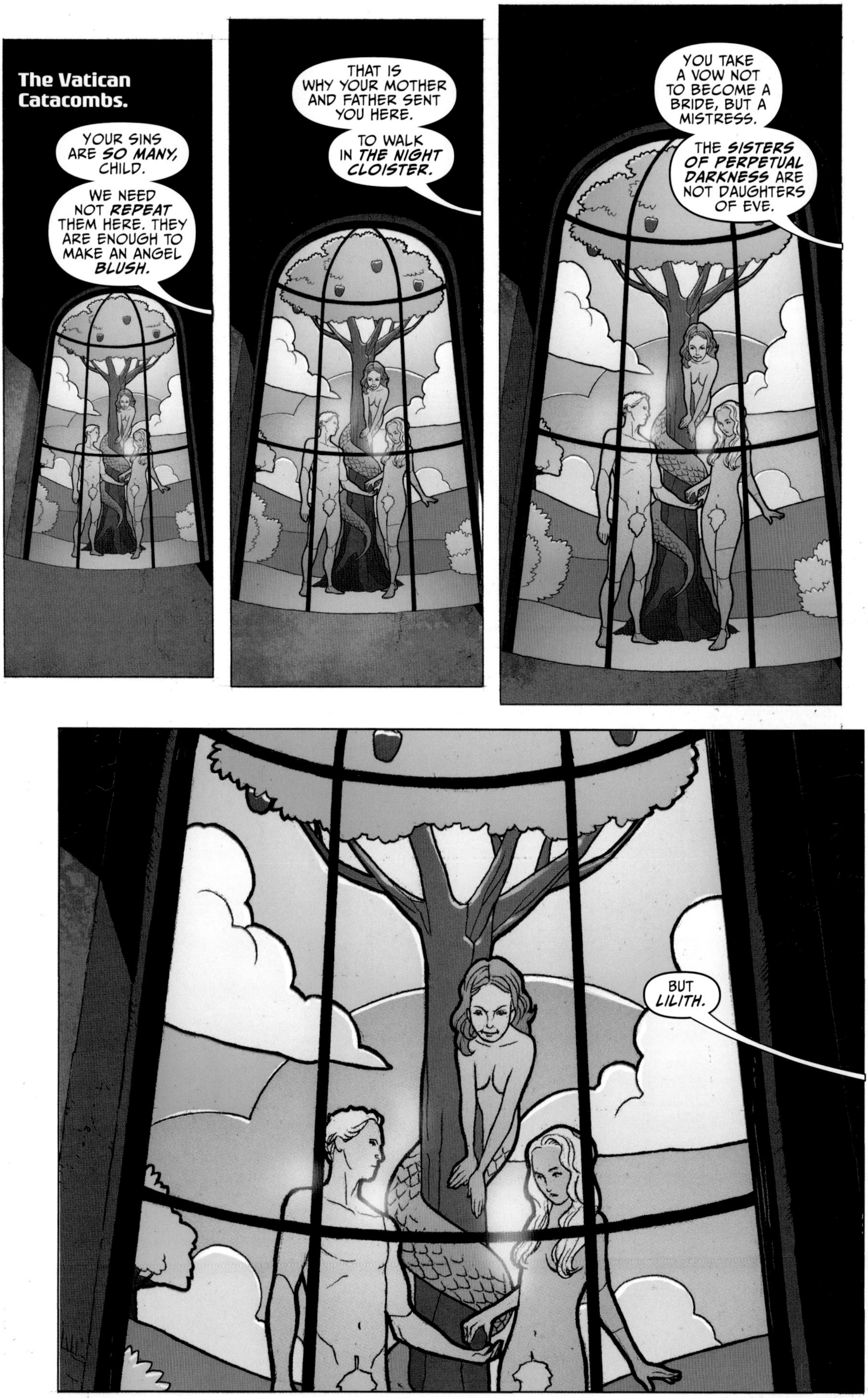
The Vatican Catacombs.
YOUR SINS ARE SO MANY, CHILD.
WE NEED NOT REPEAT THEM HERE. THEY ARE ENOUGH TO MAKE AN ANGEL BLUSH.
THAT IS WHY YOUR MOTHER AND FATHER SENT YOU HERE.
TO WALK IN THE NIGHT CLOISTER.
YOU TAKE A VOW NOT TO BECOME A BRIDE, BUT A MISTRESS.
THE SISTERS OF PERPETUAL DARKNESS ARE NOT DAUGHTERS OF EVE.
BUT LILITH.

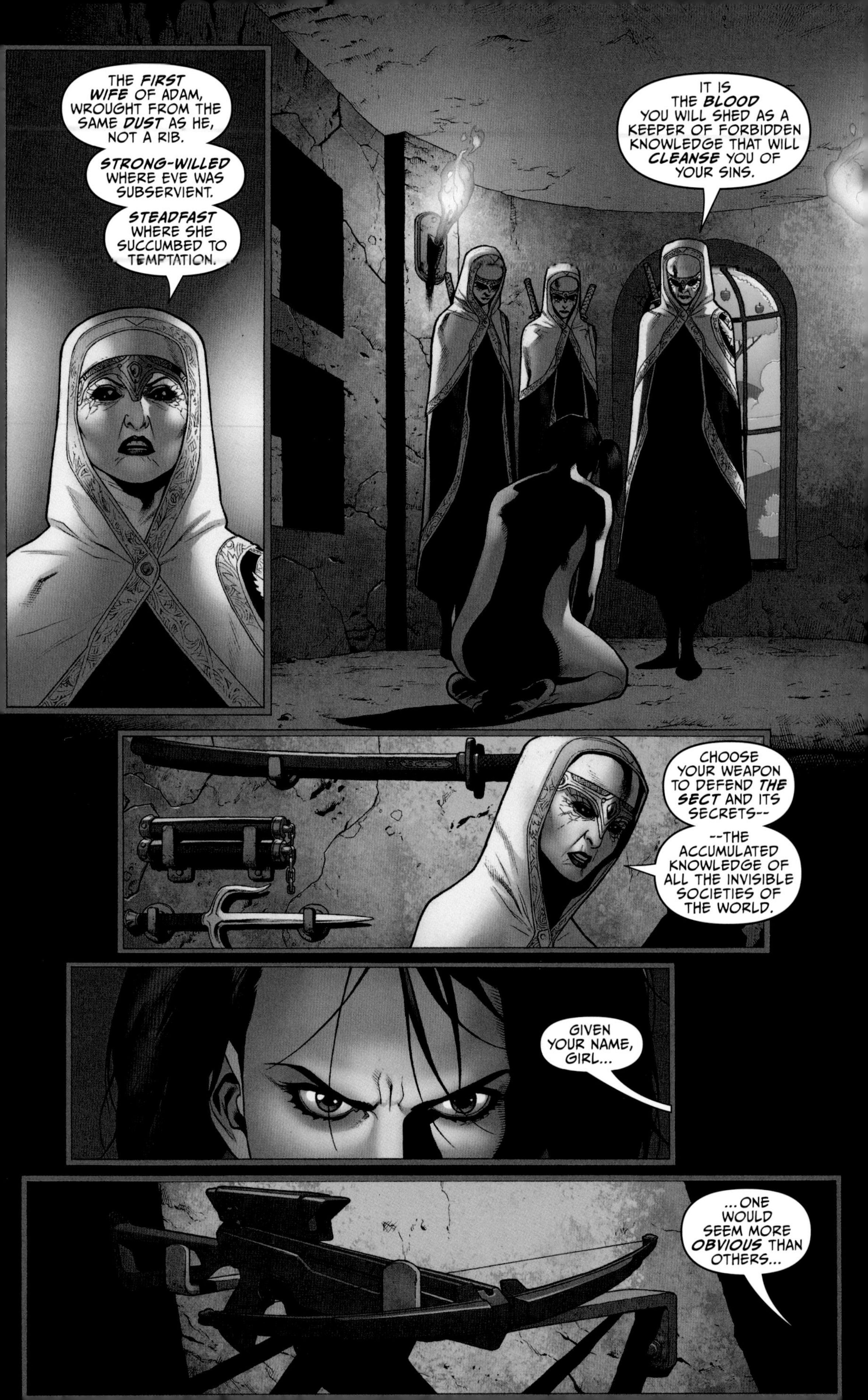
THE FIRST WIFE OF ADAM, WROUGHT FROM THE SAME DUST AS HE, NOT A RIB.
STRONG-WILLED WHERE EVE WAS SUBSERVIENT.
STEADFAST WHERE SHE SUCCUMBED TO TEMPTATION.
IT IS THE BLOOD YOU WILL SHED AS A KEEPER OF FORBIDDEN KNOWLEDGE THAT WILL CLEANSE YOU OF YOUR SINS.
CHOOSE YOUR WEAPON TO DEFEND THE SECT AND ITS SECRETS--
--THE ACCUMULATED KNOWLEDGE OF ALL THE INVISIBLE SOCIETIES OF THE WORLD.
GIVEN YOUR NAME, GIRL...
...ONE WOULD SEEM MORE OBVIOUS THAN OTHERS...

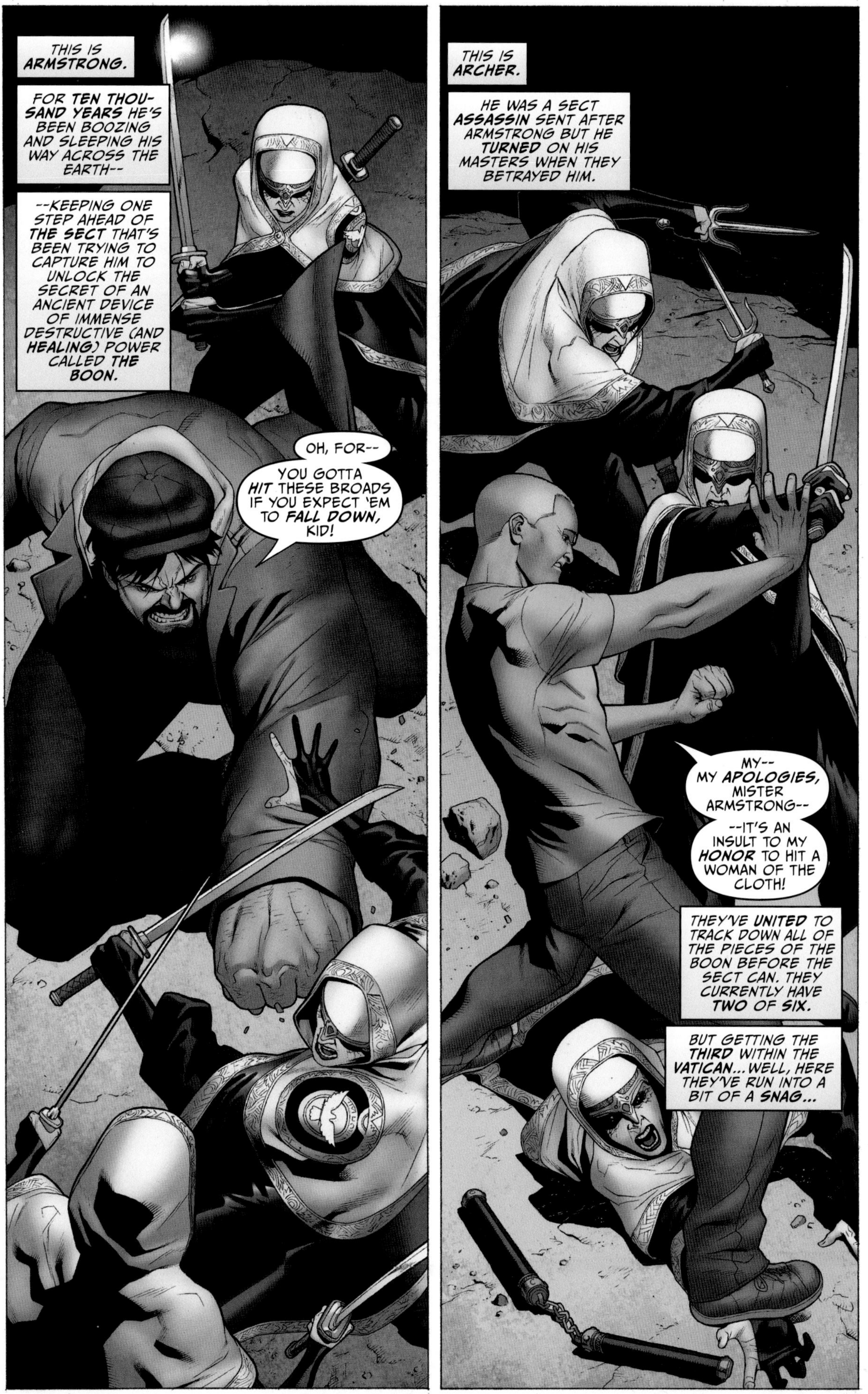
THIS IS ARMSTRONG.
FOR TEN THOUSAND YEARS HE'S BEEN BOOZING AND SLEEPING HIS WAY ACROSS THE EARTH--
--KEEPING ONE STEP AHEAD OF THE SECT THAT'S BEEN TRYING TO CAPTURE HIM TO UNLOCK THE SECRET OF AN ANCIENT DEVICE OF IMMENSE DESTRUCTIVE (AND HEALING) POWER CALLED THE BOON.
OH, FOR--
YOU GOTTA HIT THESE BROADS IF YOU EXPECT 'EM TO FALL DOWN, KID!
THIS IS ARCHER.
HE WAS A SECT ASSASSIN SENT AFTER ARMSTRONG BUT HE TURNED ON HIS MASTERS WHEN THEY BETRAYED HIM.
MY-- MY APOLOGIES, MISTER ARMSTRONG--
--IT'S AN INSULT TO MY HONOR TO HIT A WOMAN OF THE CLOTH!
THEY'VE UNITED TO TRACK DOWN ALL OF THE PIECES OF THE BOON BEFORE THE SECT CAN. THEY CURRENTLY HAVE TWO OF SIX.
BUT GETTING THE THIRD WITHIN THE VATICAN...WELL, HERE THEY'VE RUN INTO A BIT OF A SNAG...

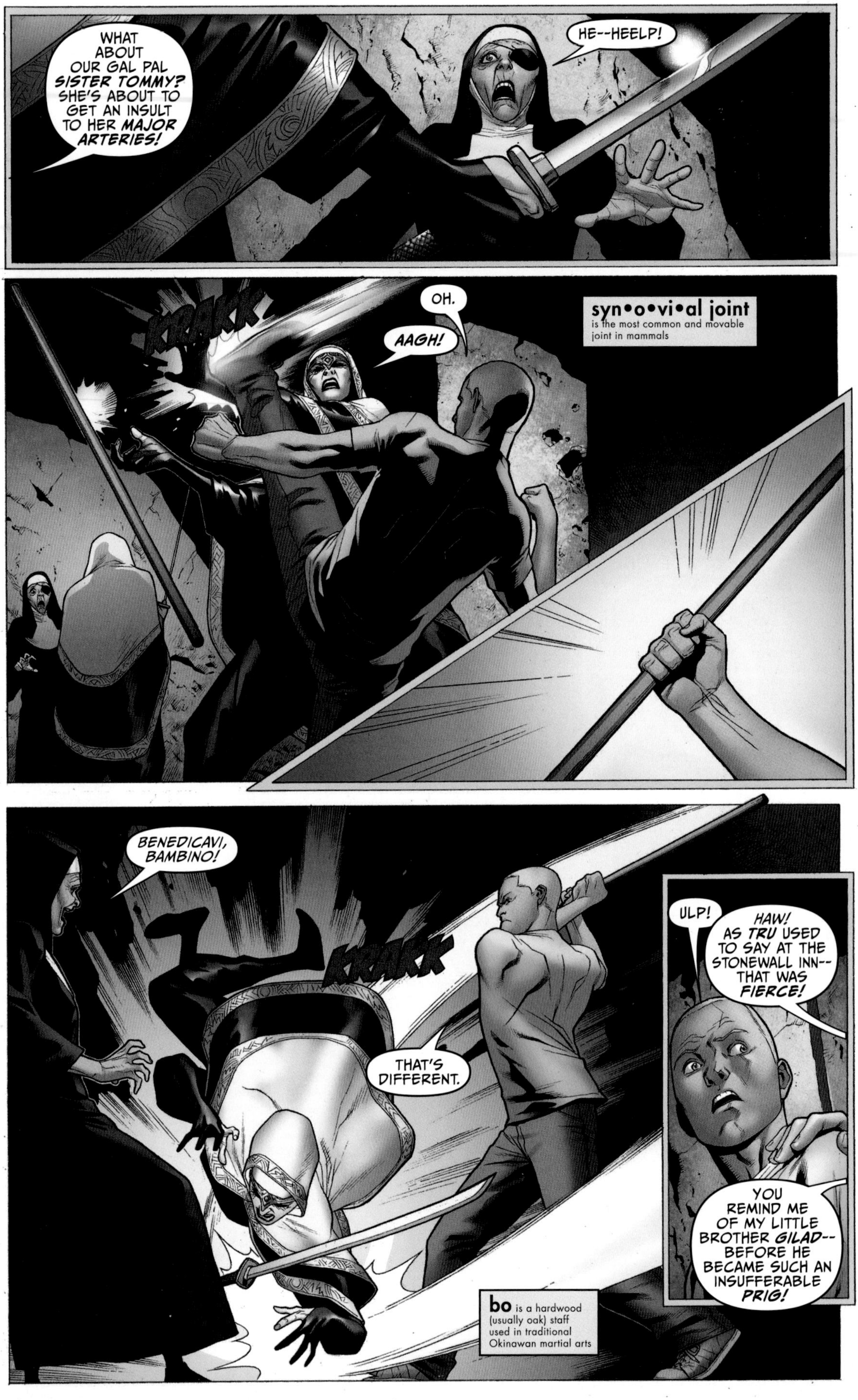

WHAT ABOUT OUR GAL PAL SISTER TOMMY? SHE'S ABOUT TO GET AN INSULT TO HER MAJOR ARTERIES!
HE--HEELP!
KRAKK
OH.
AAGH!
syn•o•vi•al joint
is the most common and movable joint in mammals
BENEDICAVI, BAMBINO!
KRAKK
THAT'S DIFFERENT.
ULP!
HAW! AS TRU USED TO SAY AT THE STONEWALL INN-- THAT WAS FIERCE!
YOU REMIND ME OF MY LITTLE BROTHER GILAD-- BEFORE HE BECAME SUCH AN INSUFFERABLE PRIG!
bo is a hardwood (usually oak) staff used in traditional Okinawan martial arts

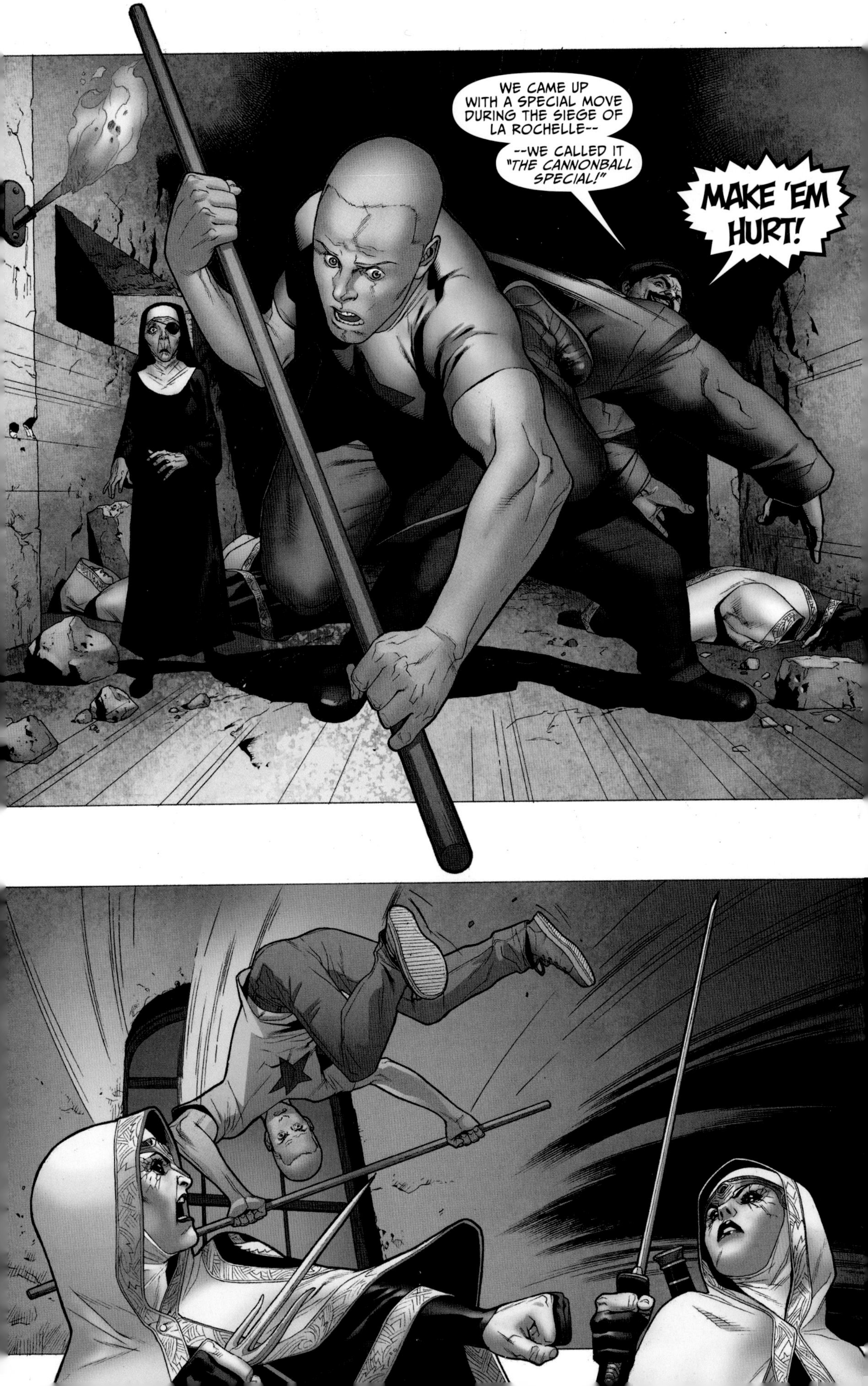
WE CAME UP WITH A SPECIAL MOVE DURING THE SIEGE OF LA ROCHELLE--
--WE CALLED IT "THE CANNONBALL SPECIAL!"
MAKE 'EM HURT!

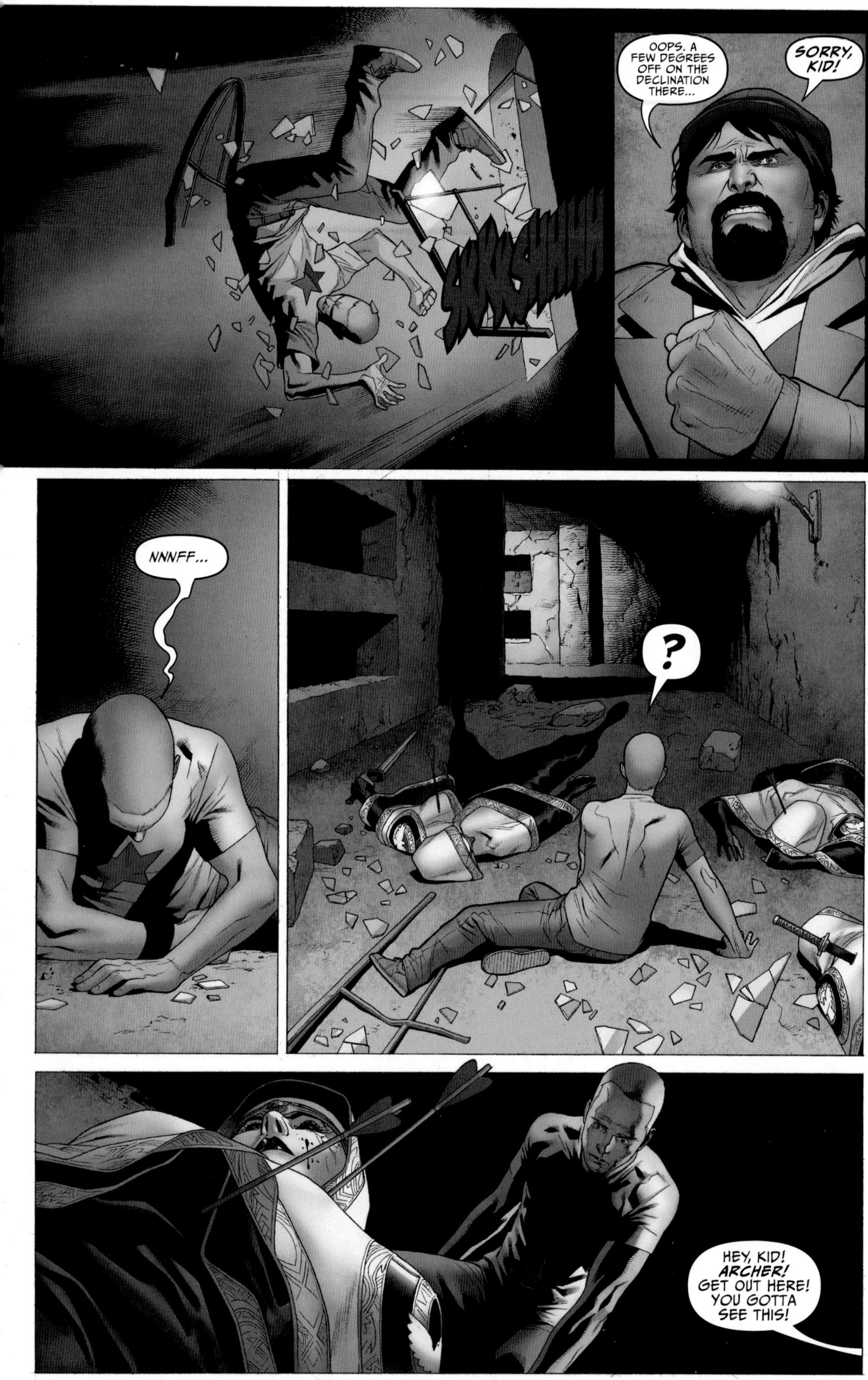
OOPS. A FEW DEGREES OFF ON THE DECLINATION THERE...
SORRY, KID!
NNNFF...
?
HEY, KID! ARCHER! GET OUT HERE! YOU GOTTA SEE THIS!

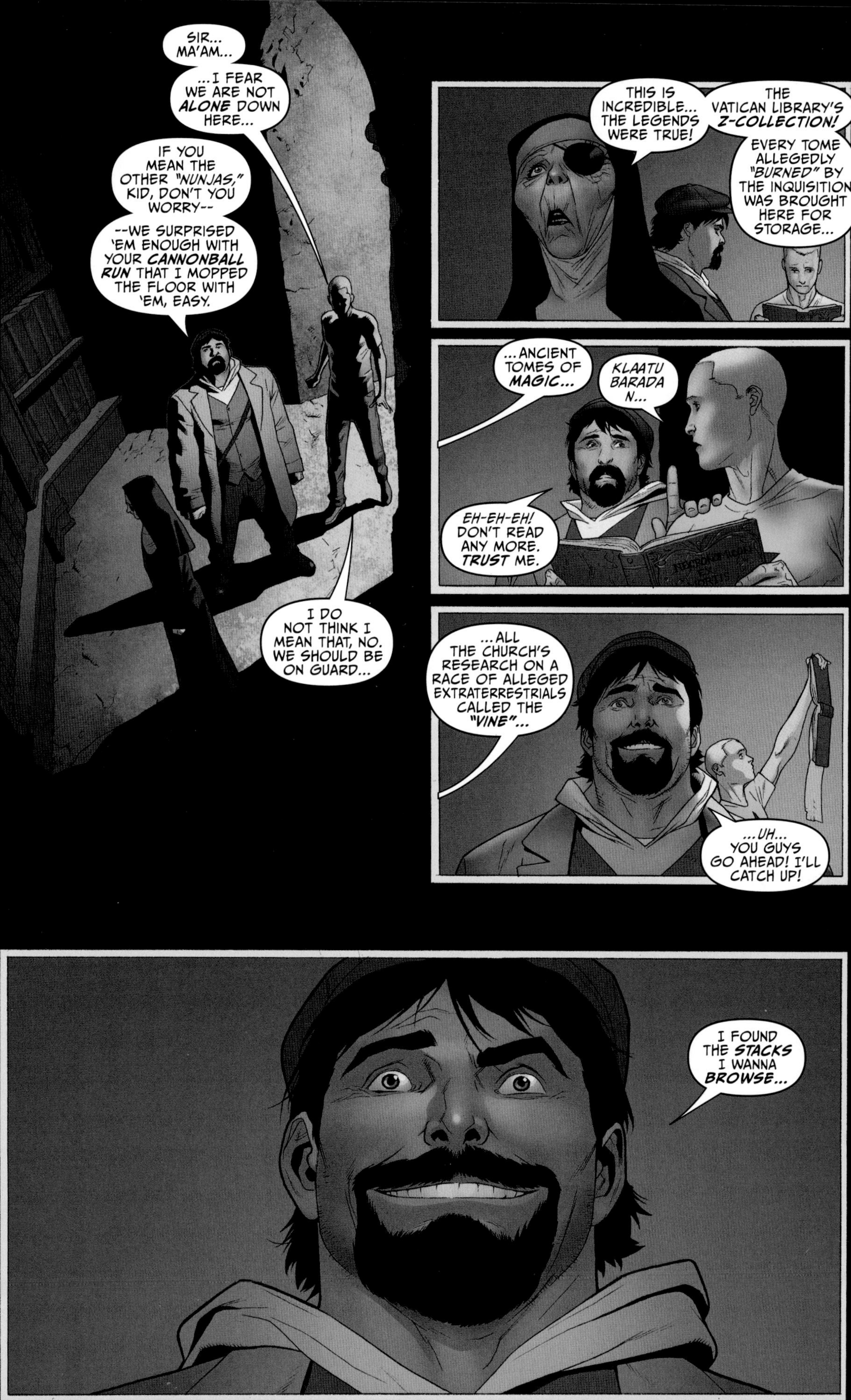
SIR... MA'AM...
...I FEAR WE ARE NOT ALONE DOWN HERE...
IF YOU MEAN THE OTHER "NUNJAS," KID, DON'T YOU WORRY--
--WE SURPRISED 'EM ENOUGH WITH YOUR CANNONBALL RUN THAT I MOPPED THE FLOOR WITH 'EM, EASY.
I DO NOT THINK I MEAN THAT, NO. WE SHOULD BE ON GUARD...
THIS IS INCREDIBLE... THE LEGENDS WERE TRUE!
THE VATICAN LIBRARY'S Z-COLLECTION!
EVERY TOME ALLEGEDLY "BURNED" BY THE INQUISITION WAS BROUGHT HERE FOR STORAGE...
...ANCIENT TOMES OF MAGIC...
KLAATU BARADA N...
EH-EH-EH! DON'T READ ANY MORE. TRUST ME.
...ALL THE CHURCH'S RESEARCH ON A RACE OF ALLEGED EXTRATERRESTRIALS CALLED THE "VINE"...
...UH... YOU GUYS GO AHEAD! I'LL CATCH UP!
I FOUND THE STACKS I WANNA BROWSE...

NO WAY! THEY'VE GOT A 1787 CHATEAU LAFITE-- *AND* A MONTRACHET 1978 FROM DOMAINE DE LA ROMANÉE-CONTI?

WHAT ARE THE *ODDS?!*

INFINE! THE SECT'S SECRETS ARE ALSO KEPT SAFE HERE...

...SUCH AS THESE SECRET PLANS FOR THE REMODELING OF THE VATICAN UNDER ONE OF THEIR MOST POWERFUL MEMBERS, *GIULIANO DELLA ROVERE...*

JUST *LOOK* AT THE COLOR ON THIS ROMANÉE-CONTI BURGUNDY...

THESE NINJA NUNS MAY BE *WACKOS,* BUT THEY KNOW HOW TO *LIVE...*

I REALLY *SHOULDN'T,* BUT... A *TASTE* COULDN'T HURT...*RIGHT?*

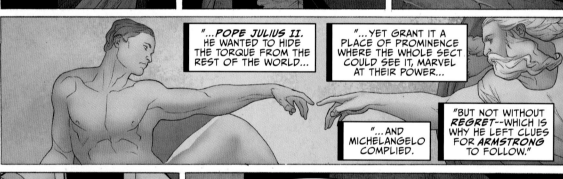

"...*POPE JULIUS II.* HE WANTED TO HIDE THE TORQUE FROM THE REST OF THE WORLD...

"...YET GRANT IT A PLACE OF PROMINENCE WHERE THE WHOLE SECT COULD SEE IT, MARVEL AT THEIR POWER...

"...AND MICHELANGELO COMPLIED.

"BUT NOT WITHOUT *REGRET*--WHICH IS WHY HE LEFT CLUES FOR *ARMSTRONG* TO FOLLOW."

GLUG GLUG GLUG GLUG GLUG

MISTER ARMSTRONG! SISTER THOMAS AQUINAS HAS DISCOVERED THE TORQUE'S HIDING PLACE! IT'S IN THE MOST OBVIOUS--

"OH KARMA, DHARMA, PUDDING AND PIE...≥HIC!≤

"GIMME A BREAK BEFORE I DIE... (SOMETHING, SOMETHING)

"AND BEFORE OUR WORLD GOES OVER THE BRINK...

"TEACH THE BELIEVERS HOW TO THINK!" HAW!

PHILIP APPLEMAN, YOU'RE THE GREATEST...

UH-OH. HE'S QUOTING POETRY.

HE ONLY DOES THAT WHEN HE'S REALLY DRUNK...

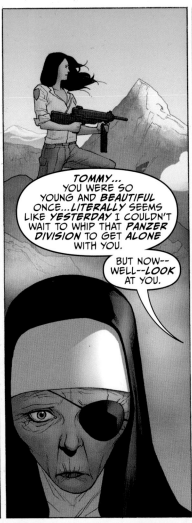

TOMMY... YOU WERE SO YOUNG AND BEAUTIFUL ONCE...LITERALLY SEEMS LIKE YESTERDAY I COULDN'T WAIT TO WHIP THAT PANZER DIVISION TO GET ALONE WITH YOU.

BUT NOW-- WELL--LOOK AT YOU.

SIR! THAT'S JUST RUDE.

IF YOU COULD SEE YOURSELVES THE WAY I DO...YOU WOULDN'T WASTE ALL YOUR TIME ON THIS "FAITH" NONSENSE!

YOU'D SEE HOW BEAUTIFUL THE WORLD IS ON ITS OWN WITHOUT BEING POLLUTED BY YOUR BELIEFS...

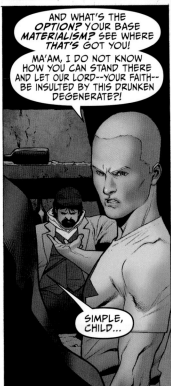

AND WHAT'S THE OPTION? YOUR BASE MATERIALISM? SEE WHERE THAT'S GOT YOU!

MA'AM, I DO NOT KNOW HOW YOU CAN STAND THERE AND LET OUR LORD--YOUR FAITH-- BE INSULTED BY THIS DRUNKEN DEGENERATE?!

SIMPLE, CHILD...

...MY FAITH IS NOT SO WEAK IT CAN BE THREATENED BY A DIFFERING OPINION.

OH, FLIP THIS! WE'RE ON A FLIPPING MISSION, HERE!

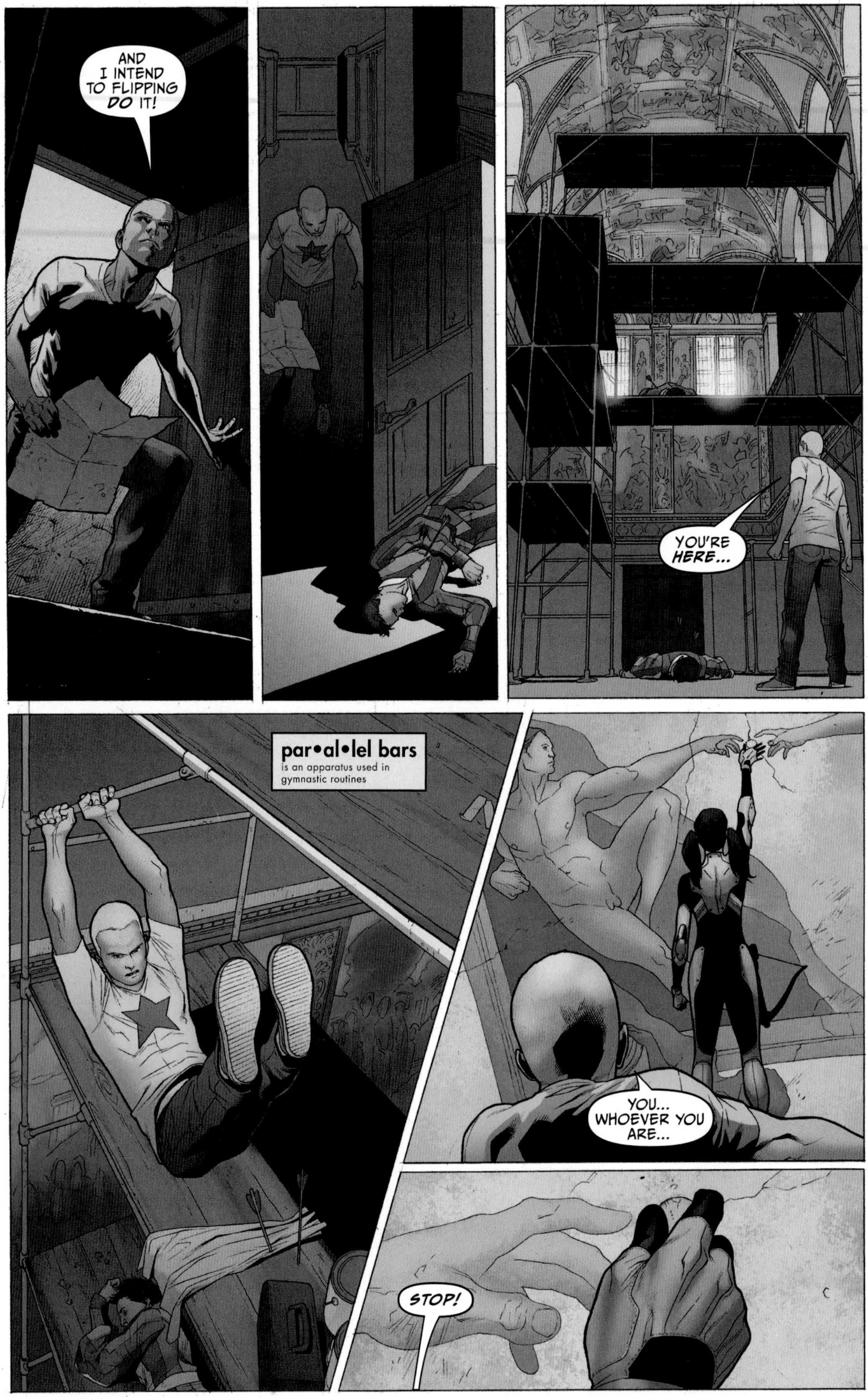
AND I INTEND TO FLIPPING DO IT!
YOU'RE HERE...
par•al•lel bars
is an apparatus used in gymnastic routines
YOU... WHOEVER YOU ARE...
STOP!

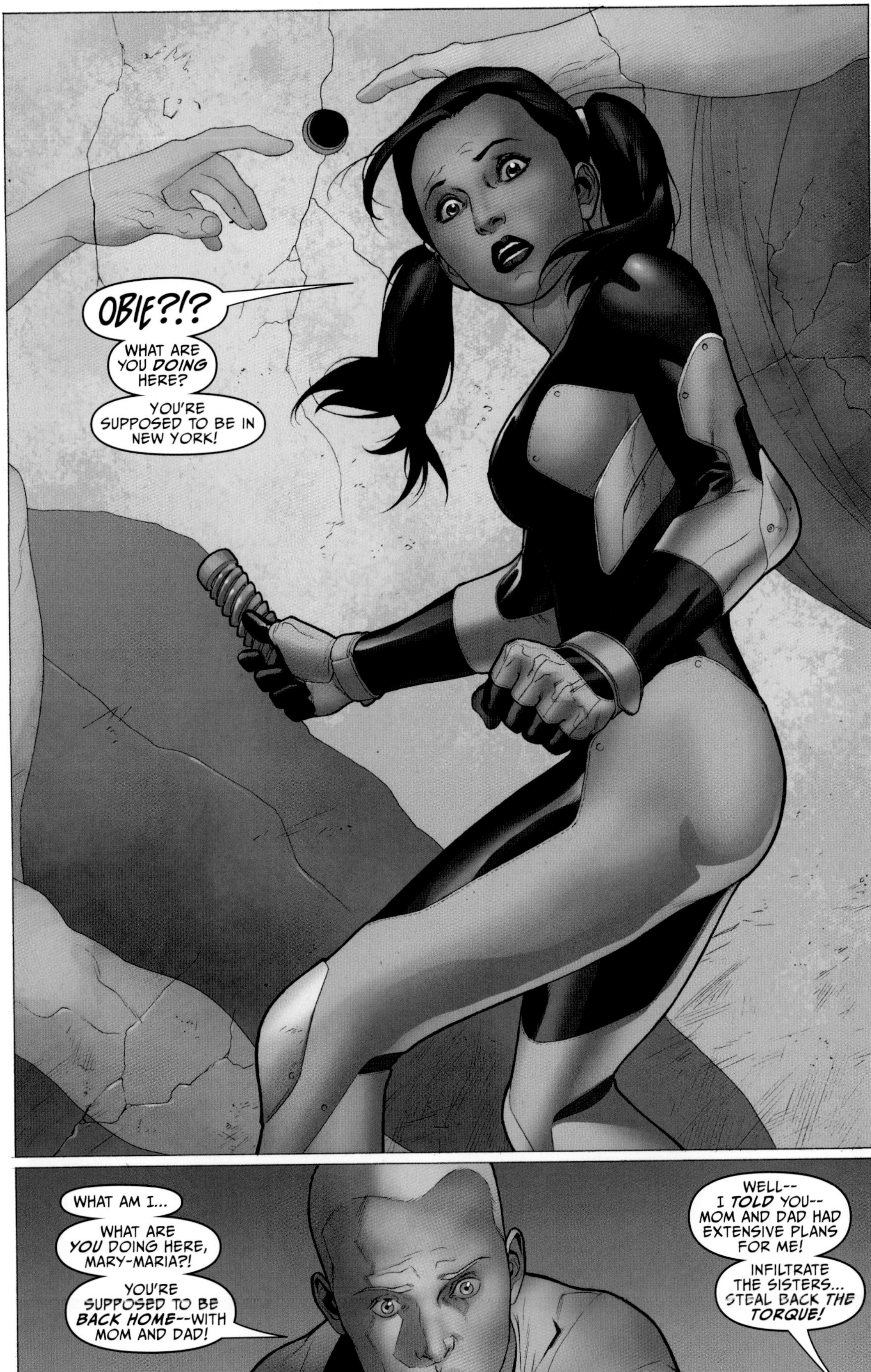
OBIE?!?
WHAT ARE YOU DOING HERE?
YOU'RE SUPPOSED TO BE IN NEW YORK!
WHAT AM I...
WHAT ARE YOU DOING HERE, MARY-MARIA?!
YOU'RE SUPPOSED TO BE BACK HOME--WITH MOM AND DAD!
WELL-- I TOLD YOU-- MOM AND DAD HAD EXTENSIVE PLANS FOR ME!
INFILTRATE THE SISTERS... STEAL BACK THE TORQUE!

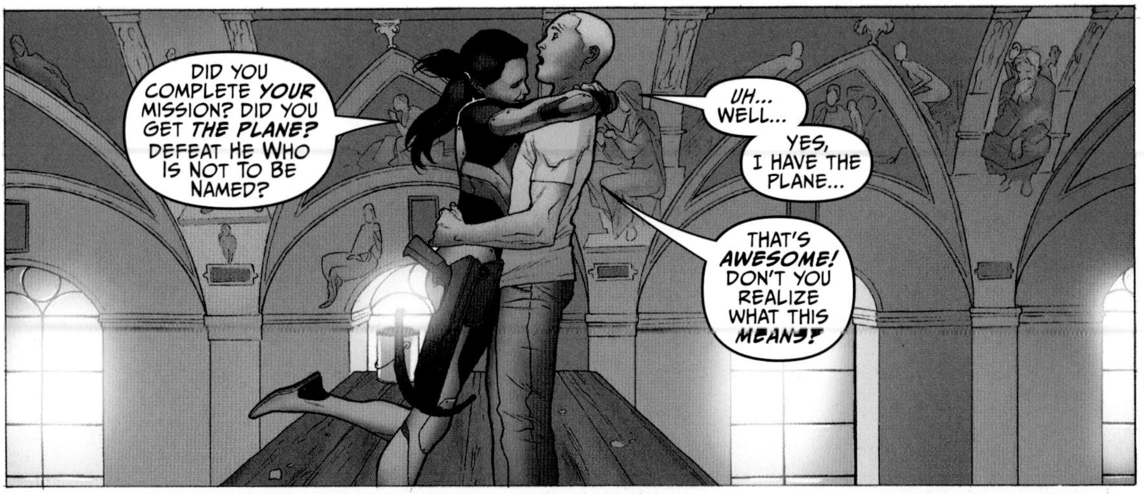
DID YOU COMPLETE YOUR MISSION? DID YOU GET THE PLANE? DEFEAT HE WHO IS NOT TO BE NAMED?
UH... WELL...
YES, I HAVE THE PLANE...
THAT'S AWESOME! DON'T YOU REALIZE WHAT THIS MEANS?!

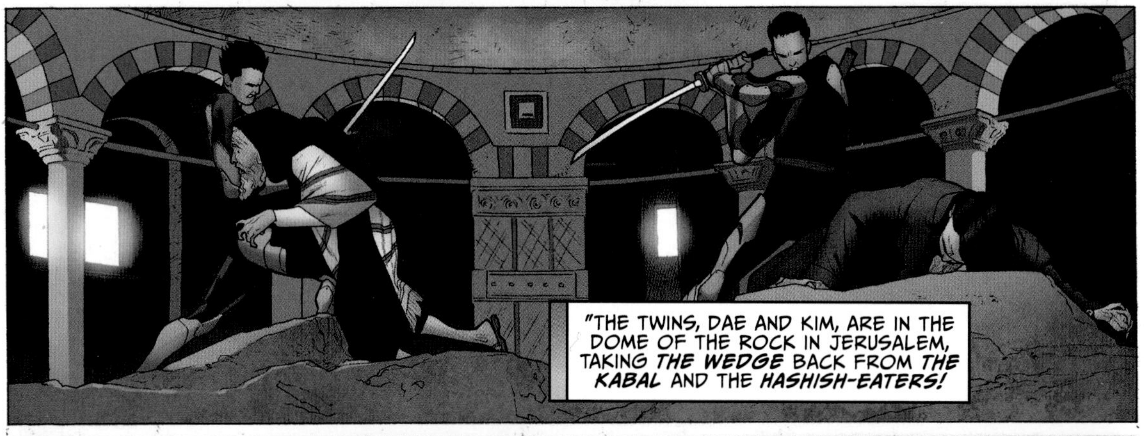
"THE TWINS, DAE AND KIM, ARE IN THE DOME OF THE ROCK IN JERUSALEM, TAKING THE WEDGE BACK FROM THE KABAL AND THE HASHISH-EATERS!

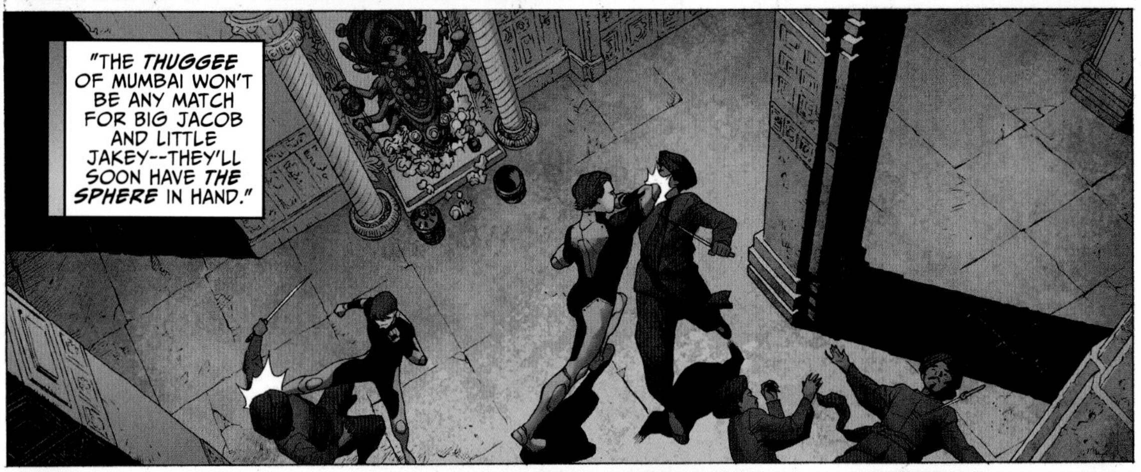
"THE THUGGEE OF MUMBAI WON'T BE ANY MATCH FOR BIG JACOB AND LITTLE JAKEY--THEY'LL SOON HAVE THE SPHERE IN HAND."

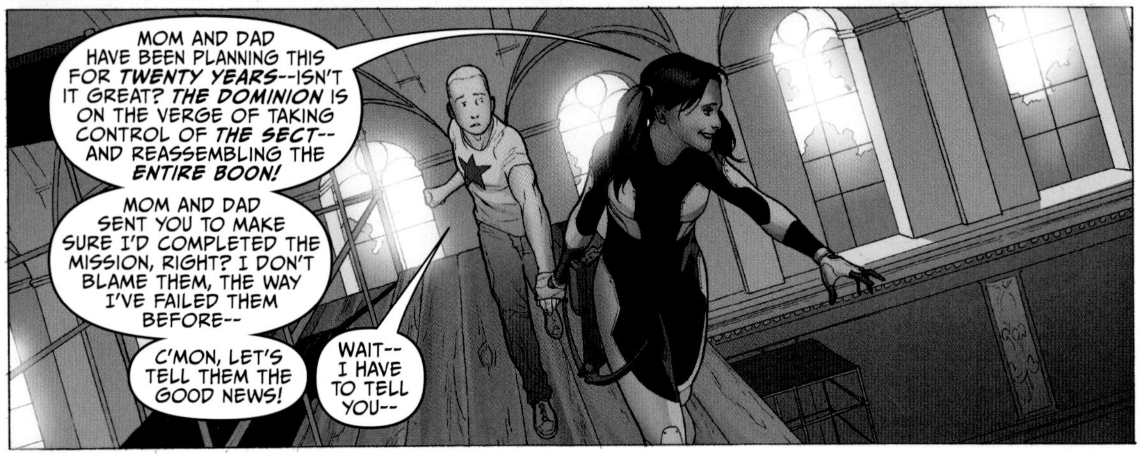
MOM AND DAD HAVE BEEN PLANNING THIS FOR TWENTY YEARS--ISN'T IT GREAT? THE DOMINION IS ON THE VERGE OF TAKING CONTROL OF THE SECT--AND REASSEMBLING THE ENTIRE BOON!
MOM AND DAD SENT YOU TO MAKE SURE I'D COMPLETED THE MISSION, RIGHT? I DON'T BLAME THEM, THE WAY I'VE FAILED THEM BEFORE--
C'MON, LET'S TELL THEM THE GOOD NEWS!
WAIT--I HAVE TO TELL YOU--

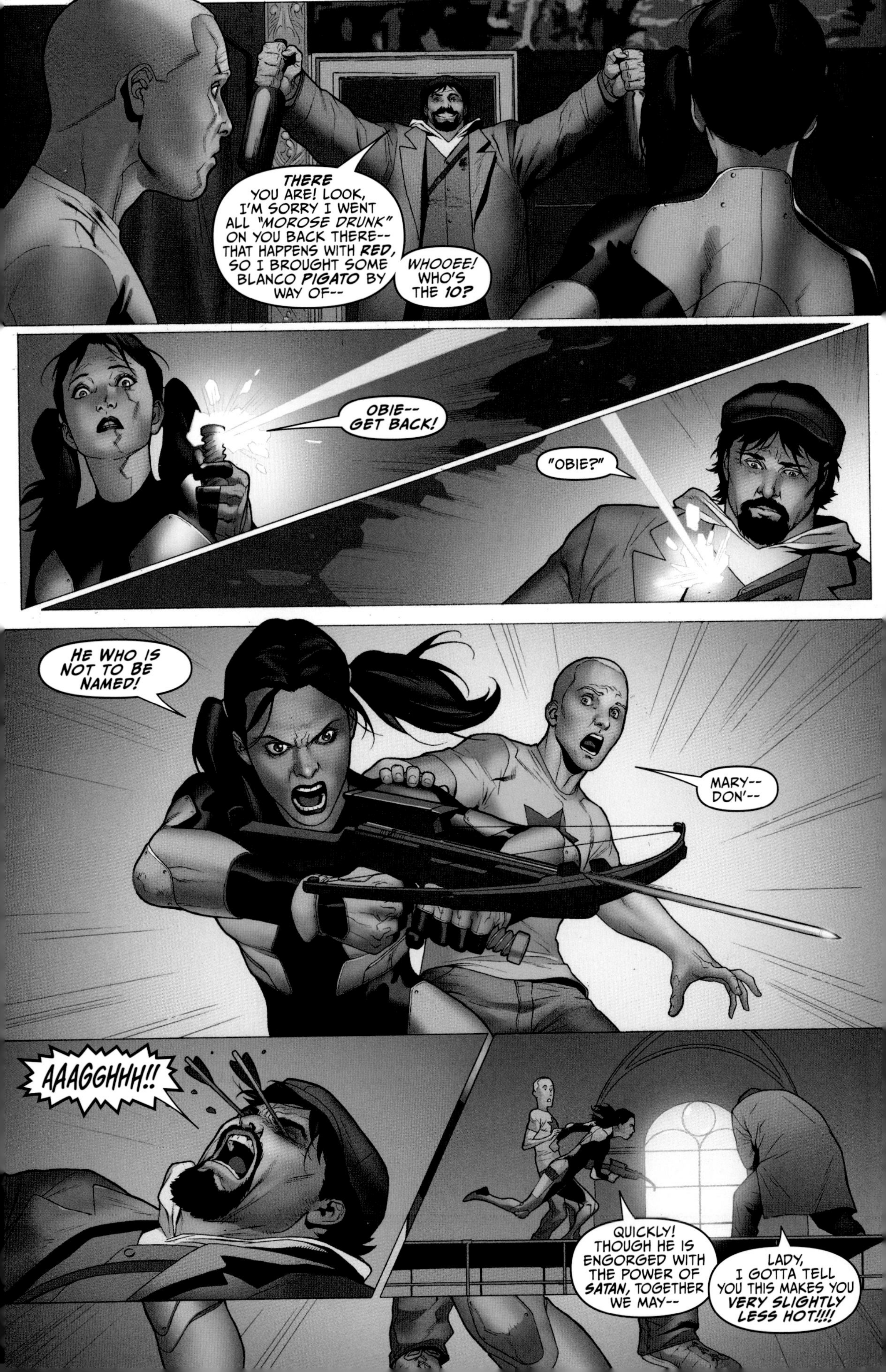
THERE YOU ARE! LOOK, I'M SORRY I WENT ALL "MOROSE DRUNK" ON YOU BACK THERE-- THAT HAPPENS WITH RED, SO I BROUGHT SOME BLANCO PIGATO BY WAY OF--
WHOOEE! WHO'S THE 10?
OBIE-- GET BACK!
"OBIE?"
HE WHO IS NOT TO BE NAMED!
MARY-- DON'--
AAAGGHHH!!
QUICKLY! THOUGH HE IS ENGORGED WITH THE POWER OF SATAN, TOGETHER WE MAY--
LADY, I GOTTA TELL YOU THIS MAKES YOU VERY SLIGHTLY LESS HOT!!!!

SISTER. NO.

WHAT? WHY NOT?

ARMSTRONG MAY BE A LOUT--AND A DRUNK--AND A BLASPHEMER--

HEY, I CAN STILL *HEAR* JUST FINE!!

BUT HE IS *NOT* EVIL.

RATHER... THOUGH THE WORDS ARE *ASHES* IN MY MOUTH...

...I MUST SAY IT IS OUR *PARENTS* WHO ARE.

WHAT... WHAT ARE YOU SAYING?

THEY'RE *USING* US. YOU, ME--*ALL* OUR BROTHERS AND SISTERS.

THEY DON'T CARE ABOUT US, OR THE *LORD*, OR JUSTICE.

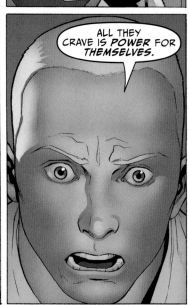

ALL THEY CRAVE IS *POWER* FOR *THEMSELVES.*

I HEARD IT WITH *MY OWN* EARS.

YOU *HAVE* TO BELIEVE ME.

OKAY. I SEE WHAT THE PROBLEM IS HERE.

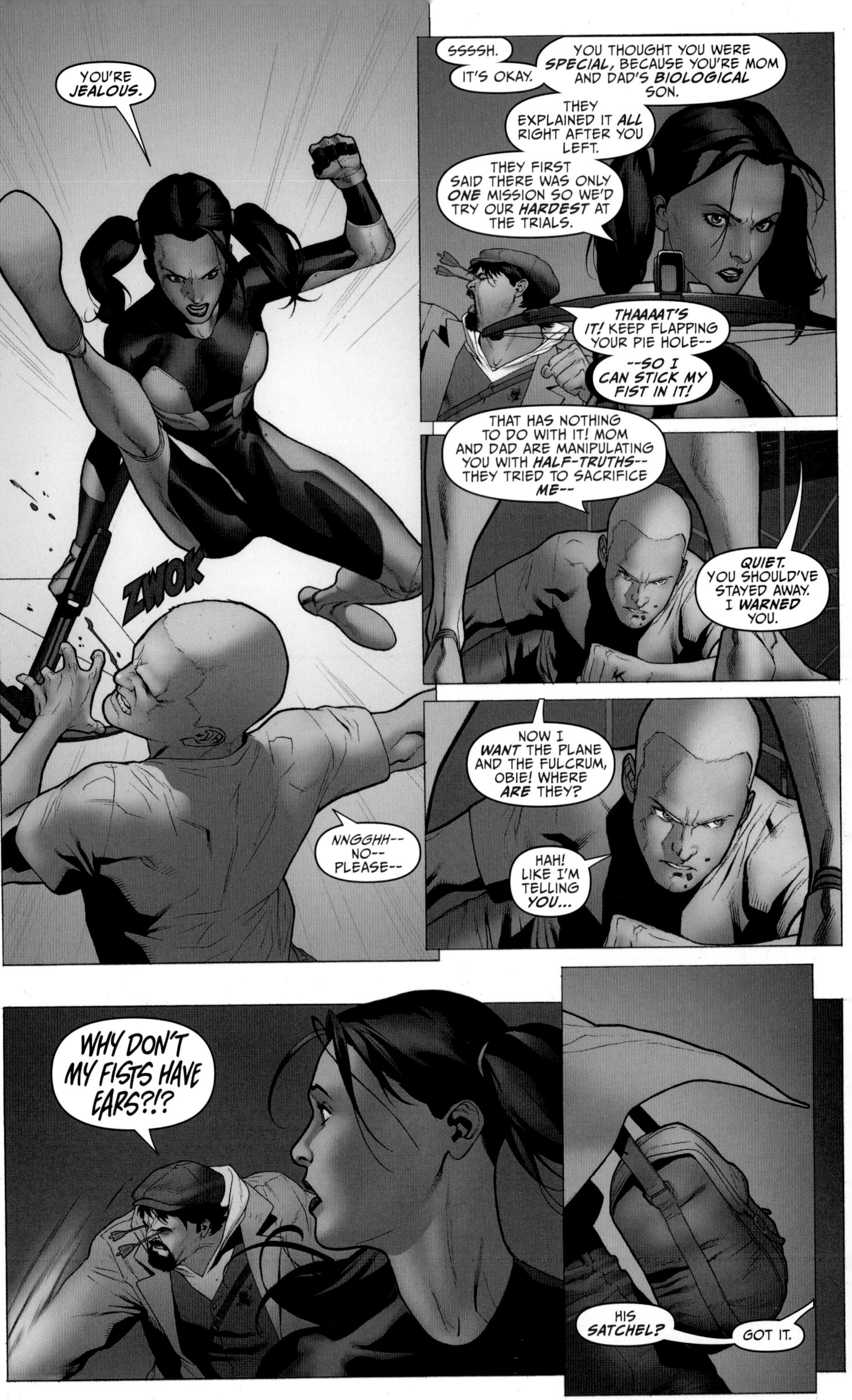
YOU'RE JEALOUS.
ZWOK
NNGGHH-- NO-- PLEASE--
SSSSH.
IT'S OKAY.
YOU THOUGHT YOU WERE SPECIAL, BECAUSE YOU'RE MOM AND DAD'S BIOLOGICAL SON.
THEY EXPLAINED IT ALL RIGHT AFTER YOU LEFT.
THEY FIRST SAID THERE WAS ONLY ONE MISSION SO WE'D TRY OUR HARDEST AT THE TRIALS.
THAAAAT'S IT! KEEP FLAPPING YOUR PIE HOLE--
--SO I CAN STICK MY FIST IN IT!
THAT HAS NOTHING TO DO WITH IT! MOM AND DAD ARE MANIPULATING YOU WITH HALF-TRUTHS-- THEY TRIED TO SACRIFICE ME--
QUIET. YOU SHOULD'VE STAYED AWAY. I WARNED YOU.
NOW I WANT THE PLANE AND THE FULCRUM, OBIE! WHERE ARE THEY?
HAH! LIKE I'M TELLING YOU...
WHY DON'T MY FISTS HAVE EARS?!?
HIS SATCHEL?
GOT IT.

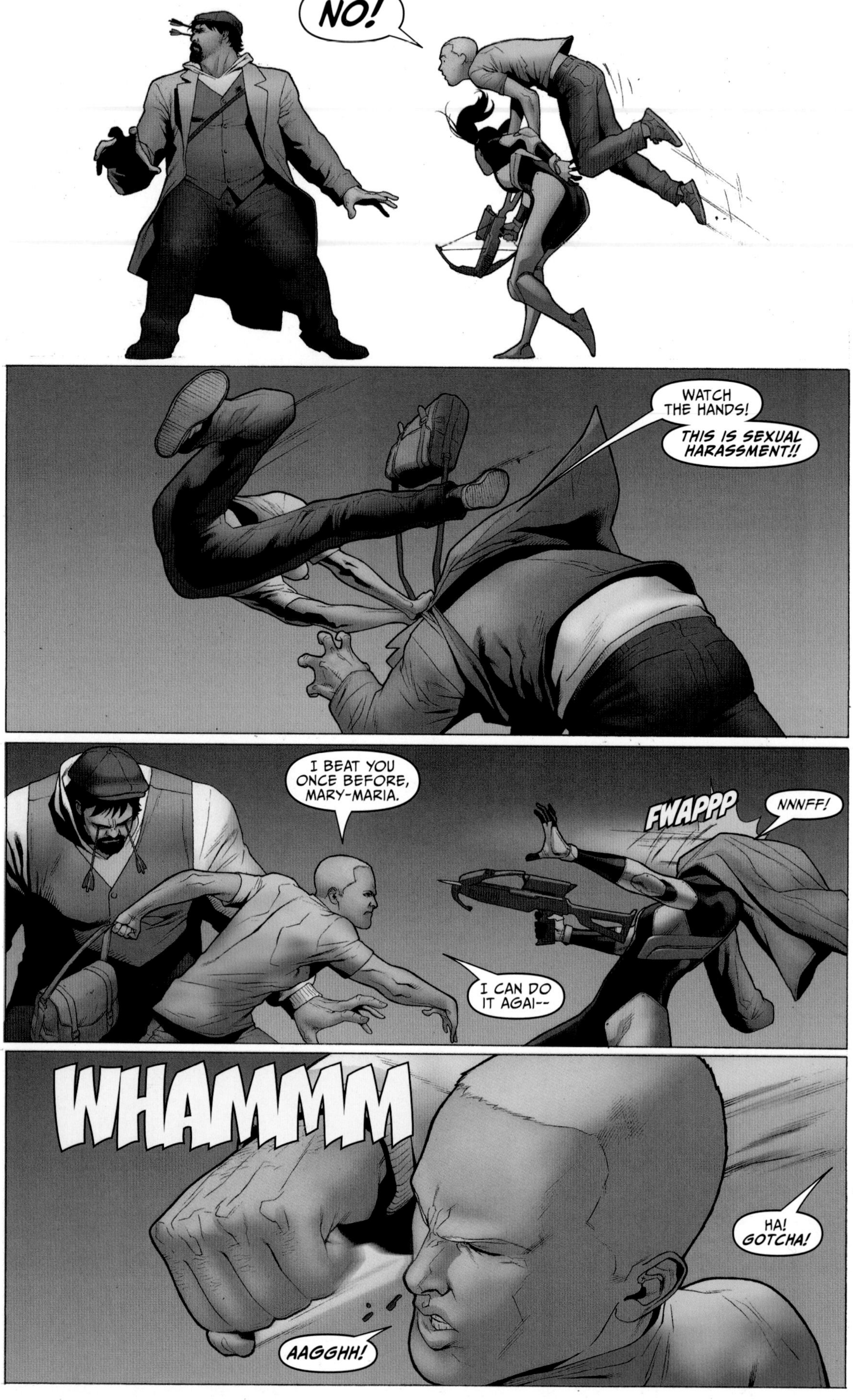
NO!
WATCH THE HANDS!
THIS IS SEXUAL HARASSMENT!!
I BEAT YOU ONCE BEFORE, MARY-MARIA.
FWAPPP
NNNFF!
I CAN DO IT AGAI--
WHAMMM
HA! GOTCHA!
AAGGHH!

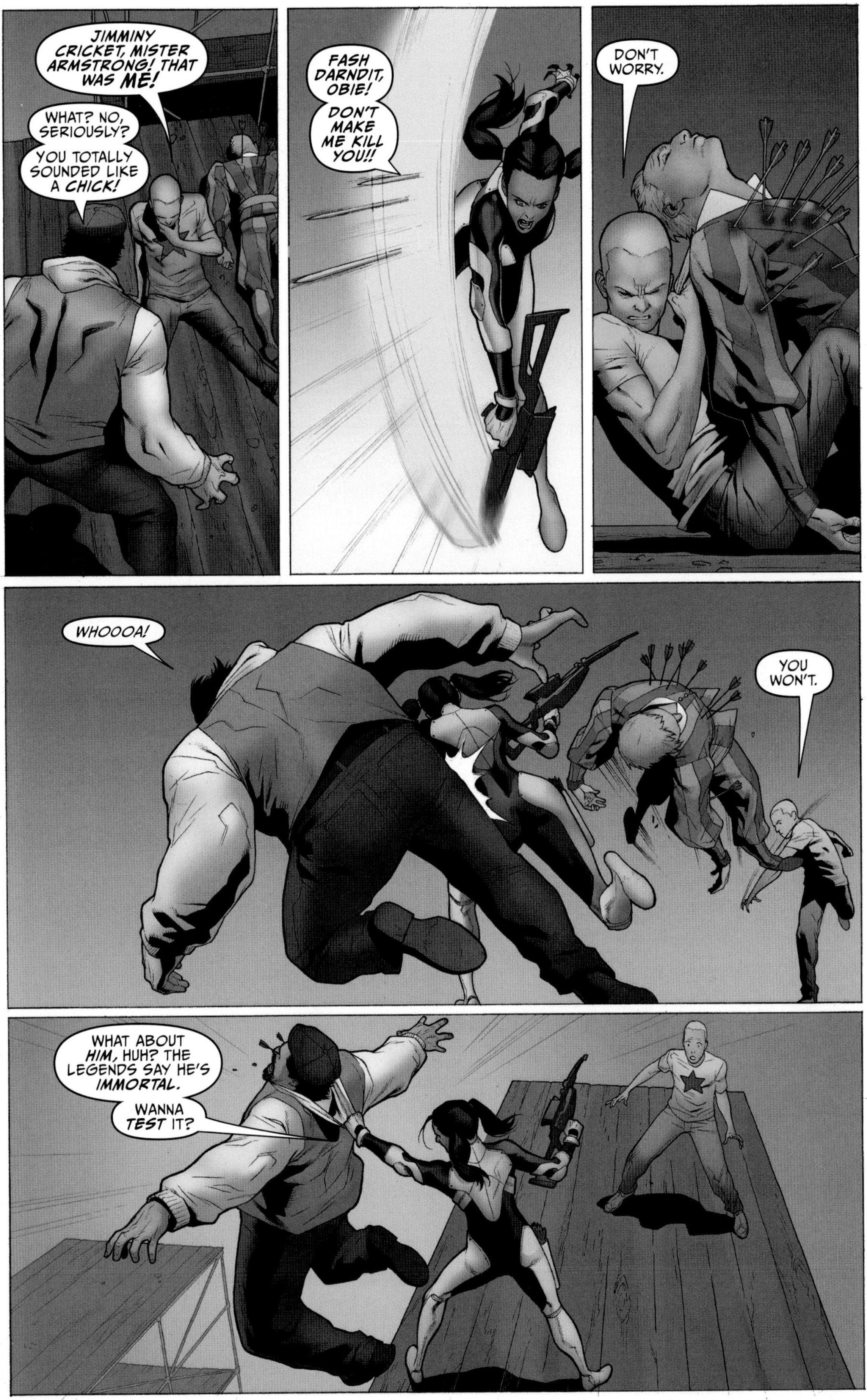
JIMMINY CRICKET, MISTER ARMSTRONG! THAT WAS ME!
WHAT? NO, SERIOUSLY?
YOU TOTALLY SOUNDED LIKE A CHICK!
FASH DARNDIT, OBIE!
DON'T MAKE ME KILL YOU!!
DON'T WORRY.
WHOOOA!
YOU WON'T.
WHAT ABOUT HIM, HUH? THE LEGENDS SAY HE'S IMMORTAL.
WANNA TEST IT?

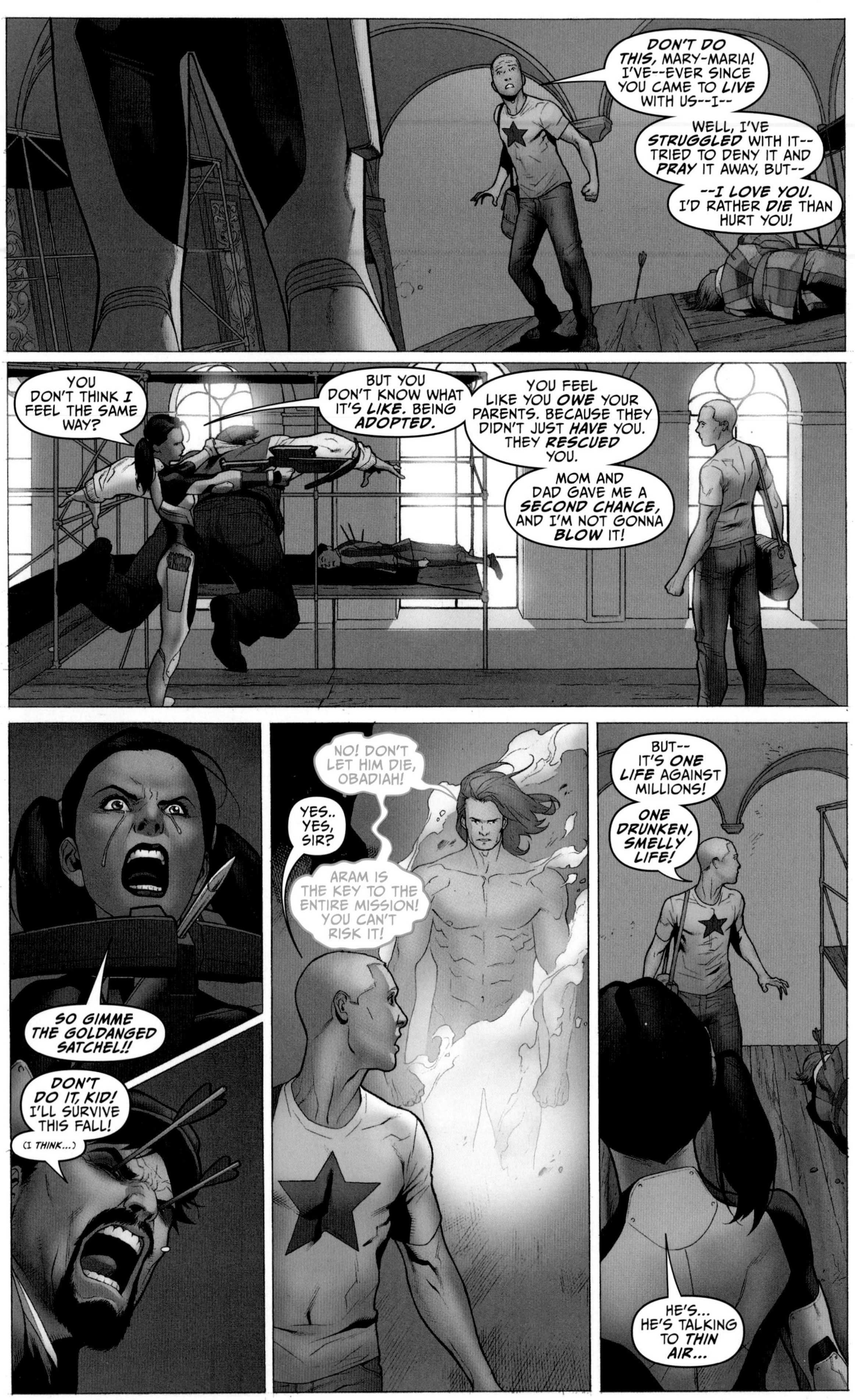
DON'T DO THIS, MARY-MARIA! I'VE--EVER SINCE YOU CAME TO LIVE WITH US--I--
WELL, I'VE STRUGGLED WITH IT-- TRIED TO DENY IT AND PRAY IT AWAY, BUT--
--I LOVE YOU. I'D RATHER DIE THAN HURT YOU!
YOU DON'T THINK I FEEL THE SAME WAY?
BUT YOU DON'T KNOW WHAT IT'S LIKE. BEING ADOPTED.
YOU FEEL LIKE YOU OWE YOUR PARENTS. BECAUSE THEY DIDN'T JUST HAVE YOU. THEY RESCUED YOU.
MOM AND DAD GAVE ME A SECOND CHANCE, AND I'M NOT GONNA BLOW IT!
SO GIMME THE GOLDANGED SATCHEL!!
DON'T DO IT, KID! I'LL SURVIVE THIS FALL!
(I THINK...)
NO! DON'T LET HIM DIE, OBADIAH!
YES.. YES, SIR?
ARAM IS THE KEY TO THE ENTIRE MISSION! YOU CAN'T RISK IT!
BUT-- IT'S ONE LIFE AGAINST MILLIONS!
ONE DRUNKEN, SMELLY LIFE!
HE'S... HE'S TALKING TO THIN AIR...

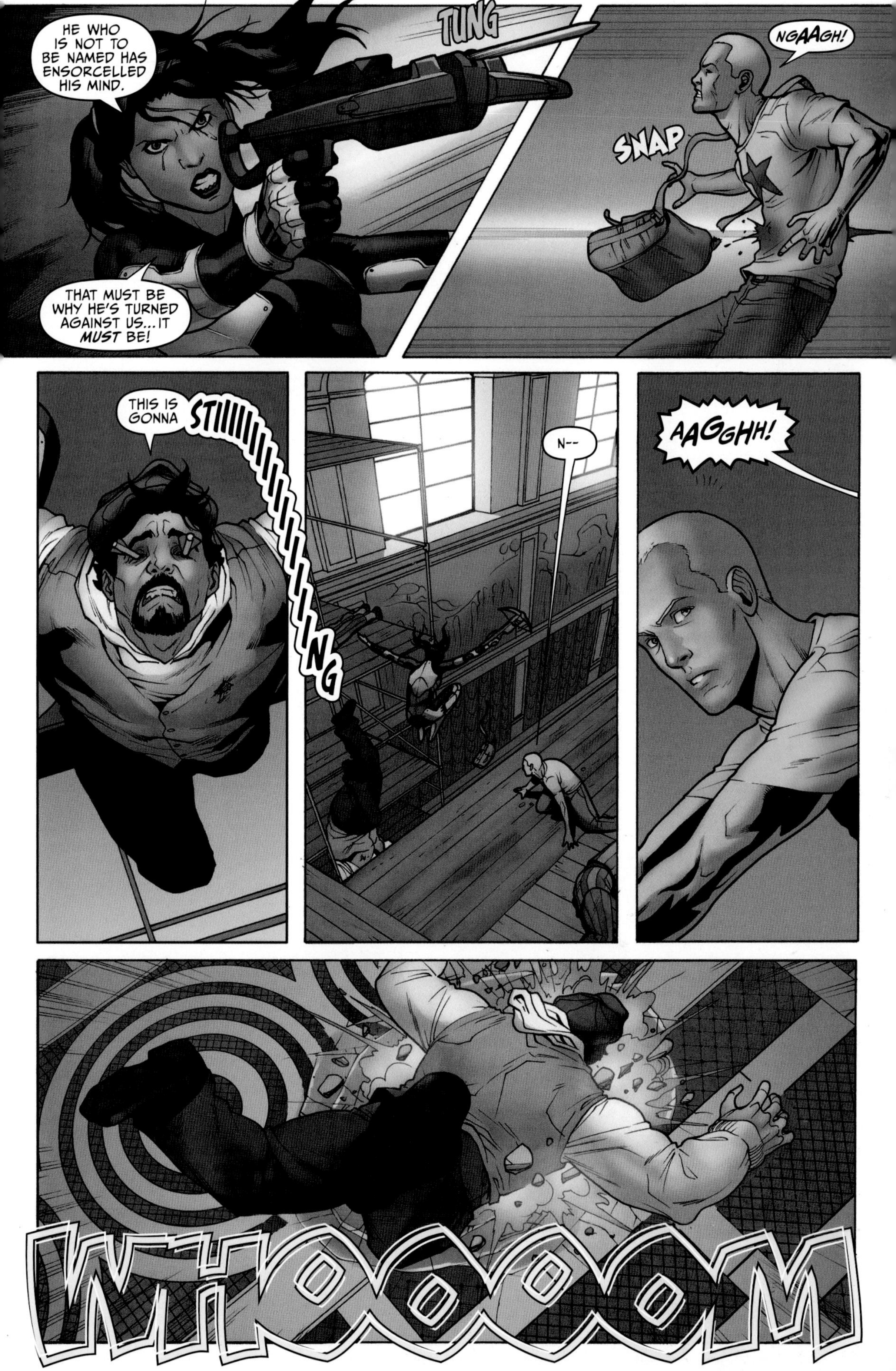
HE WHO IS NOT TO BE NAMED HAS ENSORCELLED HIS MIND.
THAT MUST BE WHY HE'S TURNED AGAINST US... IT MUST BE!
TUNG
NGAAGH!
SNAP
THIS IS GONNA
STIIIIIIIIIIIIIING
N--
AAGGHH!
WHOOOOOM

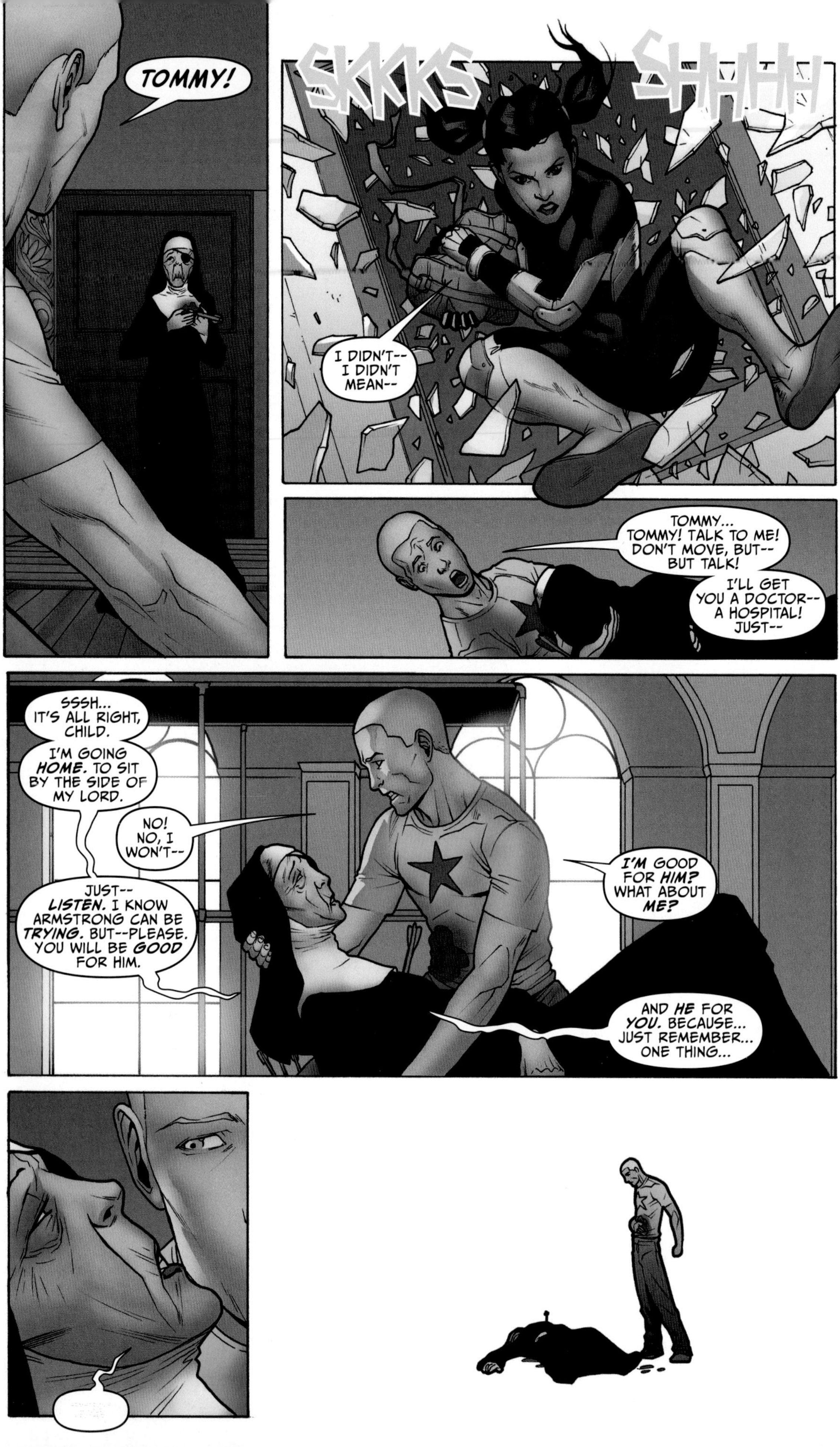
TOMMY!
SKKKS
SHHHH
I DIDN'T-- I DIDN'T MEAN--
TOMMY... TOMMY! TALK TO ME! DON'T MOVE, BUT-- BUT TALK!
I'LL GET YOU A DOCTOR-- A HOSPITAL! JUST--
SSSH... IT'S ALL RIGHT, CHILD.
I'M GOING HOME. TO SIT BY THE SIDE OF MY LORD.
NO! NO, I WON'T--
JUST-- LISTEN. I KNOW ARMSTRONG CAN BE TRYING. BUT--PLEASE. YOU WILL BE GOOD FOR HIM.
I'M GOOD FOR HIM? WHAT ABOUT ME?
AND HE FOR YOU. BECAUSE... JUST REMEMBER... ONE THING...

TOMMY...?

NO.

BASTARDS.
SIS GOT THE SATCHEL?

YES.

SO YOUR 'RENTS GOT THE TORQUE, AND THE PLANE, AND THE FULCRUM...

...AND THE SPHERE AND THE WEDGE. FIVE OF SIX.

GOOD.

GOOD?

YEAH. MEANS WE KNOW EXACTLY WHERE THEY'RE GOIN' NEXT.

LA-CHEN MONASTERY, IN THE HIMALAYAS. LAST PIECE THEY NEED IS THE AXLE. AND THAT'S WHERE I LEFT IT.

MY EYES SHOULD GROW BACK BY THE TIME WE GET THERE.

WHAT, YOU SUDDENLY CARE AGAIN? ABOUT THE WORLD?

THE WORLD CAN GO SCREW. THE SECT KILLED THE BEST WOMAN I'VE KNOWN FOR TEN THOUSAND YEARS.

NOW IT'S PERSONAL...

...IF YOU'LL LET ME COME WITH.

I HAVE TO. I PROMISED TOMMY. HER DYING WISH.

SHE SAID...

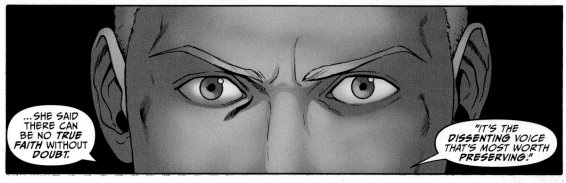

...SHE SAID THERE CAN BE NO TRUE FAITH WITHOUT DOUBT.

"IT'S THE DISSENTING VOICE THAT'S MOST WORTH PRESERVING."

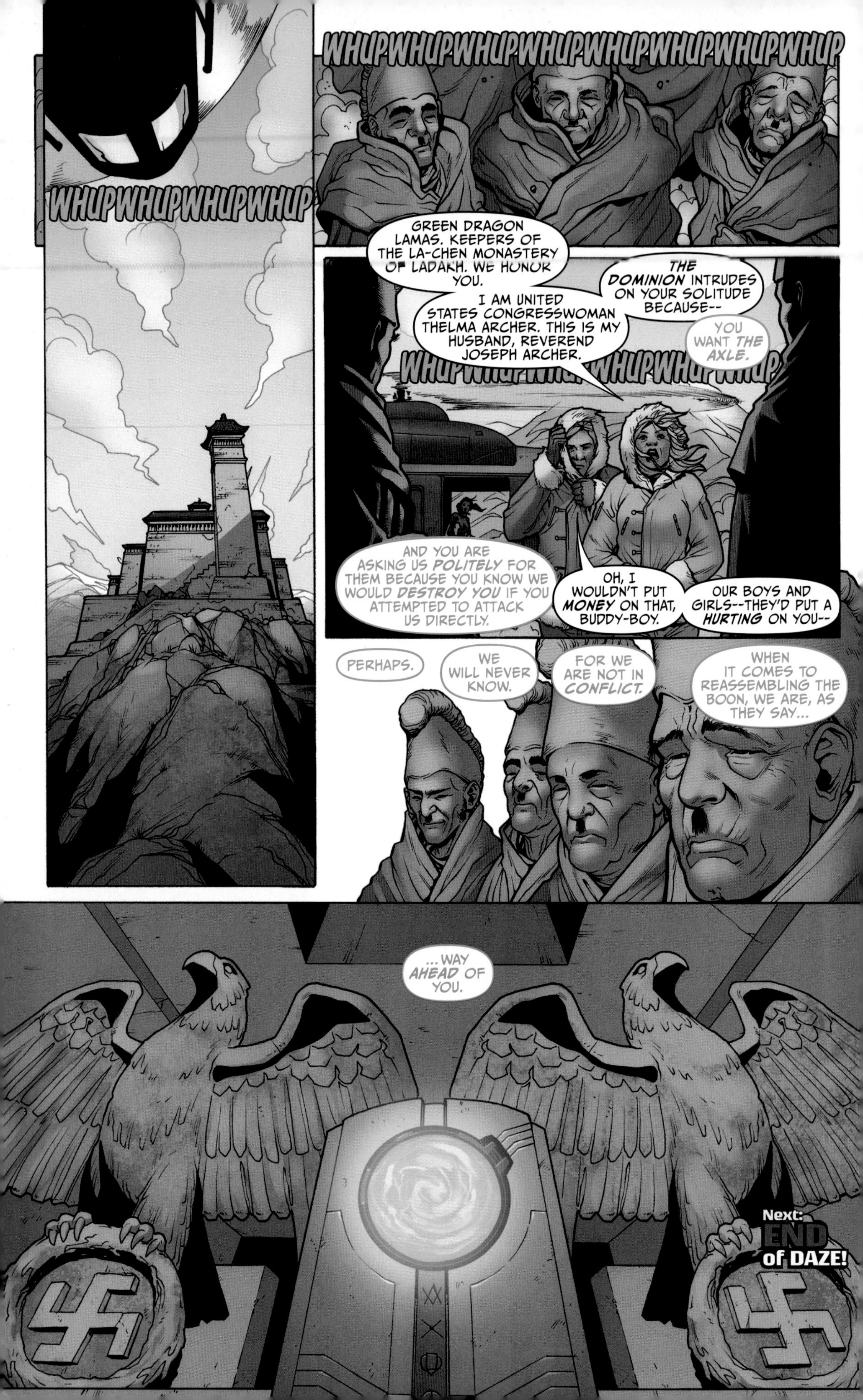
WHUPWHUPWHUPWHUP
WHUPWHUPWHUPWHUPWHUPWHUPWHUPWHUP
GREEN DRAGON LAMAS. KEEPERS OF THE LA-CHEN MONASTERY OF LADAKH. WE HONOR YOU.
I AM UNITED STATES CONGRESSWOMAN THELMA ARCHER. THIS IS MY HUSBAND, REVEREND JOSEPH ARCHER.
THE DOMINION INTRUDES ON YOUR SOLITUDE BECAUSE--
YOU WANT THE AXLE.
AND YOU ARE ASKING US POLITELY FOR THEM BECAUSE YOU KNOW WE WOULD DESTROY YOU IF YOU ATTEMPTED TO ATTACK US DIRECTLY.
OH, I WOULDN'T PUT MONEY ON THAT, BUDDY-BOY.
OUR BOYS AND GIRLS--THEY'D PUT A HURTING ON YOU--
PERHAPS.
WE WILL NEVER KNOW.
FOR WE ARE NOT IN CONFLICT.
WHEN IT COMES TO REASSEMBLING THE BOON, WE ARE, AS THEY SAY...
...WAY AHEAD OF YOU.
Next: END of DAZE!

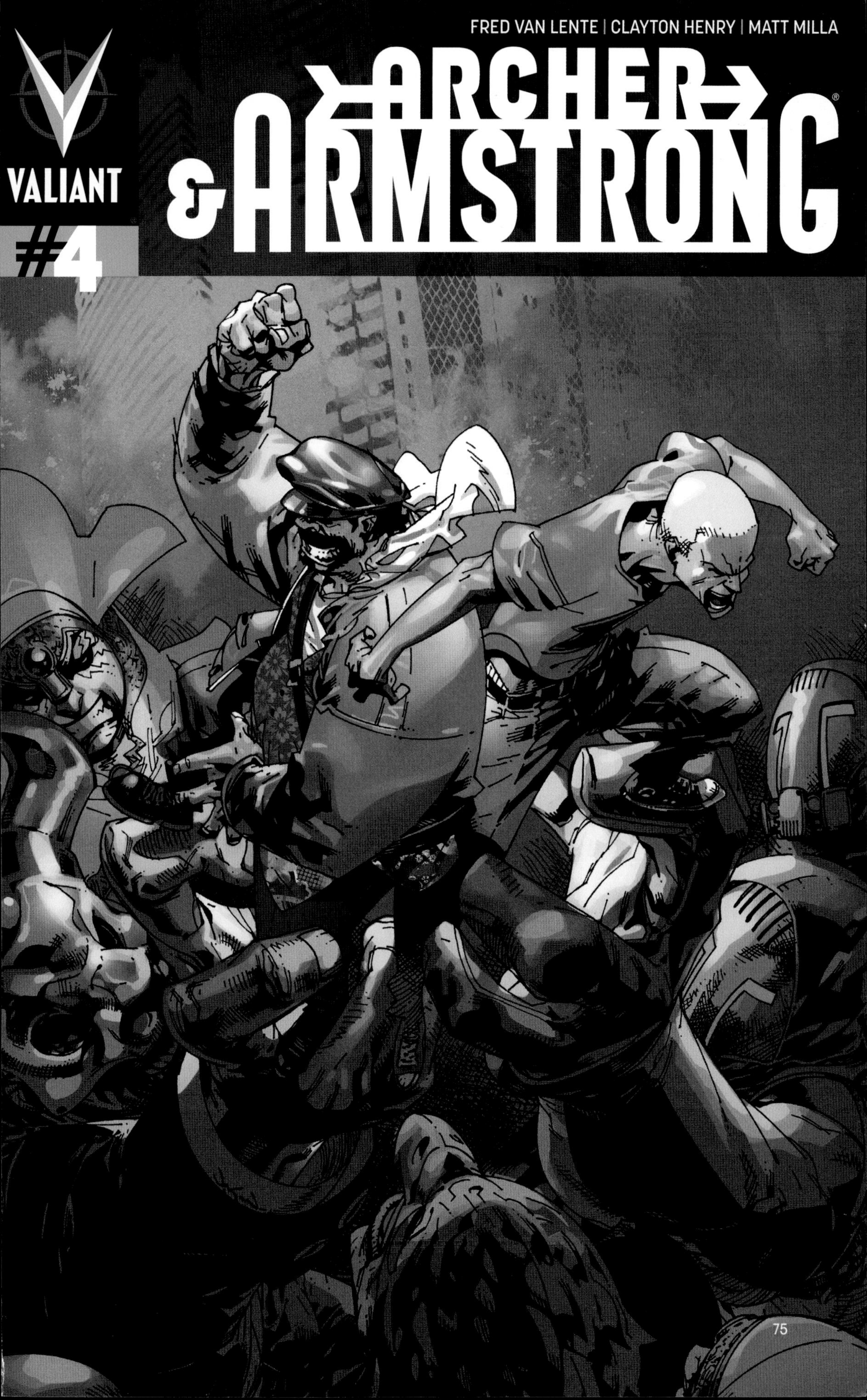
FRED VAN LENTE | CLAYTON HENRY | MATT MILLA
VALIANT
#4
ARCHER & ARMSTRONG

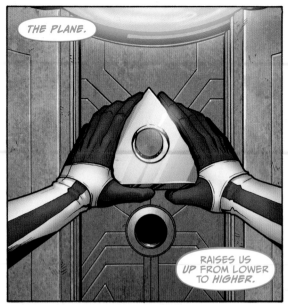

THE PLANE.

RAISES US UP FROM LOWER TO *HIGHER.*

THE TORQUE.

TWISTS THE *REVOLUTIONARY* INTO THE *STRAIGHT-AND-NARROW.*

THE WEDGE.

SPLITS THE TWAIN *APART...* OR HOLDS THEM *TOGETHER.*

THE SPHERE.

SPINNING WITH THE TRANSFERENCE OF *POWER.*

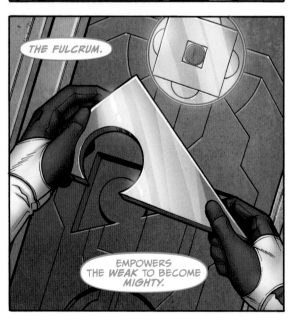

THE FULCRUM.

EMPOWERS THE *WEAK* TO BECOME *MIGHTY.*

AND THE AXLE.

BEARS ANY *BURDEN...* MOVES ANY *MOUNTAIN.*

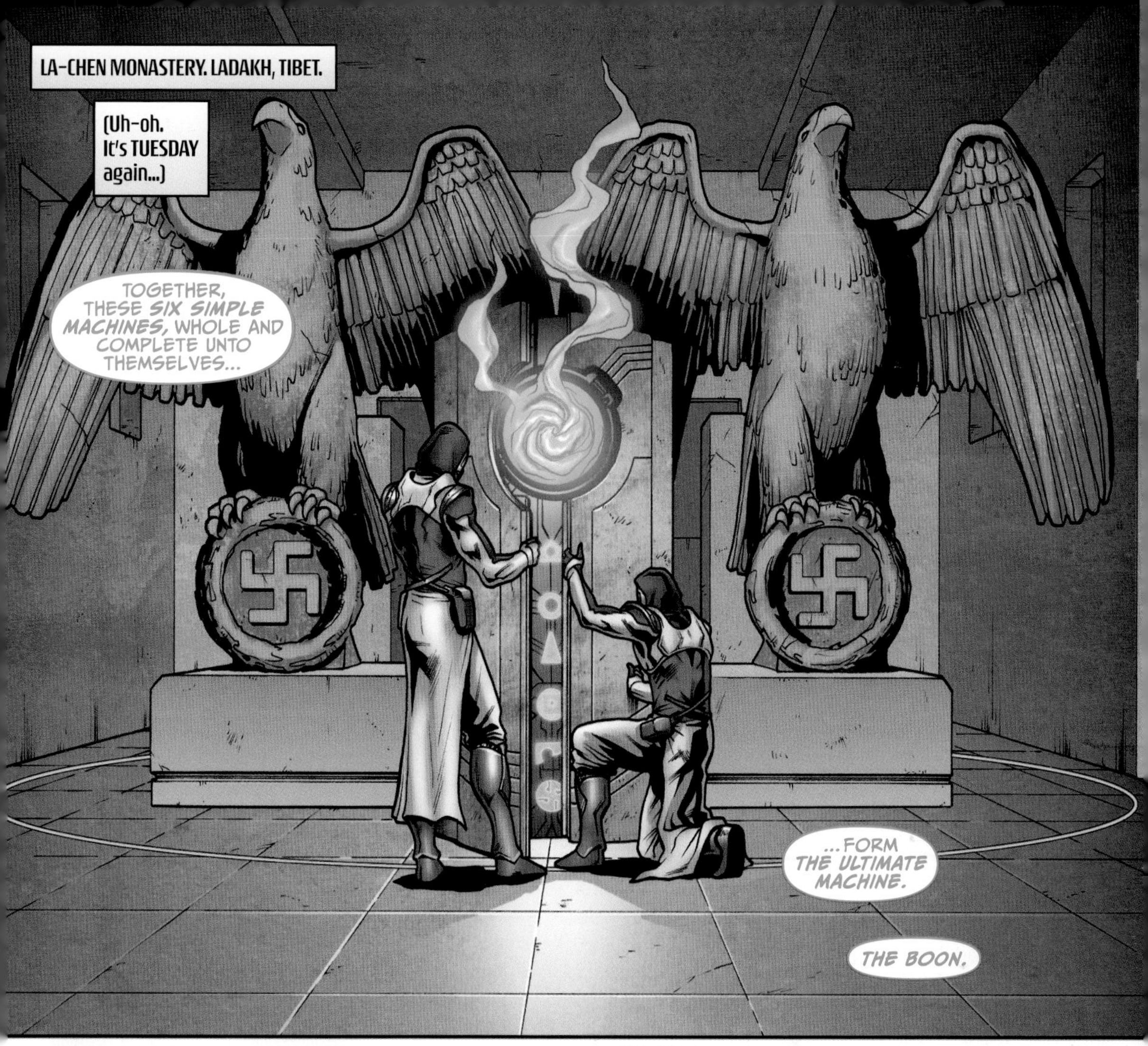
LA-CHEN MONASTERY. LADAKH, TIBET.
(Uh-oh. It's TUESDAY again...)
TOGETHER, THESE SIX SIMPLE MACHINES, WHOLE AND COMPLETE UNTO THEMSELVES...
...FORM THE ULTIMATE MACHINE.
THE BOON.

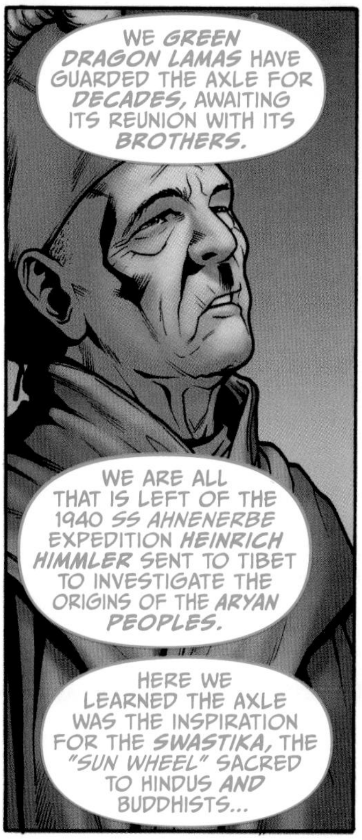
WE GREEN DRAGON LAMAS HAVE GUARDED THE AXLE FOR DECADES, AWAITING ITS REUNION WITH ITS BROTHERS.
WE ARE ALL THAT IS LEFT OF THE 1940 SS AHNENERBE EXPEDITION HEINRICH HIMMLER SENT TO TIBET TO INVESTIGATE THE ORIGINS OF THE ARYAN PEOPLES.
HERE WE LEARNED THE AXLE WAS THE INSPIRATION FOR THE SWASTIKA, THE "SUN WHEEL" SACRED TO HINDUS AND BUDDHISTS...

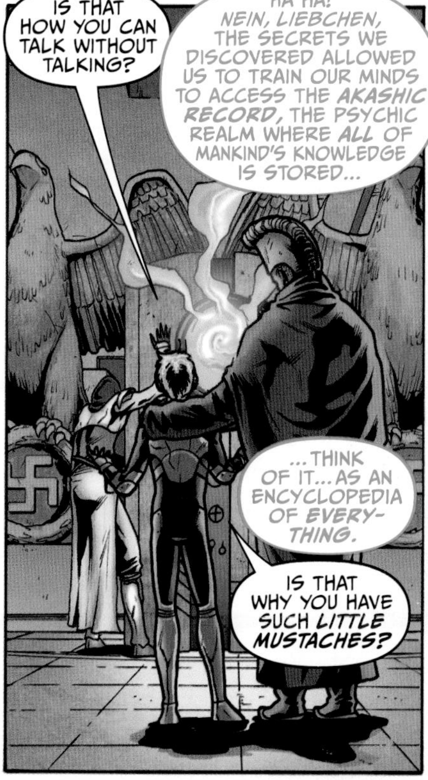
IS THAT HOW YOU CAN TALK WITHOUT TALKING?
HA HA! NEIN, LIEBCHEN, THE SECRETS WE DISCOVERED ALLOWED US TO TRAIN OUR MINDS TO ACCESS THE AKASHIC RECORD, THE PSYCHIC REALM WHERE ALL OF MANKIND'S KNOWLEDGE IS STORED...
...THINK OF IT...AS AN ENCYCLOPEDIA OF EVERYTHING.
IS THAT WHY YOU HAVE SUCH LITTLE MUSTACHES?

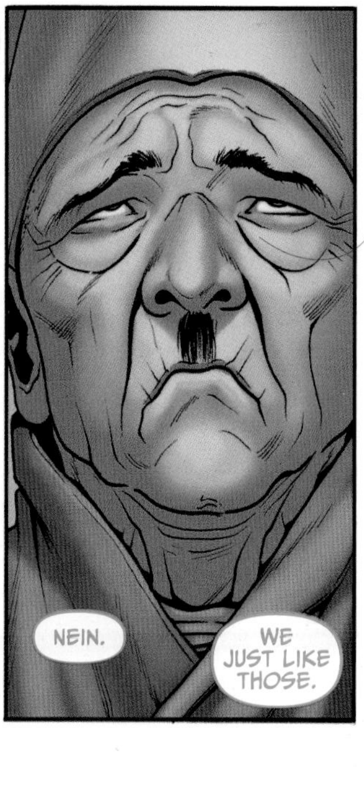
NEIN.
WE JUST LIKE THOSE.

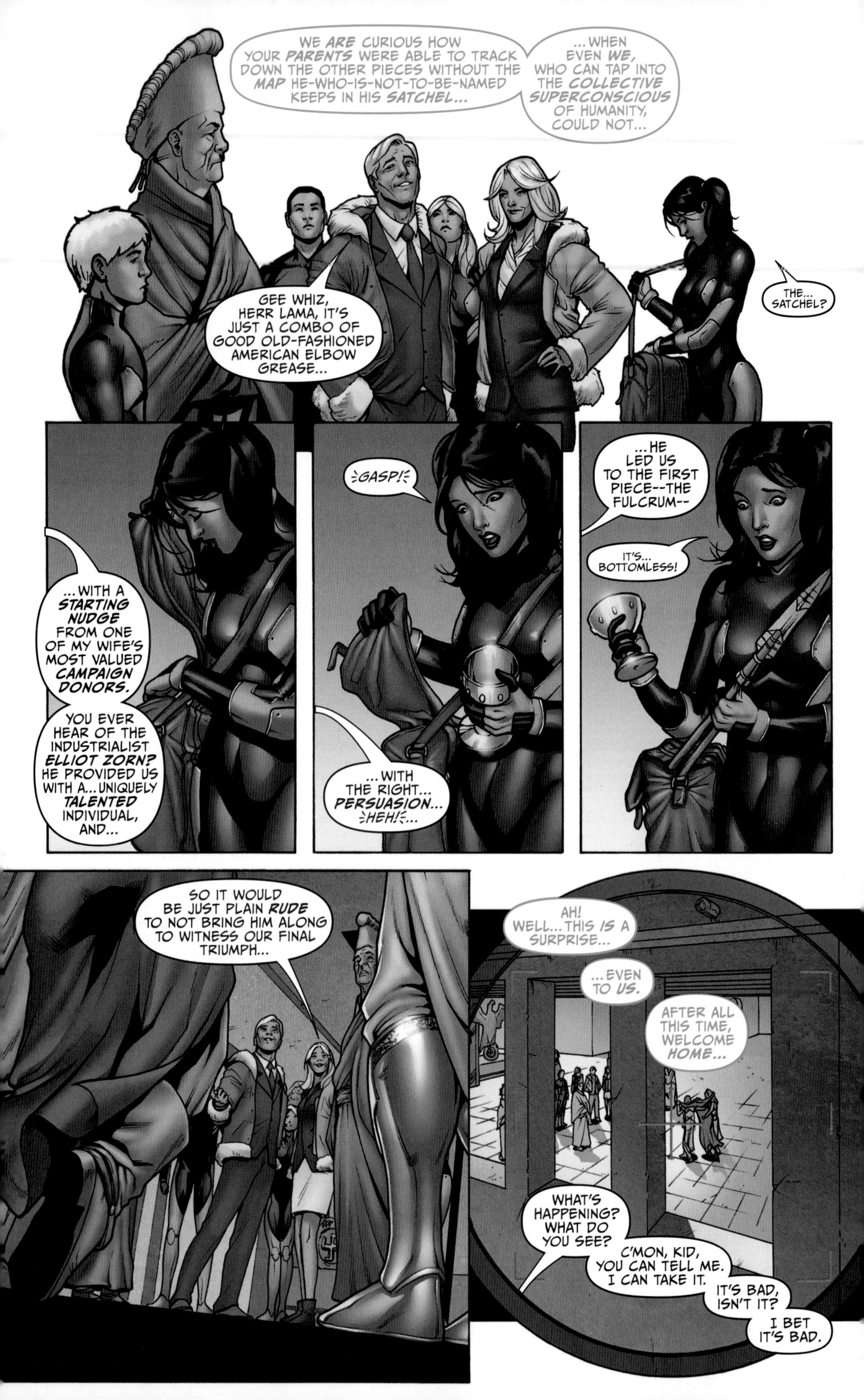
WE ARE CURIOUS HOW YOUR PARENTS WERE ABLE TO TRACK DOWN THE OTHER PIECES WITHOUT THE MAP HE-WHO-IS-NOT-TO-BE-NAMED KEEPS IN HIS SATCHEL...
...WHEN EVEN WE, WHO CAN TAP INTO THE COLLECTIVE SUPERCONSCIOUS OF HUMANITY, COULD NOT...
GEE WHIZ, HERR LAMA, IT'S JUST A COMBO OF GOOD OLD-FASHIONED AMERICAN ELBOW GREASE...
THE... SATCHEL?
...WITH A STARTING NUDGE FROM ONE OF MY WIFE'S MOST VALUED CAMPAIGN DONORS.
YOU EVER HEAR OF THE INDUSTRIALIST ELLIOT ZORN? HE PROVIDED US WITH A...UNIQUELY TALENTED INDIVIDUAL, AND...
GASP!
...WITH THE RIGHT... PERSUASION... HEH!...
...HE LED US TO THE FIRST PIECE--THE FULCRUM--
IT'S... BOTTOMLESS!
SO IT WOULD BE JUST PLAIN RUDE TO NOT BRING HIM ALONG TO WITNESS OUR FINAL TRIUMPH...
AH! WELL...THIS IS A SURPRISE...
...EVEN TO US.
AFTER ALL THIS TIME, WELCOME HOME...
WHAT'S HAPPENING? WHAT DO YOU SEE?
C'MON, KID, YOU CAN TELL ME. I CAN TAKE IT.
IT'S BAD, ISN'T IT?
I BET IT'S BAD.

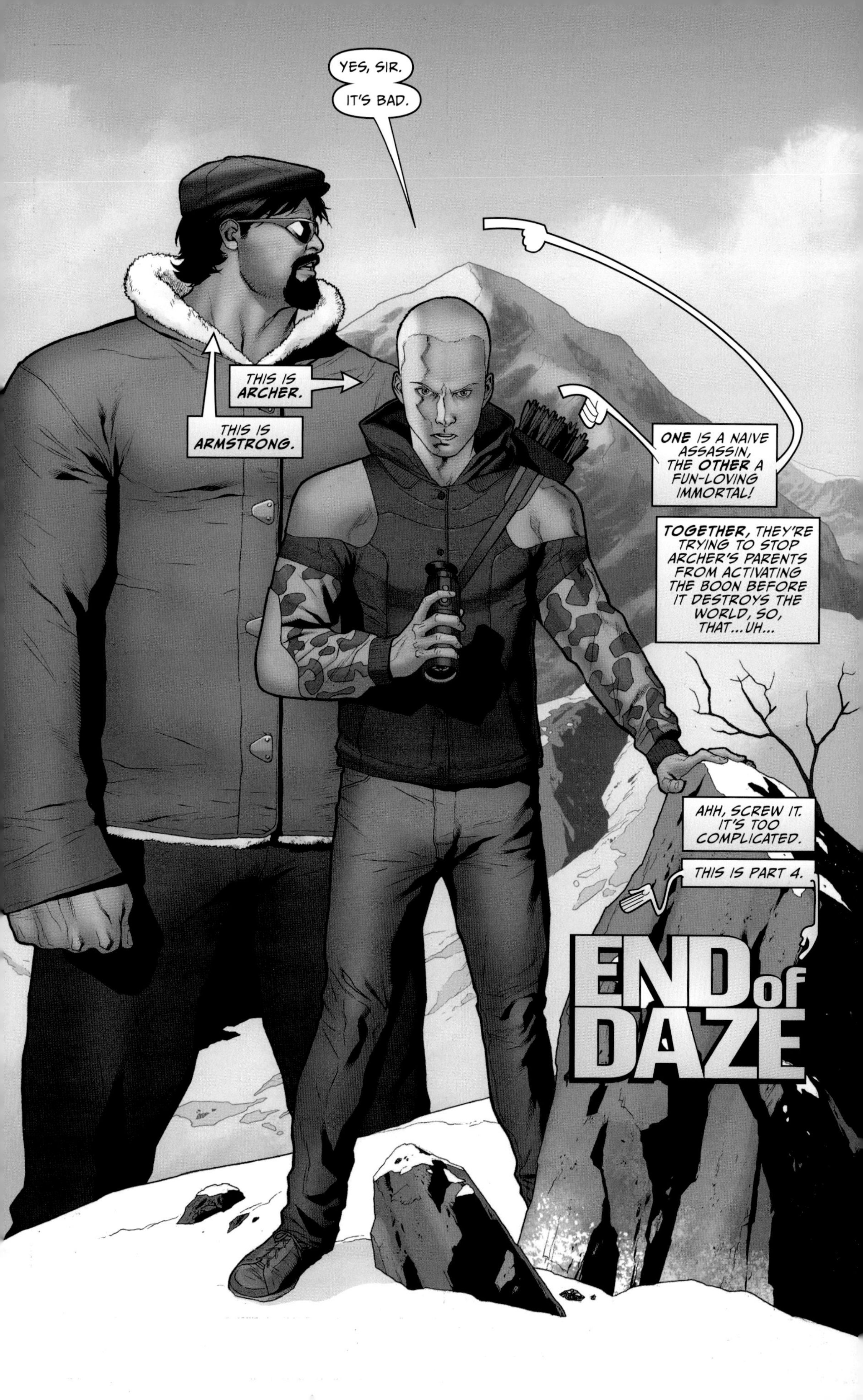
YES, SIR.
IT'S BAD.
THIS IS ARCHER.
THIS IS ARMSTRONG.
ONE IS A NAIVE ASSASSIN, THE OTHER A FUN-LOVING IMMORTAL!
TOGETHER, THEY'RE TRYING TO STOP ARCHER'S PARENTS FROM ACTIVATING THE BOON BEFORE IT DESTROYS THE WORLD, SO, THAT...UH...
AHH, SCREW IT. IT'S TOO COMPLICATED.
THIS IS PART 4.
END of DAZE

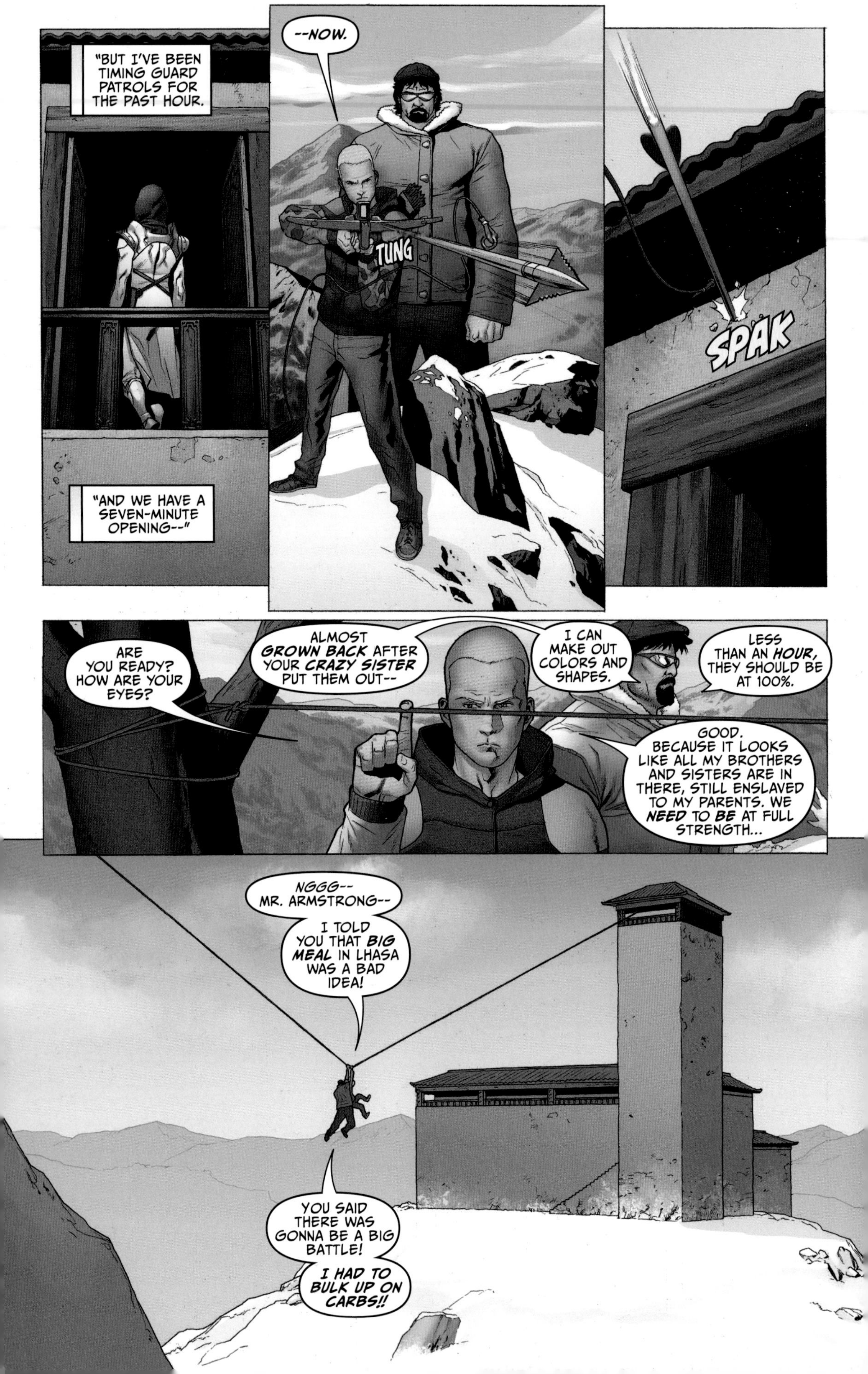
"BUT I'VE BEEN TIMING GUARD PATROLS FOR THE PAST HOUR.
"AND WE HAVE A SEVEN-MINUTE OPENING--"
--NOW.
TUNG
SPAK
ARE YOU READY? HOW ARE YOUR EYES?
ALMOST GROWN BACK AFTER YOUR CRAZY SISTER PUT THEM OUT--
I CAN MAKE OUT COLORS AND SHAPES.
LESS THAN AN HOUR, THEY SHOULD BE AT 100%.
GOOD. BECAUSE IT LOOKS LIKE ALL MY BROTHERS AND SISTERS ARE IN THERE, STILL ENSLAVED TO MY PARENTS. WE NEED TO BE AT FULL STRENGTH...
NGGG-- MR. ARMSTRONG--
I TOLD YOU THAT BIG MEAL IN LHASA WAS A BAD IDEA!
YOU SAID THERE WAS GONNA BE A BIG BATTLE!
I HAD TO BULK UP ON CARBS!!

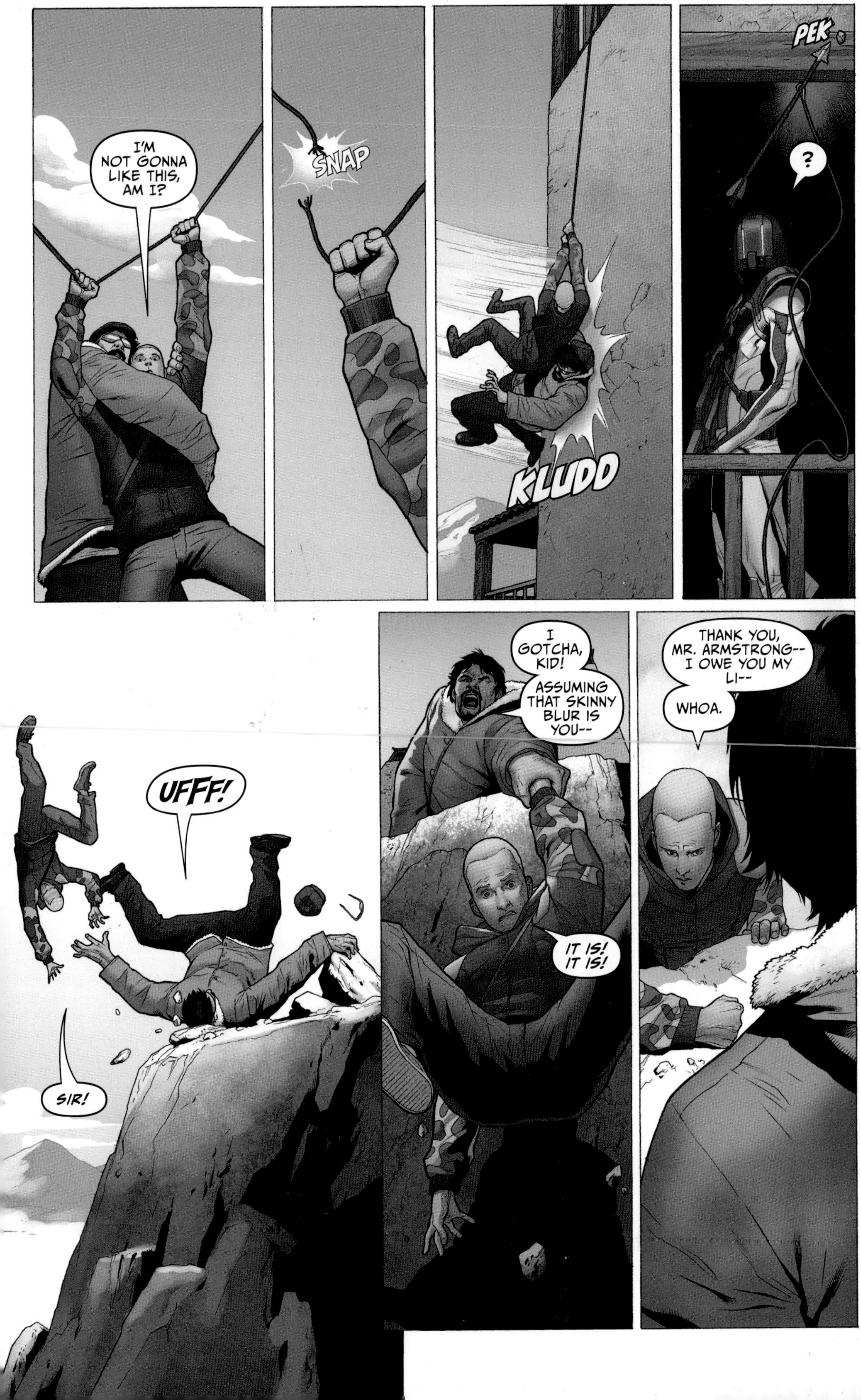
I'M NOT GONNA LIKE THIS, AM I?
SNAP
KLUDD
PEK
?
UFFF!
SIR!
I GOTCHA, KID!
ASSUMING THAT SKINNY BLUR IS YOU--
IT IS! IT IS!
THANK YOU, MR. ARMSTRONG-- I OWE YOU MY LI--
WHOA.

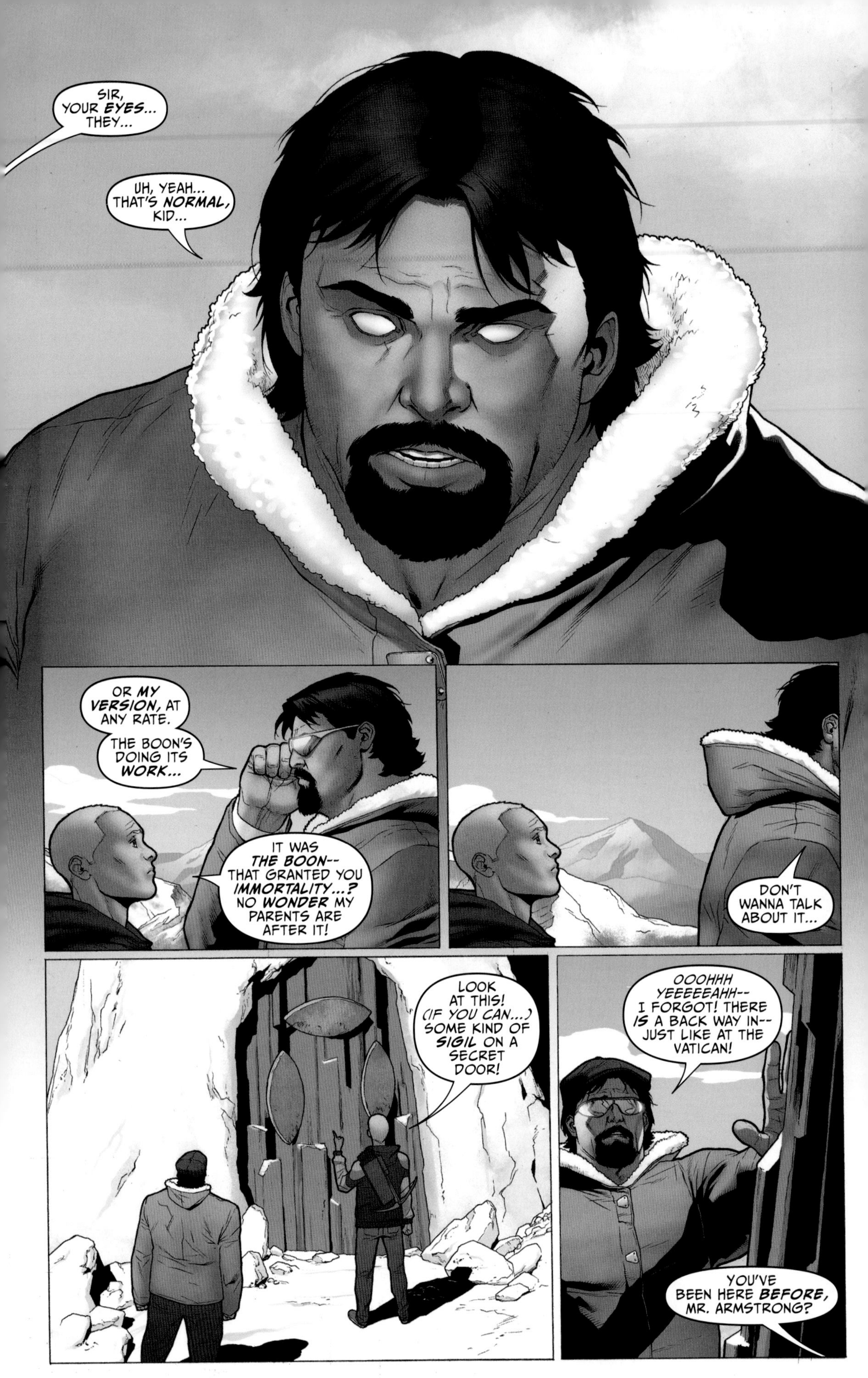
SIR, YOUR *EYES*... THEY...
UH, YEAH... THAT'S *NORMAL*, KID...
OR *MY VERSION*, AT ANY RATE.
THE BOON'S DOING ITS *WORK*...
IT WAS *THE BOON*-- THAT GRANTED YOU *IMMORTALITY...?* NO *WONDER* MY PARENTS ARE AFTER IT!
DON'T WANNA TALK ABOUT IT...
LOOK AT THIS! (*IF YOU CAN...*) SOME KIND OF *SIGIL* ON A SECRET DOOR!
OOOHHH YEEEEEAHH-- I FORGOT! THERE *IS* A BACK WAY IN-- JUST LIKE AT THE VATICAN!
YOU'VE BEEN HERE *BEFORE*, MR. ARMSTRONG?

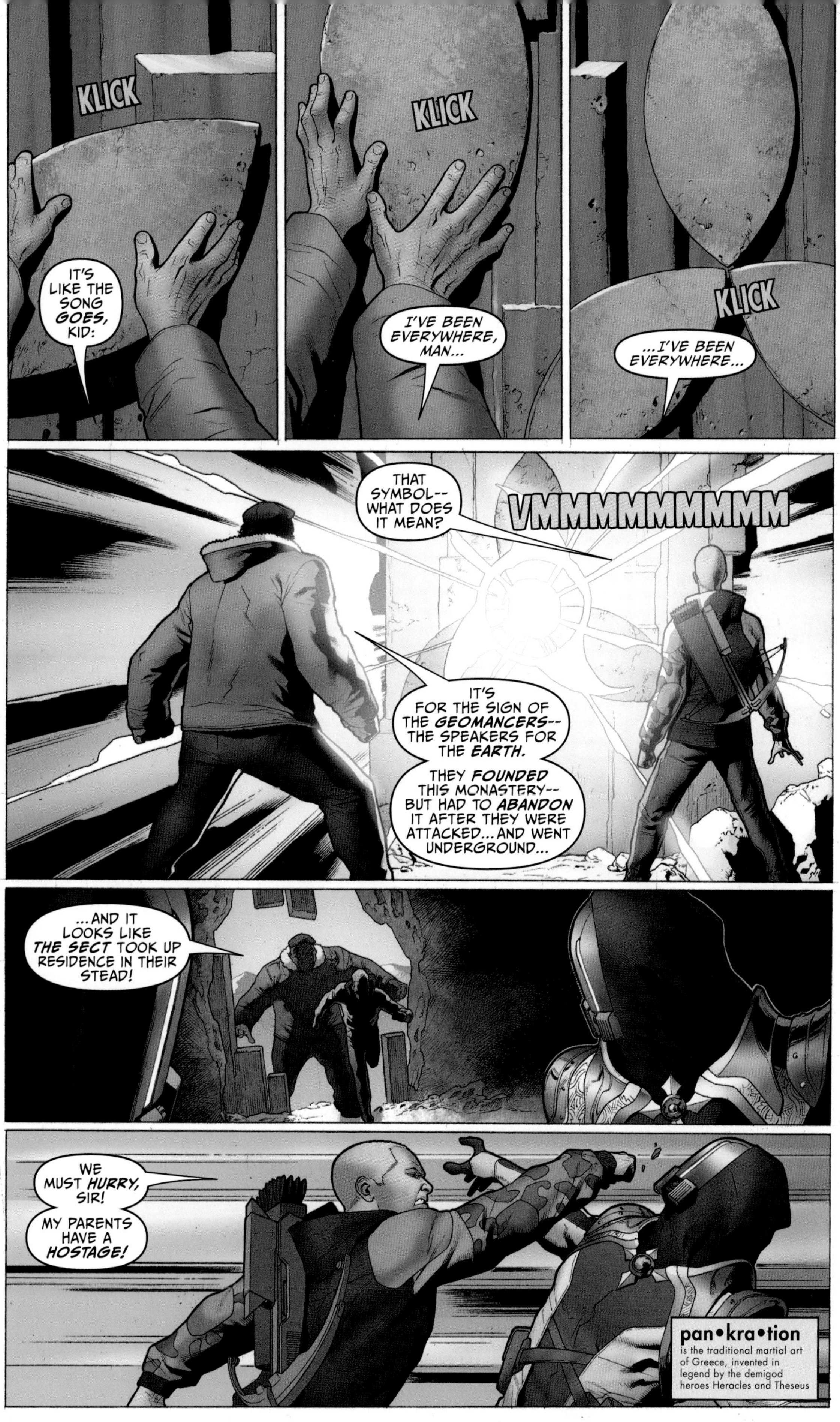
KLICK
IT'S LIKE THE SONG GOES, KID:
KLICK
I'VE BEEN EVERYWHERE, MAN...
KLICK
...I'VE BEEN EVERYWHERE...
THAT SYMBOL--WHAT DOES IT MEAN?
VMMMMMMMMMM
IT'S FOR THE SIGN OF THE GEOMANCERS--THE SPEAKERS FOR THE EARTH.
THEY FOUNDED THIS MONASTERY--BUT HAD TO ABANDON IT AFTER THEY WERE ATTACKED...AND WENT UNDERGROUND...
...AND IT LOOKS LIKE THE SECT TOOK UP RESIDENCE IN THEIR STEAD!
WE MUST HURRY, SIR!
MY PARENTS HAVE A HOSTAGE!
pan•kra•tion
is the traditional martial art of Greece, invented in legend by the demigod heroes Heracles and Theseus

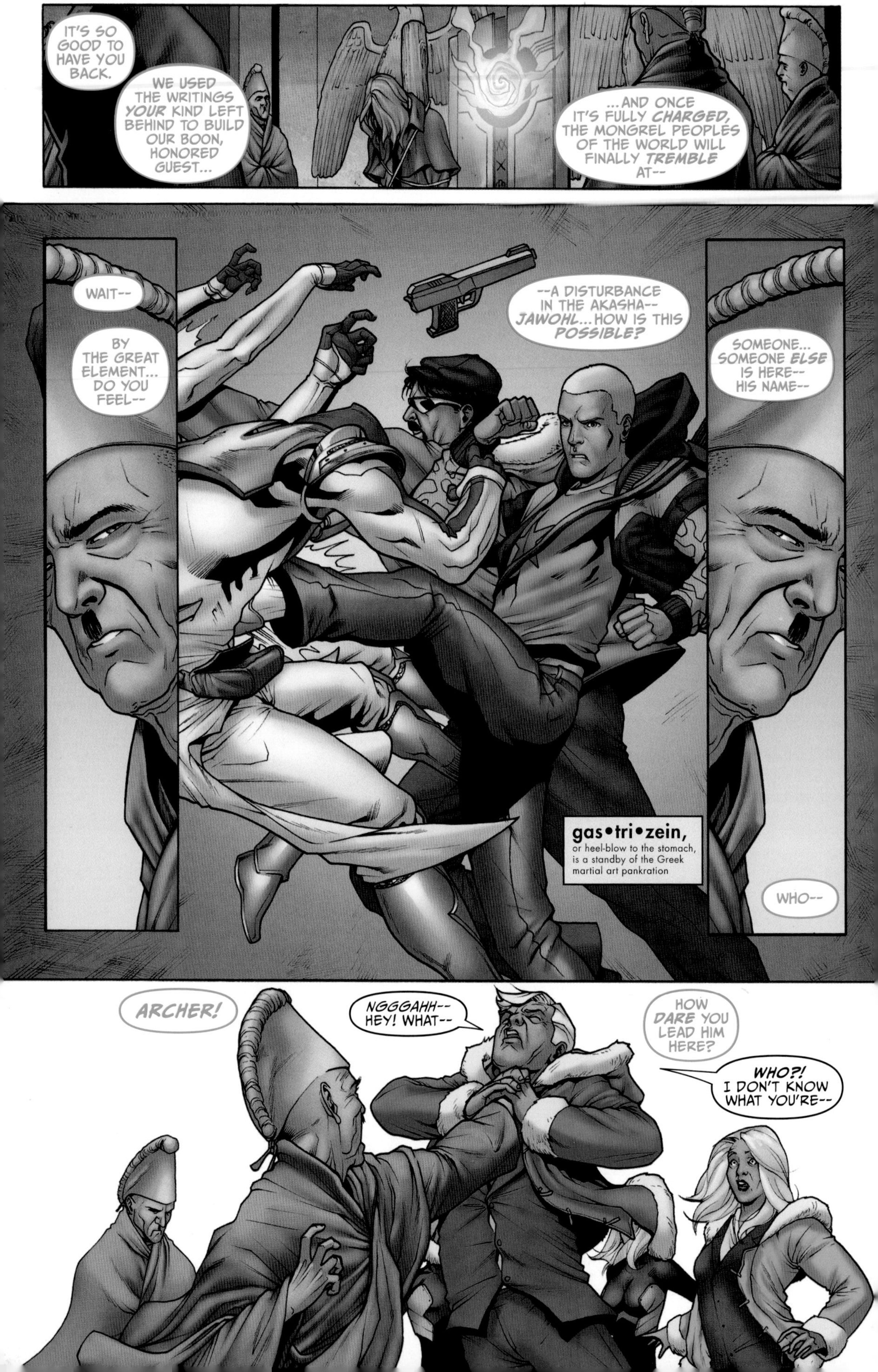
IT'S SO GOOD TO HAVE YOU BACK.
WE USED THE WRITINGS YOUR KIND LEFT BEHIND TO BUILD OUR BOON, HONORED GUEST...
...AND ONCE IT'S FULLY CHARGED, THE MONGREL PEOPLES OF THE WORLD WILL FINALLY TREMBLE AT--
WAIT--
BY THE GREAT ELEMENT... DO YOU FEEL--
--A DISTURBANCE IN THE AKASHA-- JAWOHL... HOW IS THIS POSSIBLE?
SOMEONE... SOMEONE ELSE IS HERE-- HIS NAME--
gas•tri•zein,
or heel-blow to the stomach, is a standby of the Greek martial art pankration
WHO--
ARCHER!
NGGGAHH-- HEY! WHAT--
HOW DARE YOU LEAD HIM HERE?
WHO?! I DON'T KNOW WHAT YOU'RE--

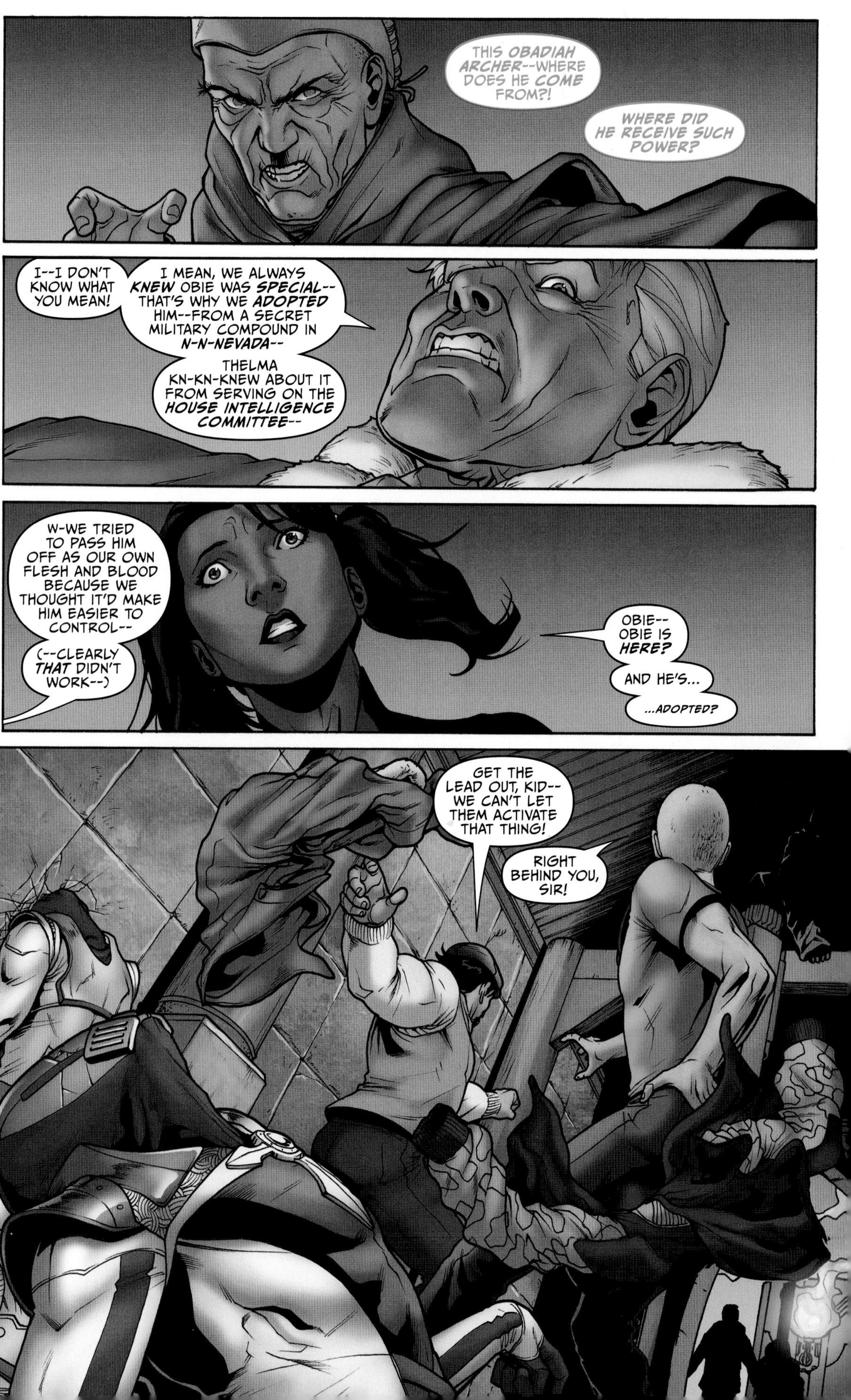
THIS OBADIAH ARCHER--WHERE DOES HE COME FROM?!
WHERE DID HE RECEIVE SUCH POWER?
I--I DON'T KNOW WHAT YOU MEAN!
I MEAN, WE ALWAYS KNEW OBIE WAS SPECIAL--THAT'S WHY WE ADOPTED HIM--FROM A SECRET MILITARY COMPOUND IN N-N-NEVADA--
THELMA KN-KN-KNEW ABOUT IT FROM SERVING ON THE HOUSE INTELLIGENCE COMMITTEE--
W-WE TRIED TO PASS HIM OFF AS OUR OWN FLESH AND BLOOD BECAUSE WE THOUGHT IT'D MAKE HIM EASIER TO CONTROL--
(--CLEARLY THAT DIDN'T WORK--)
OBIE--OBIE IS HERE?
AND HE'S...
...ADOPTED?
GET THE LEAD OUT, KID--WE CAN'T LET THEM ACTIVATE THAT THING!
RIGHT BEHIND YOU, SIR!

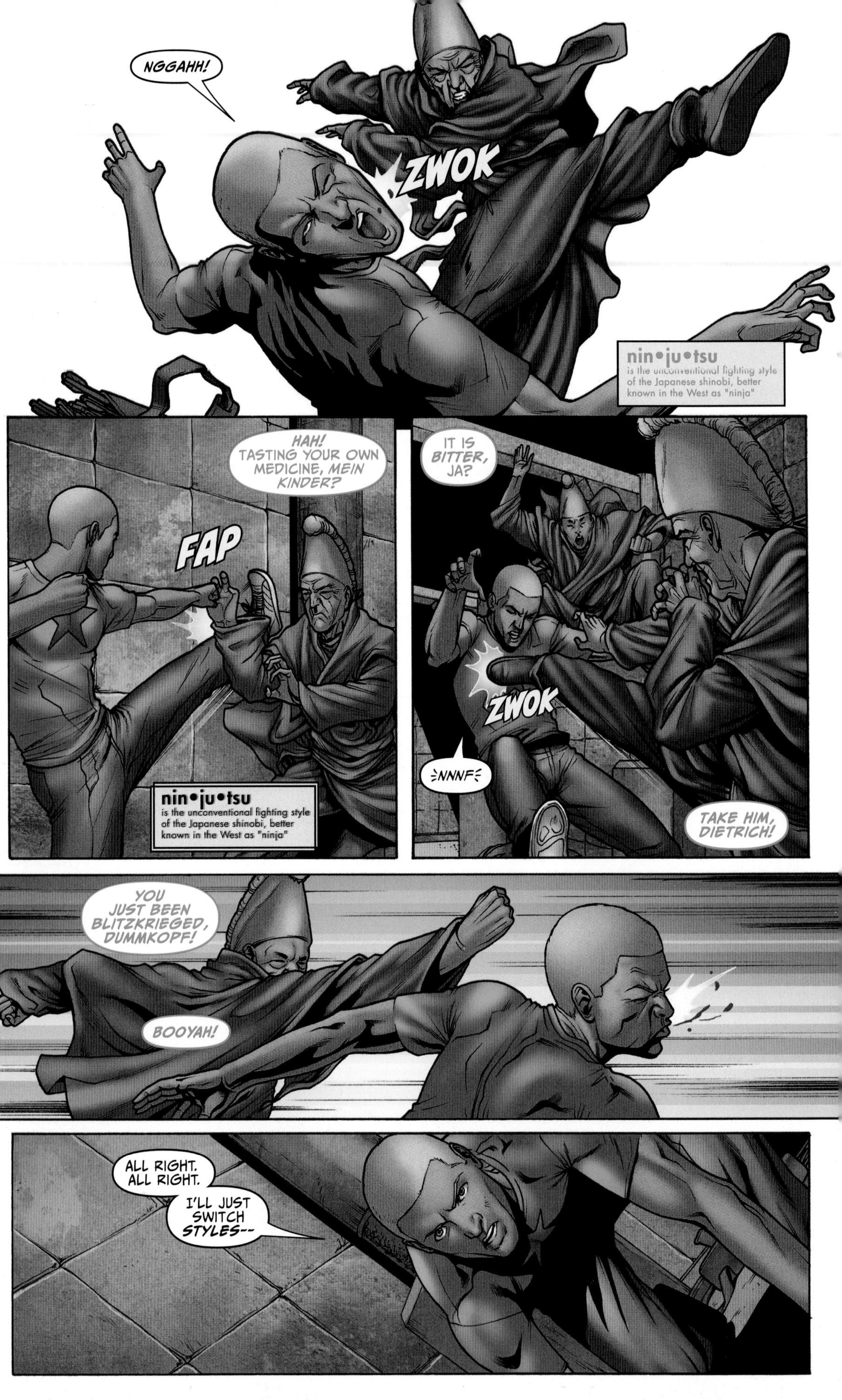
NGGAHH!
ZWOK
nin•ju•tsu
is the unconventional fighting style of the Japanese shinobi, better known in the West as "ninja"
HAH! TASTING YOUR OWN MEDICINE, MEIN KINDER?
FAP
nin•ju•tsu
is the unconventional fighting style of the Japanese shinobi, better known in the West as "ninja"
IT IS BITTER, JA?
ZWOK
NNNF
TAKE HIM, DIETRICH!
YOU JUST BEEN BLITZKRIEGED, DUMMKOPF!
BOOYAH!
ALL RIGHT. ALL RIGHT.
I'LL JUST SWITCH STYLES--

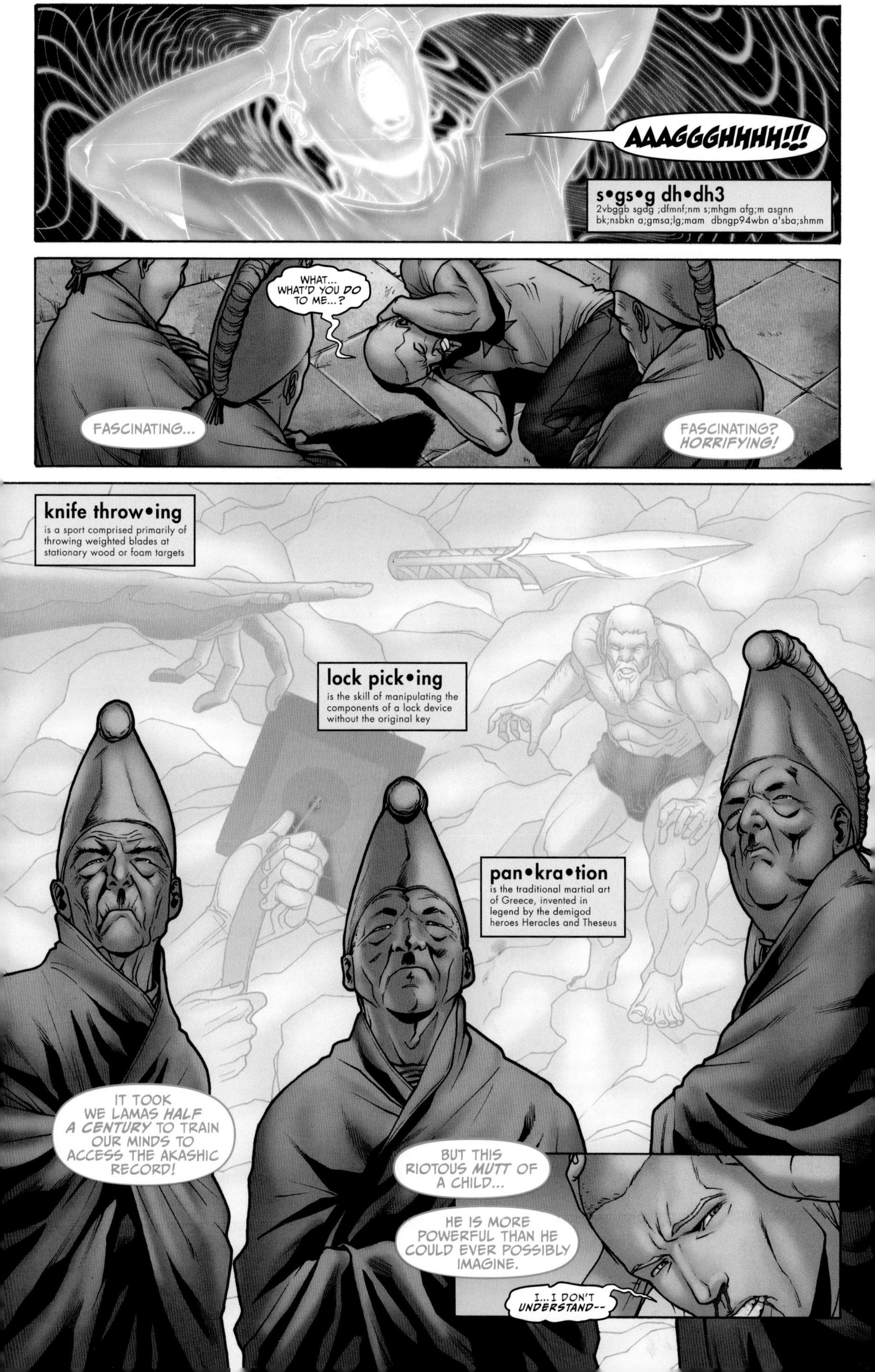
AAAGGGHHHH!!!
s•gs•g dh•dh3
2vbggb sgdg ;dfmnf;nm s;mhgm afg;m asgnn bk;nsbkn a;gmsa;lg;mam dbngp94wbn a'sba;shmm
WHAT... WHAT'D YOU *DO* TO ME...?
FASCINATING...
FASCINATING? *HORRIFYING!*
knife throw•ing
is a sport comprised primarily of throwing weighted blades at stationary wood or foam targets
lock pick•ing
is the skill of manipulating the components of a lock device without the original key
pan•kra•tion
is the traditional martial art of Greece, invented in legend by the demigod heroes Heracles and Theseus
IT TOOK WE LAMAS *HALF A CENTURY* TO TRAIN OUR MINDS TO ACCESS THE AKASHIC RECORD!
BUT THIS RIOTOUS *MUTT* OF A CHILD...
HE IS MORE POWERFUL THAN HE COULD EVER POSSIBLY IMAGINE.
I... I DON'T *UNDERSTAND*--

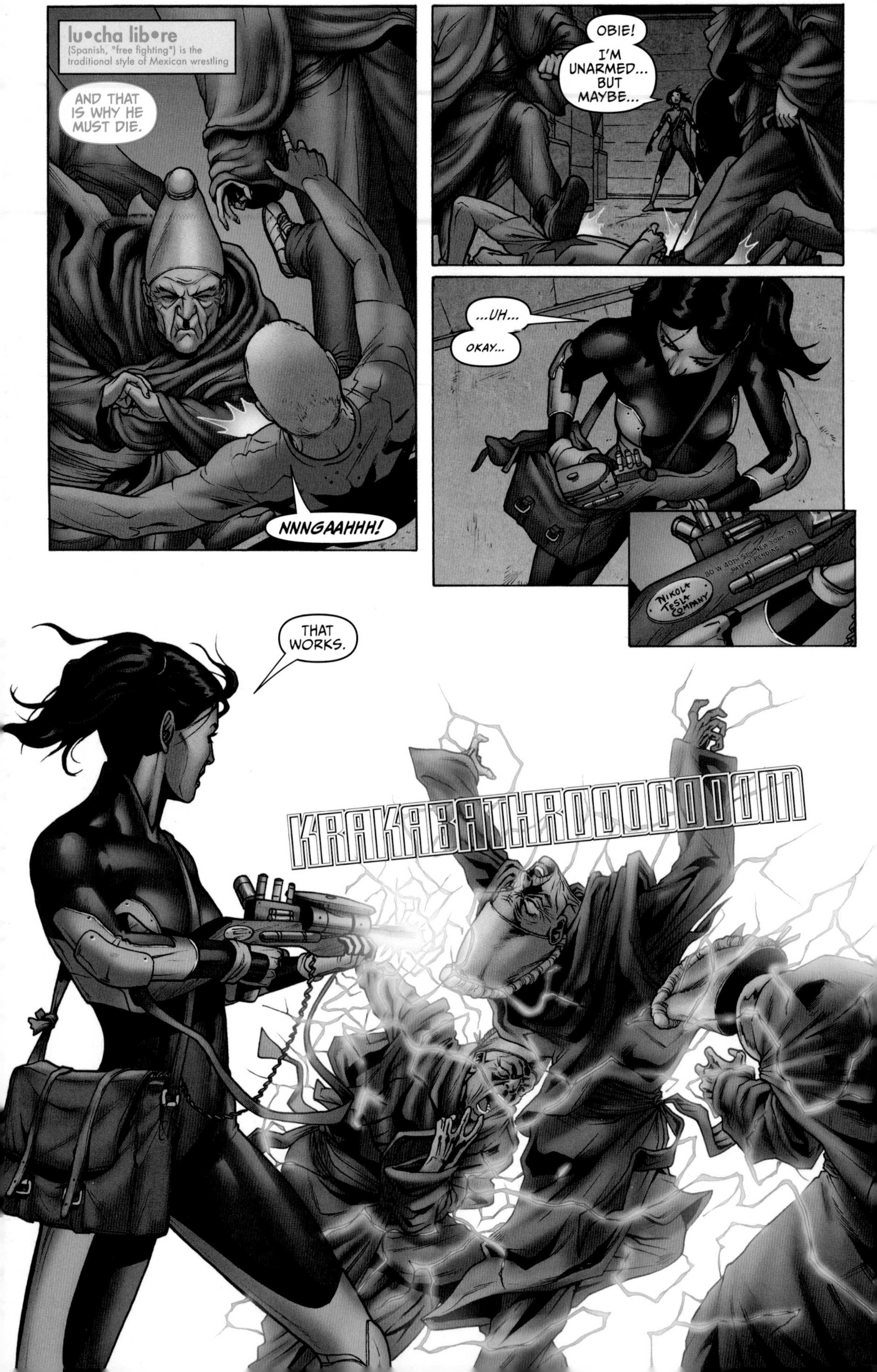
lu•cha lib•re
(Spanish, "free fighting") is the traditional style of Mexican wrestling
AND THAT IS WHY HE MUST DIE.
NNNGAAHHH!
OBIE!
I'M UNARMED... BUT MAYBE...
...UH...
OKAY...
NIKOLA TESLA COMPANY
80 W 40TH ST. NEW YORK, NY
PATENT PENDING
THAT WORKS.
KRAKABATHROOOOOOOOM

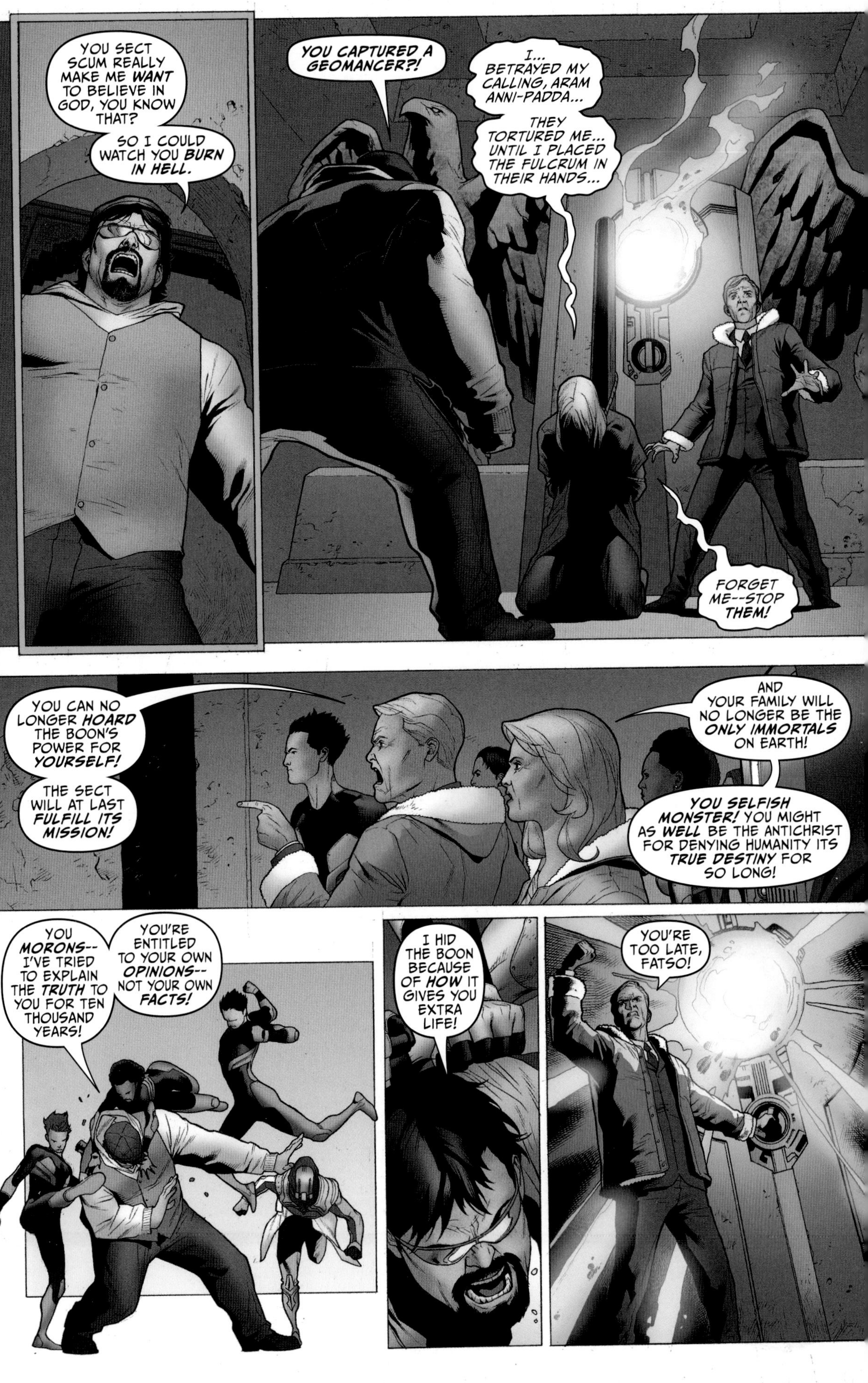

YOU SECT SCUM REALLY MAKE ME WANT TO BELIEVE IN GOD, YOU KNOW THAT?
SO I COULD WATCH YOU BURN IN HELL.
YOU CAPTURED A GEOMANCER?!
I... BETRAYED MY CALLING, ARAM ANNI-PADDA...
THEY TORTURED ME... UNTIL I PLACED THE FULCRUM IN THEIR HANDS...
FORGET ME--STOP THEM!
YOU CAN NO LONGER HOARD THE BOON'S POWER FOR YOURSELF!
THE SECT WILL AT LAST FULFILL ITS MISSION!
AND YOUR FAMILY WILL NO LONGER BE THE ONLY IMMORTALS ON EARTH!
YOU SELFISH MONSTER! YOU MIGHT AS WELL BE THE ANTICHRIST FOR DENYING HUMANITY ITS TRUE DESTINY FOR SO LONG!
YOU MORONS-- I'VE TRIED TO EXPLAIN THE TRUTH TO YOU FOR TEN THOUSAND YEARS!
YOU'RE ENTITLED TO YOUR OWN OPINIONS-- NOT YOUR OWN FACTS!
I HID THE BOON BECAUSE OF HOW IT GIVES YOU EXTRA LIFE!
YOU'RE TOO LATE, FATSO!

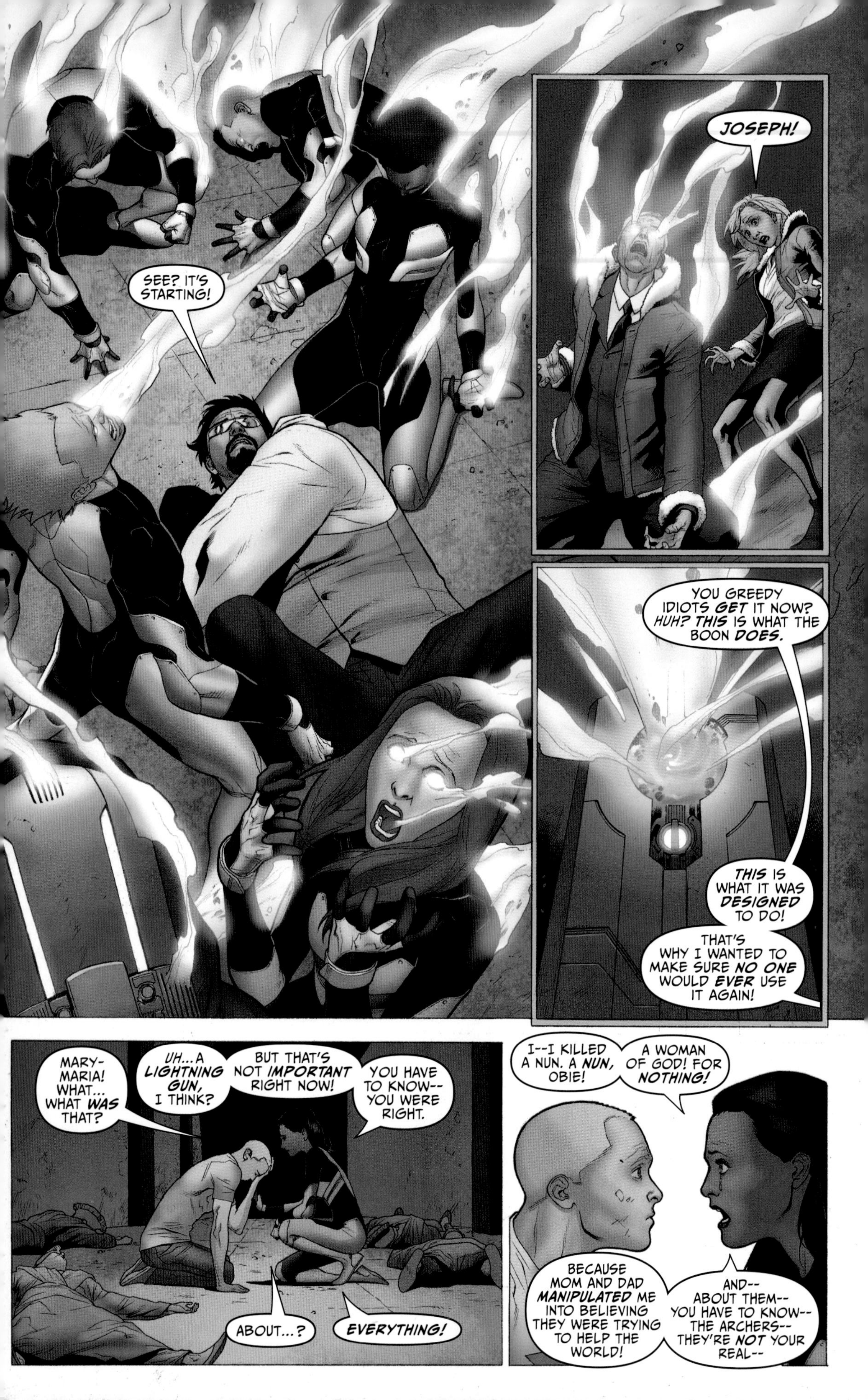

SEE? IT'S STARTING!
JOSEPH!
YOU GREEDY IDIOTS GET IT NOW? HUH? THIS IS WHAT THE BOON DOES.
THIS IS WHAT IT WAS DESIGNED TO DO!
THAT'S WHY I WANTED TO MAKE SURE NO ONE WOULD EVER USE IT AGAIN!
MARY-MARIA! WHAT... WHAT WAS THAT?
UH...A LIGHTNING GUN, I THINK?
BUT THAT'S NOT IMPORTANT RIGHT NOW!
YOU HAVE TO KNOW-- YOU WERE RIGHT.
ABOUT...?
EVERYTHING!
I--I KILLED A NUN. A NUN, OBIE!
A WOMAN OF GOD! FOR NOTHING!
BECAUSE MOM AND DAD MANIPULATED ME INTO BELIEVING THEY WERE TRYING TO HELP THE WORLD!
AND-- ABOUT THEM-- YOU HAVE TO KNOW-- THE ARCHERS-- THEY'RE NOT YOUR REAL--

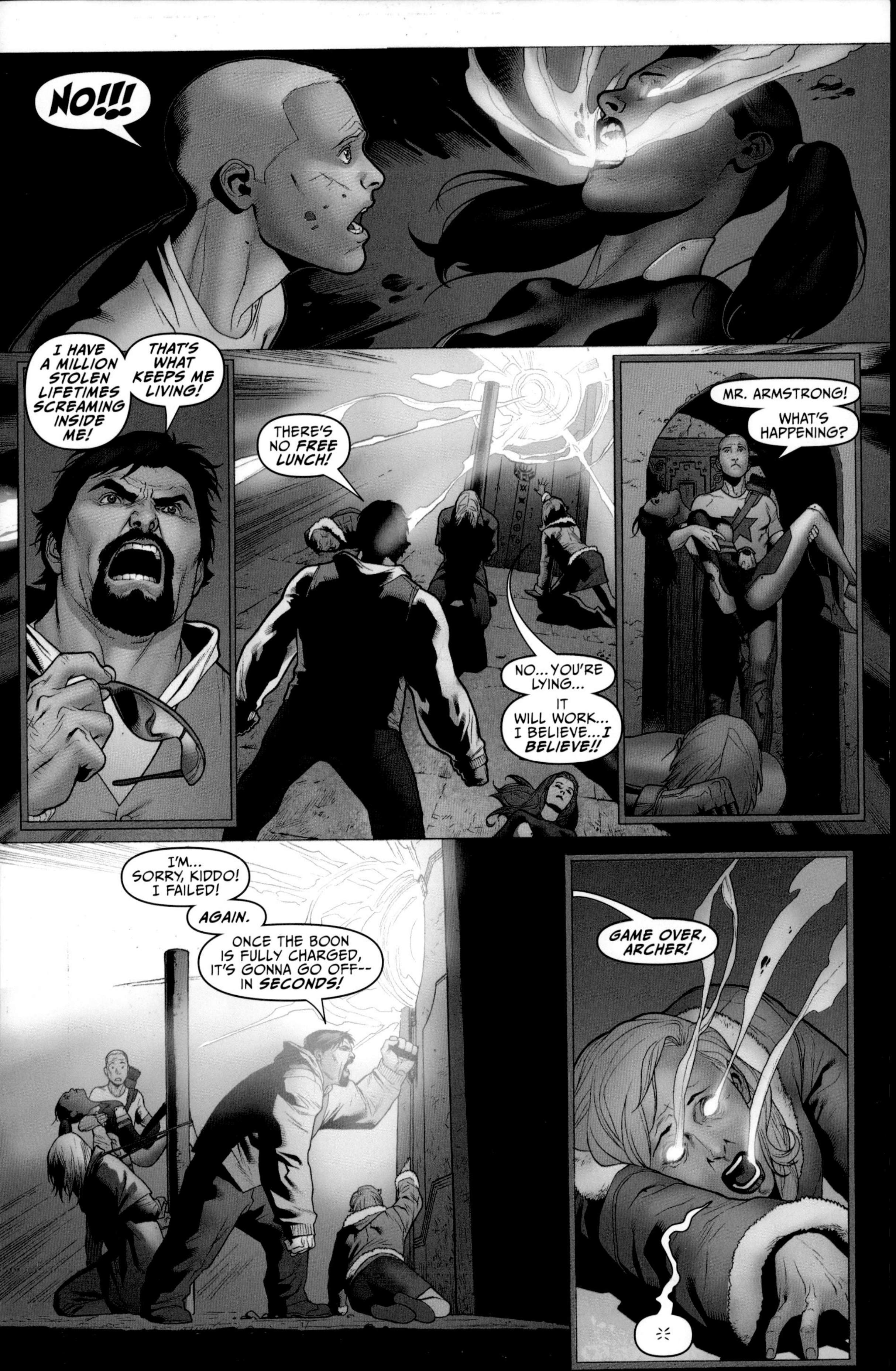
NO!!!
I HAVE A MILLION STOLEN LIFETIMES SCREAMING INSIDE ME!
THAT'S WHAT KEEPS ME LIVING!
THERE'S NO FREE LUNCH!
NO...YOU'RE LYING...
IT WILL WORK... I BELIEVE...I BELIEVE!!
MR. ARMSTRONG!
WHAT'S HAPPENING?
I'M... SORRY, KIDDO! I FAILED!
AGAIN.
ONCE THE BOON IS FULLY CHARGED, IT'S GONNA GO OFF-- IN SECONDS!
GAME OVER, ARCHER!

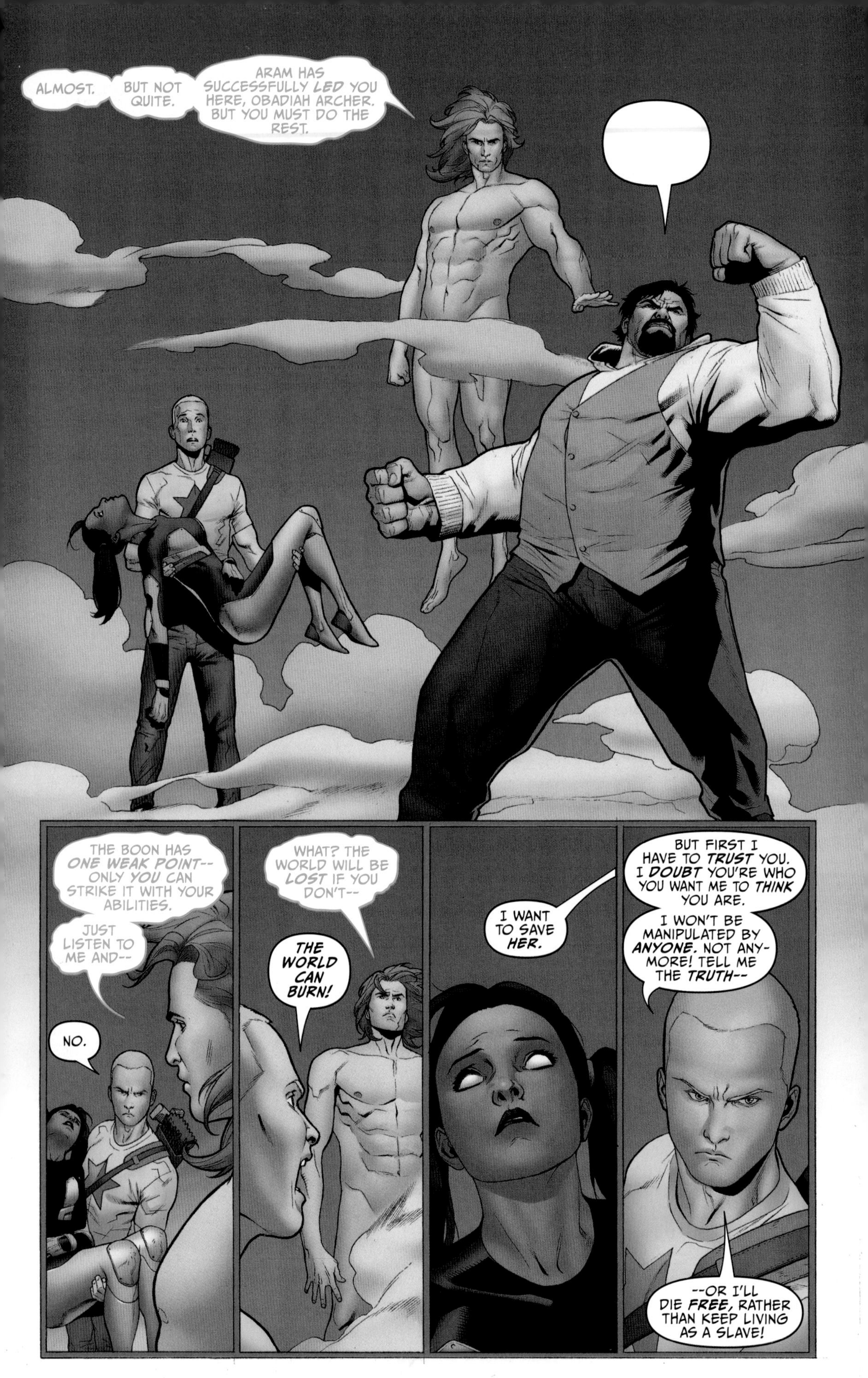
ALMOST.
BUT NOT QUITE.
ARAM HAS SUCCESSFULLY LED YOU HERE, OBADIAH ARCHER. BUT YOU MUST DO THE REST.
THE BOON HAS ONE WEAK POINT-- ONLY YOU CAN STRIKE IT WITH YOUR ABILITIES.
JUST LISTEN TO ME AND--
NO.
WHAT? THE WORLD WILL BE LOST IF YOU DON'T--
THE WORLD CAN BURN!
I WANT TO SAVE HER.
BUT FIRST I HAVE TO TRUST YOU. I DOUBT YOU'RE WHO YOU WANT ME TO THINK YOU ARE.
I WON'T BE MANIPULATED BY ANYONE. NOT ANY-MORE! TELL ME THE TRUTH--
--OR I'LL DIE FREE, RATHER THAN KEEP LIVING AS A SLAVE!

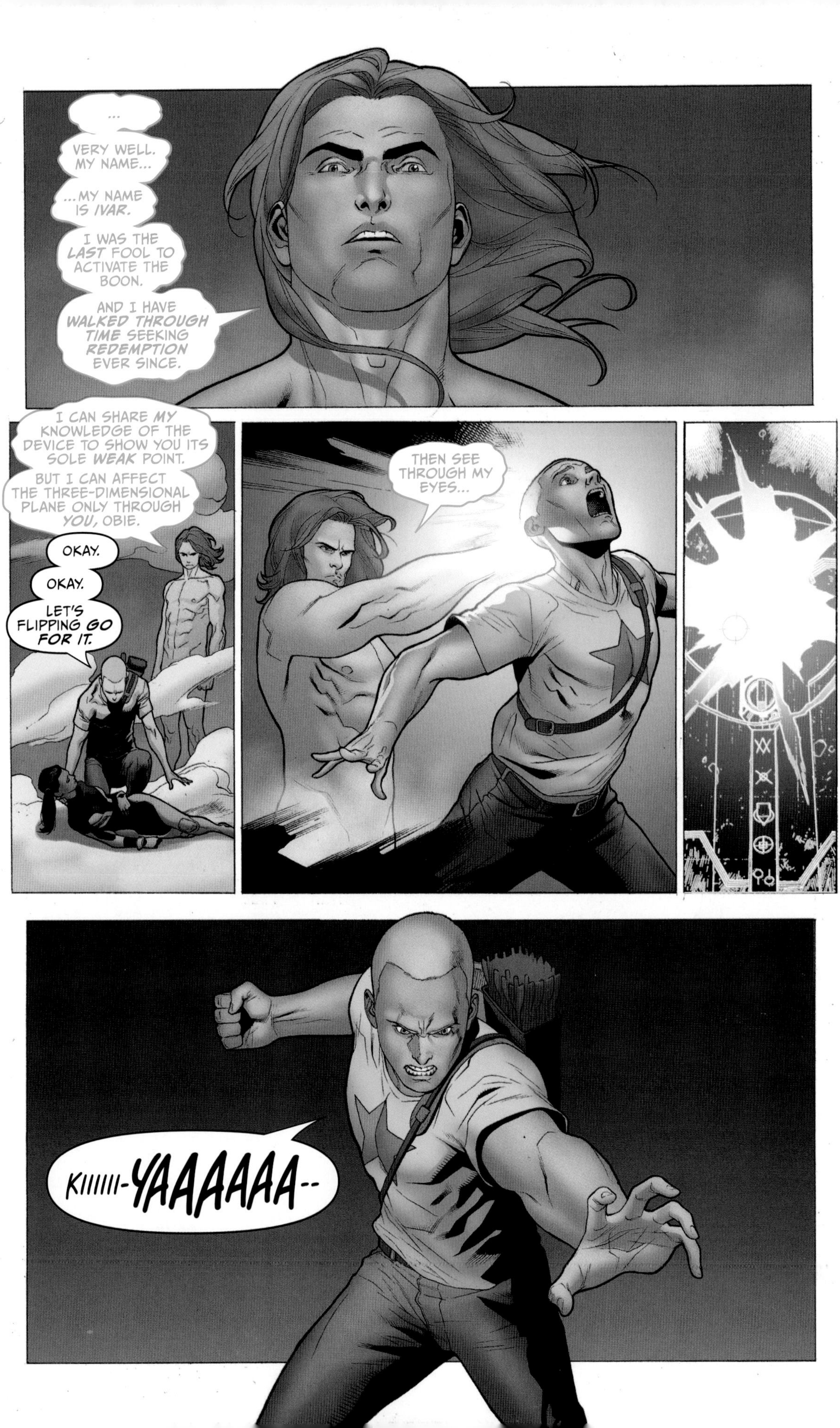
...
VERY WELL. MY NAME...
...MY NAME IS IVAR.
I WAS THE LAST FOOL TO ACTIVATE THE BOON.
AND I HAVE WALKED THROUGH TIME SEEKING REDEMPTION EVER SINCE.
I CAN SHARE MY KNOWLEDGE OF THE DEVICE TO SHOW YOU ITS SOLE WEAK POINT.
BUT I CAN AFFECT THE THREE-DIMENSIONAL PLANE ONLY THROUGH YOU, OBIE.
OKAY.
OKAY.
LET'S FLIPPING GO FOR IT.
THEN SEE THROUGH MY EYES...
KIIIIII-YAAAAAA--

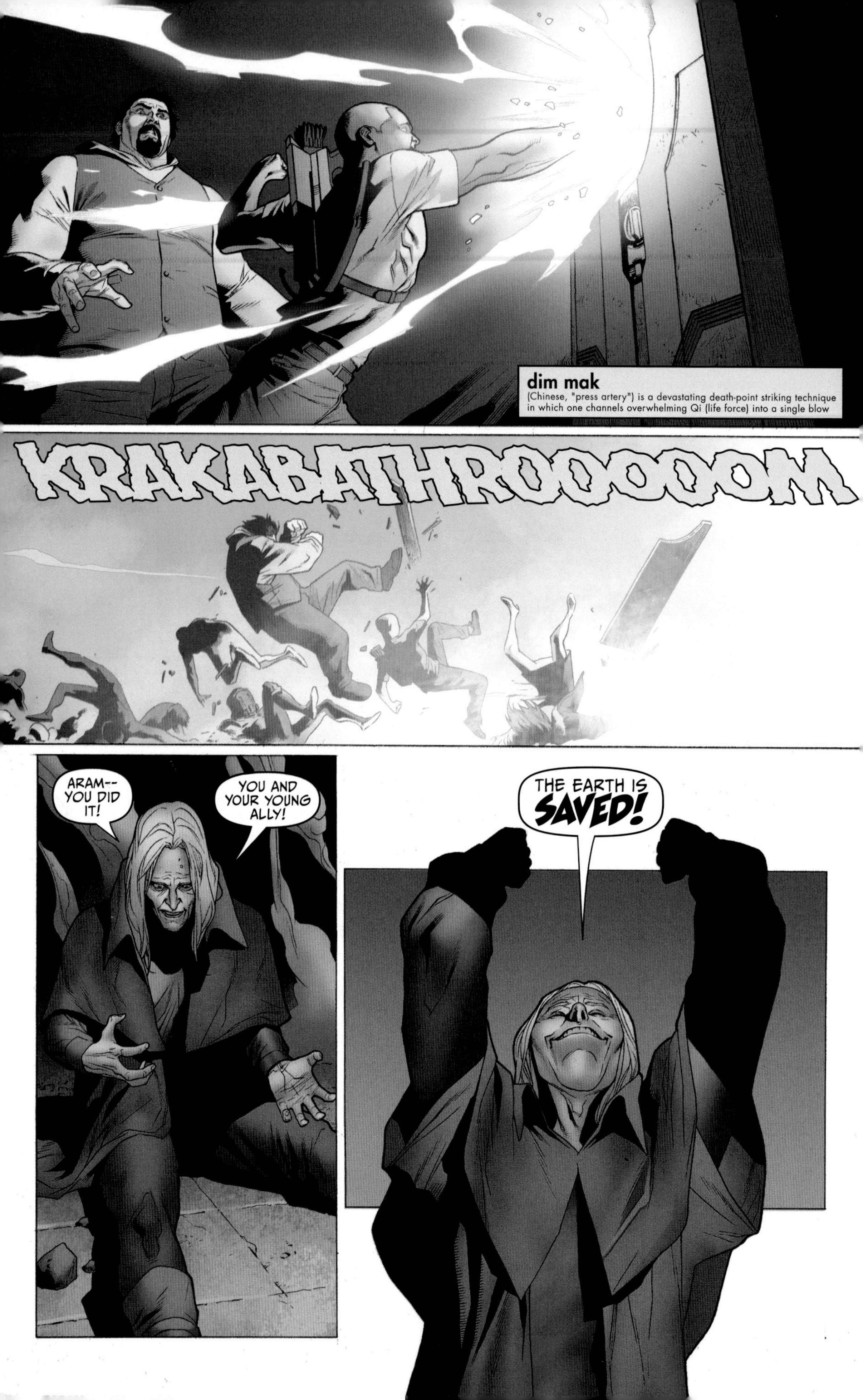
dim mak
(Chinese, "press artery") is a devastating death-point striking technique in which one channels overwhelming Qi (life force) into a single blow
KRAKABATHROOOOOOM
ARAM-- YOU DID IT!
YOU AND YOUR YOUNG ALLY!
THE EARTH IS SAVED!

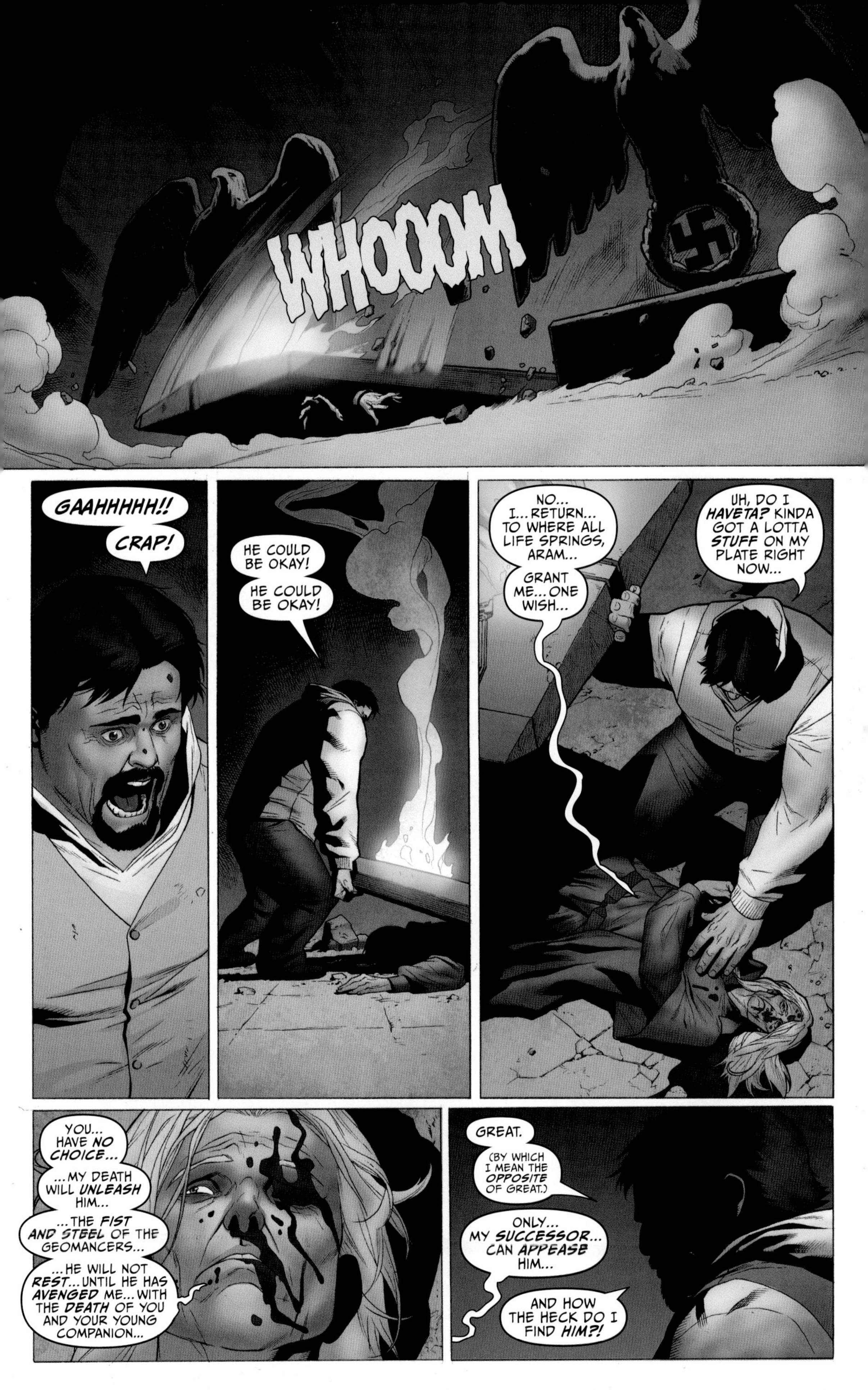
WHOOOM
GAAHHHHH!!
CRAP!
HE COULD BE OKAY!
HE COULD BE OKAY!
NO... I... RETURN... TO WHERE ALL LIFE SPRINGS, ARAM...
GRANT ME... ONE WISH...
UH, DO I HAVETA? KINDA GOT A LOTTA STUFF ON MY PLATE RIGHT NOW...
YOU... HAVE NO CHOICE...
...MY DEATH WILL UNLEASH HIM...
...THE FIST AND STEEL OF THE GEOMANCERS...
...HE WILL NOT REST... UNTIL HE HAS AVENGED ME... WITH THE DEATH OF YOU AND YOUR YOUNG COMPANION...
GREAT.
(BY WHICH I MEAN THE OPPOSITE OF GREAT.)
ONLY... MY SUCCESSOR... CAN APPEASE HIM...
AND HOW THE HECK DO I FIND HIM?!

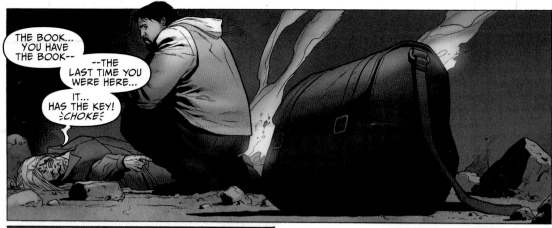

THE BOOK... YOU HAVE THE BOOK--

--THE LAST TIME YOU WERE HERE...

IT... HAS THE KEY! ≥CHOKE≤

RIIIIIIGHT... LAST TIME I WAS HERE...

...I SWIPED THE BOOK!

IT DIDN'T...IT DIDN'T WORK, SIR! I COULDN'T SAVE THEM!

YOU SAVED THE WORLD, KID. THAT MAYBE HAS TO BE ENOUGH.

MY PARENTS... I COULDN'T SAVE THEM! I KNOW-- I KNOW THEY BETRAYED ME-- BUT THEY GAVE ME LIFE!

AND-- I DON'T KNOW WHAT HAPPENED TO MARY-MARIA--HER BODY MUST HAVE BEEN BLOWN SOMEWHERE BY THE BLAST--I HAVE TO FIND--

IT'S ROUGH, I KNOW, BUT WE GOTTA HELP OURSELVES NOW! WE GOTTA GO!

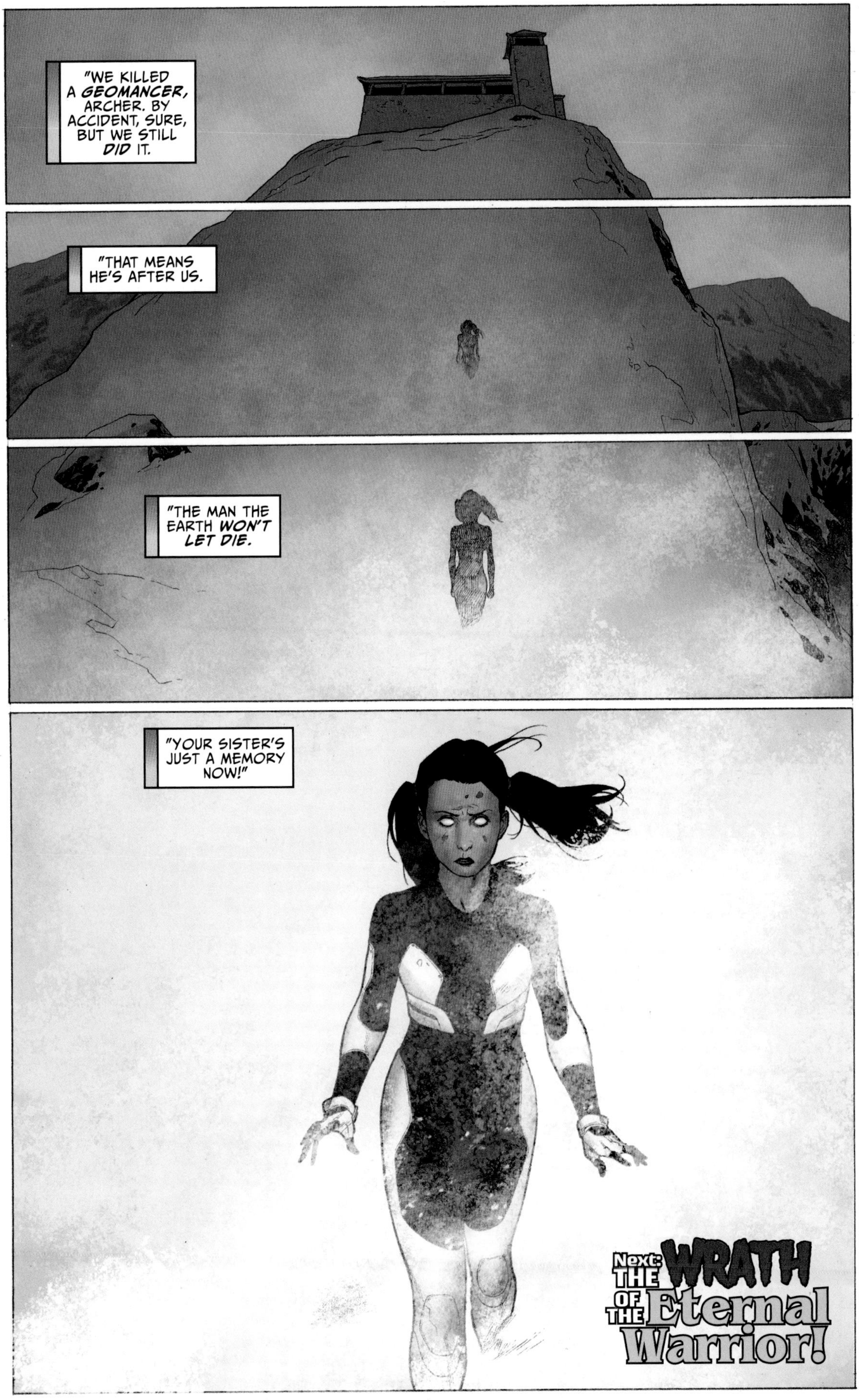
"WE KILLED A GEOMANCER, ARCHER. BY ACCIDENT, SURE, BUT WE STILL DID IT.
"THAT MEANS HE'S AFTER US.
"THE MAN THE EARTH WON'T LET DIE.
"YOUR SISTER'S JUST A MEMORY NOW!"
Next: THE WRATH OF THE Eternal Warrior!

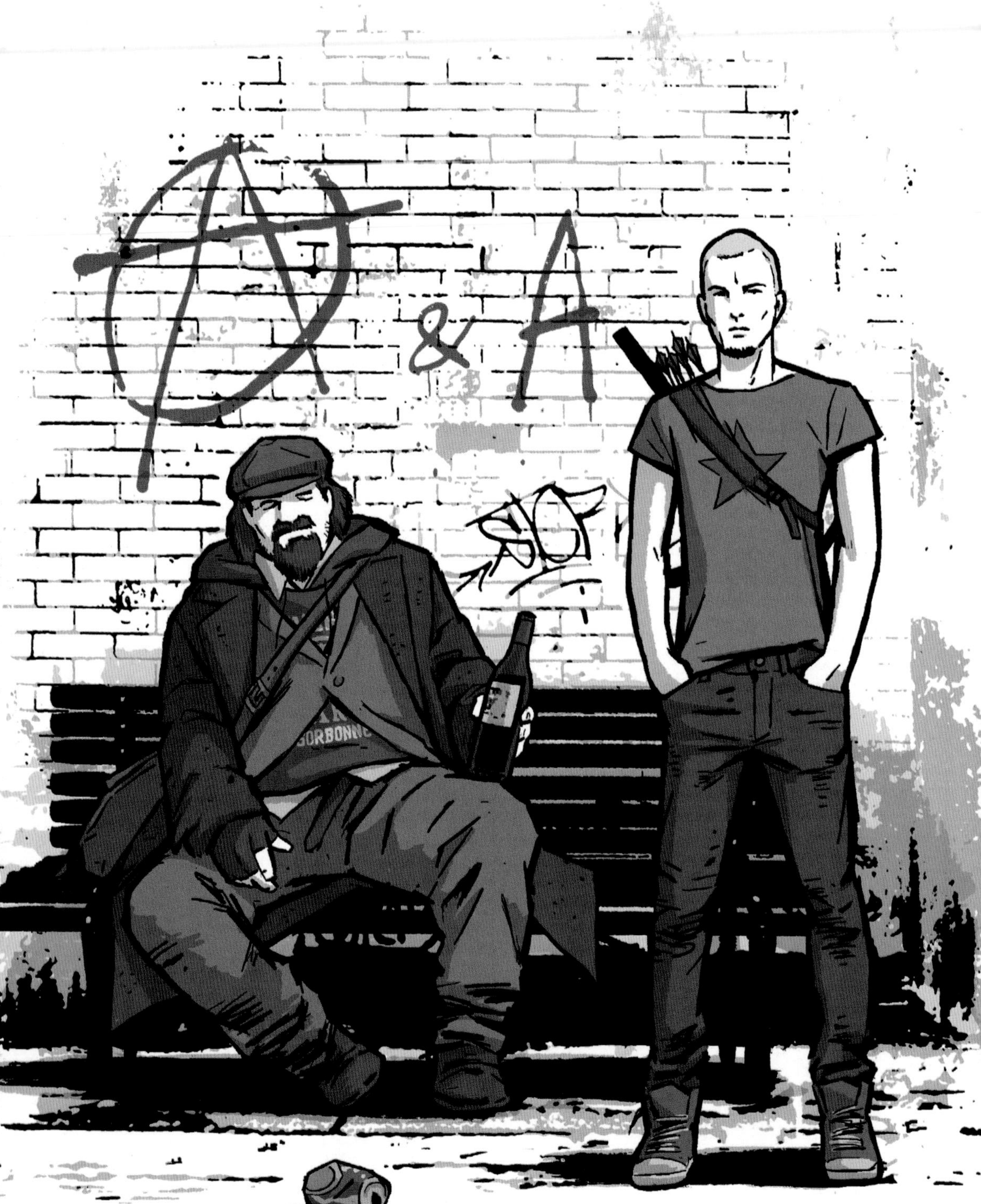
A & A

ARCHER & ARMSTRONG #1 VARIANT
by DAVID AJA

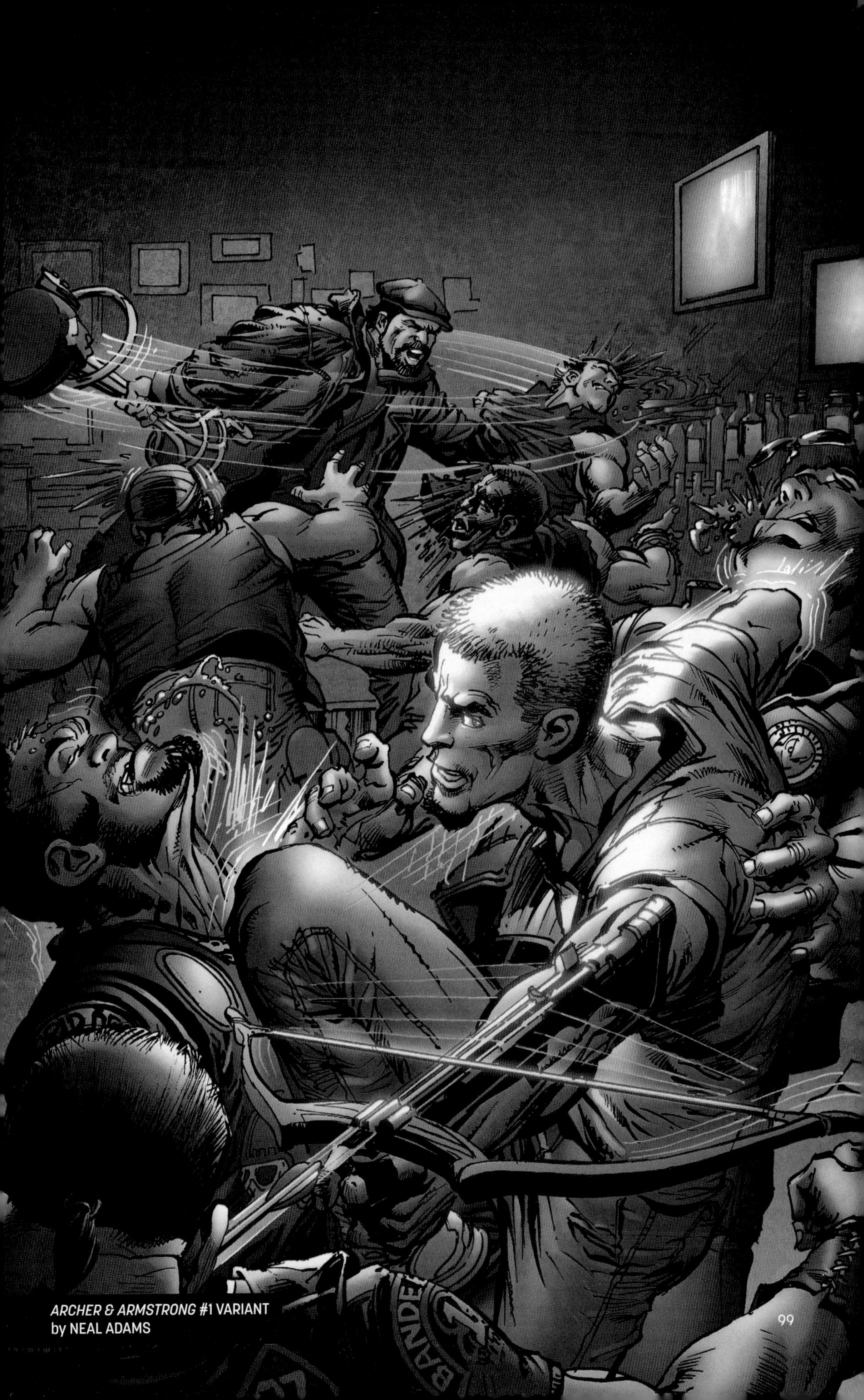

ARCHER & ARMSTRONG #1 VARIANT
by NEAL ADAMS

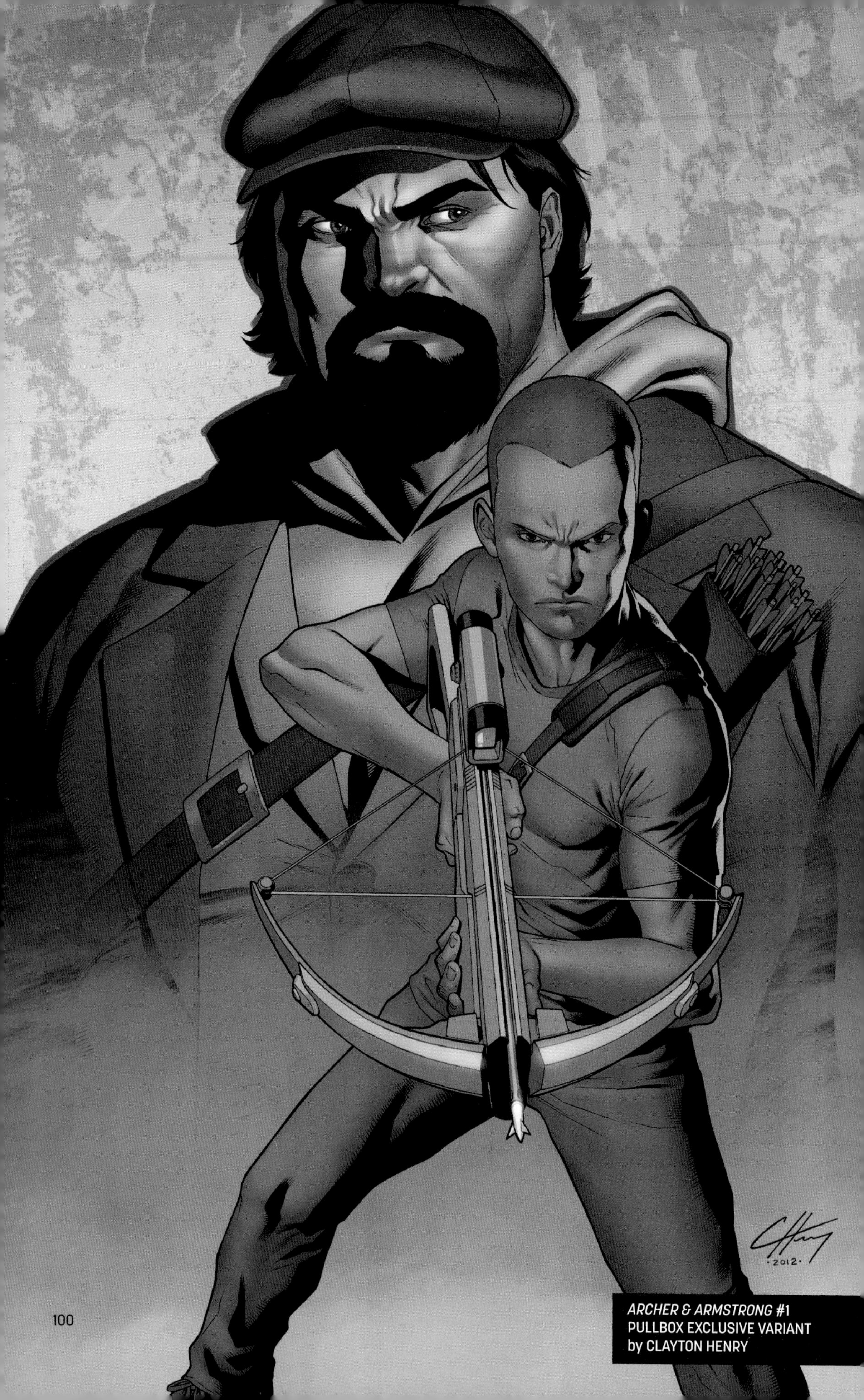

ARCHER & ARMSTRONG #1
PULLBOX EXCLUSIVE VARIANT
by CLAYTON HENRY

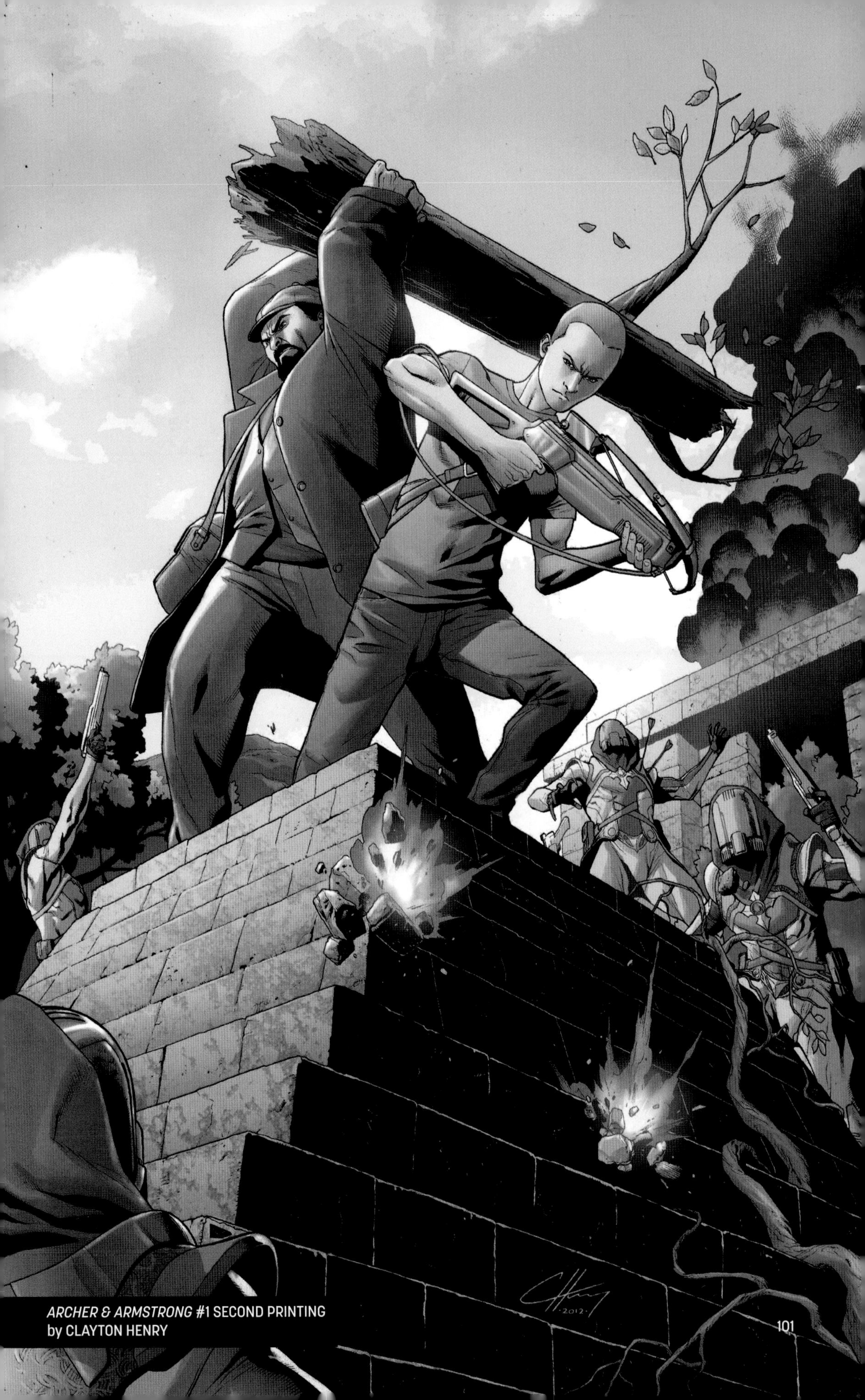

ARCHER & ARMSTRONG #1 SECOND PRINTING
by CLAYTON HENRY

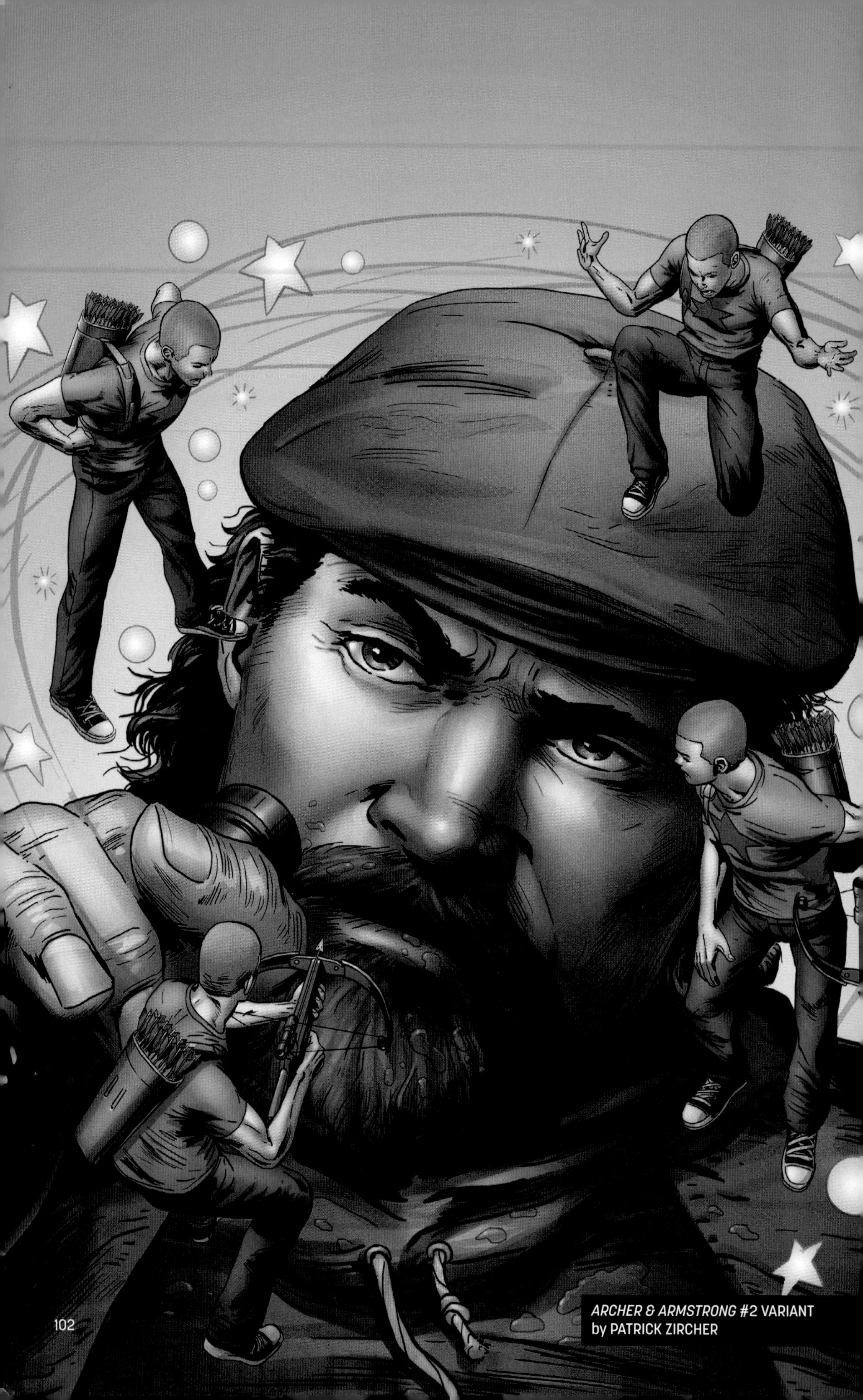

ARCHER & ARMSTRONG #2 VARIANT
by PATRICK ZIRCHER

DISHEVELED BUT CHARMING. HUMOR IN EYES, ALSO CYNICISM AND SADNESS.
OFTEN HAS A BOTTLE IN HAND. HEDONISTIC LIFESTYLE KILLS THE PAIN.
CLOSE-CROPPED HAIR, HIGH ENERGY, EAGER TO DO THE RIGHT THING. YOUNG AND HOPEFUL.
MESSENGER-BAG STYLE SATCHEL.
LOOKS GREAT
UNIVERSITE
PARIS
SORBONNE
FOREIGN UNIVERSITY SWEATSHIRT SAYS WORLDLY AND EDUCATED BUT STILL DOWN TO PARTY.
T-SHIRT AND JEANS. CLEANER, SIMPLER LOOK THAN ARMSTRONG. IN MANY WAYS HIS OPPOSITE.
MORE MODERN, POWERFUL VERSION OF CROSSBOW.

ARCHER & ARMSTRONG #3
CHARACTER DESIGN VARIANT
by DAVID AJA

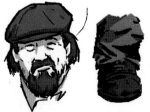

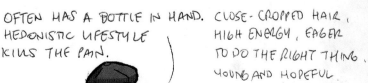

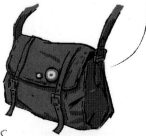

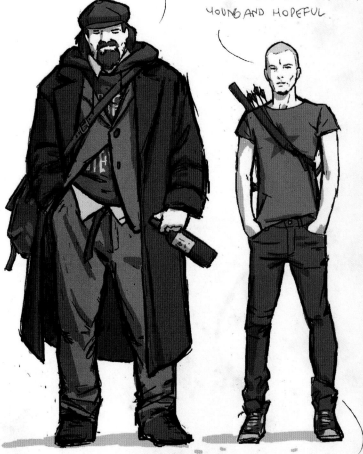

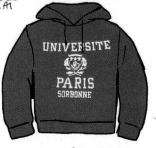

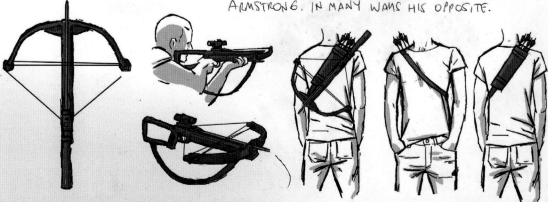

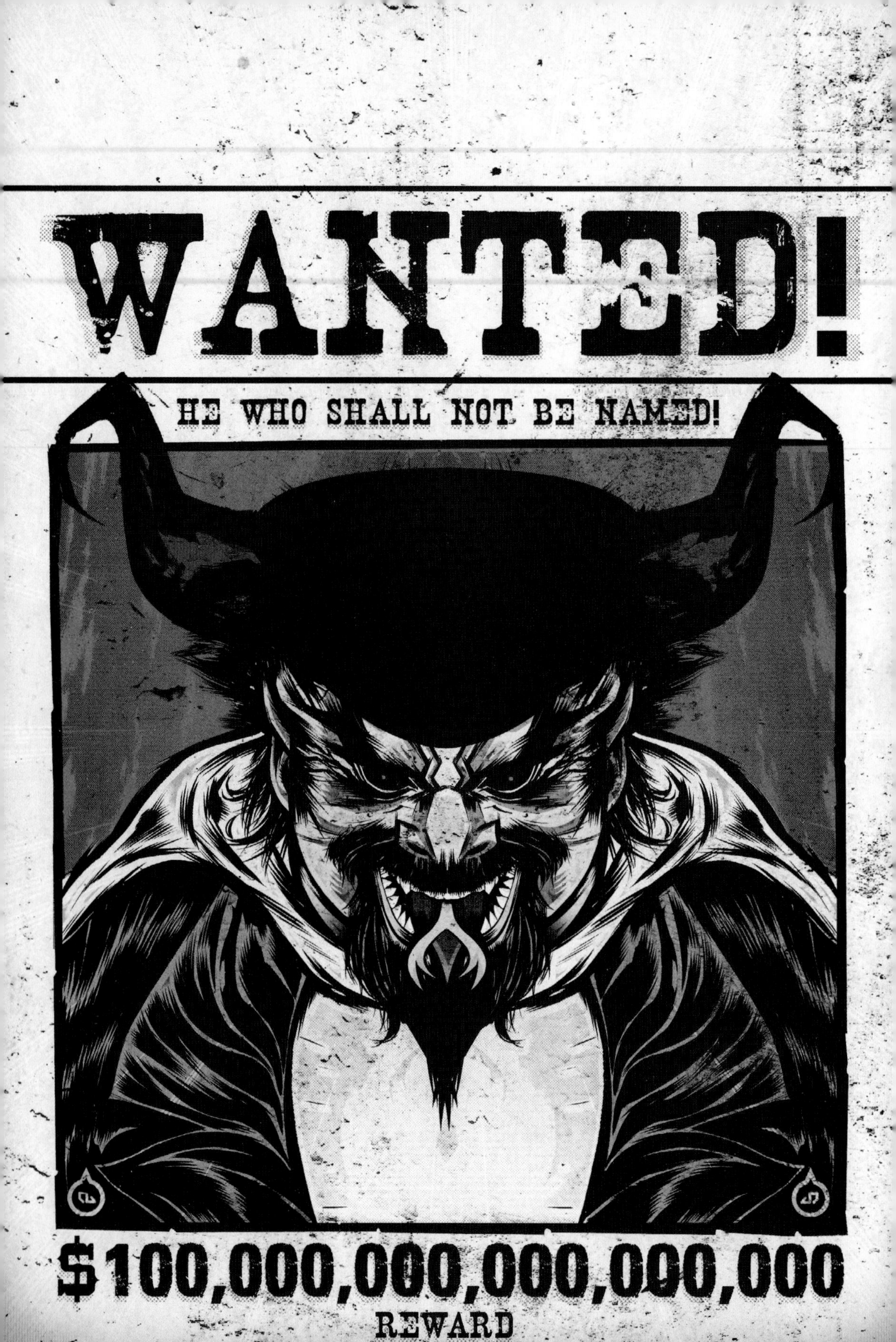
WANTED!
HE WHO SHALL NOT BE NAMED!
$100,000,000,000,000,000
REWARD

ARCHER & ARMSTRONG #4 VARIANT
by JUAN DOE

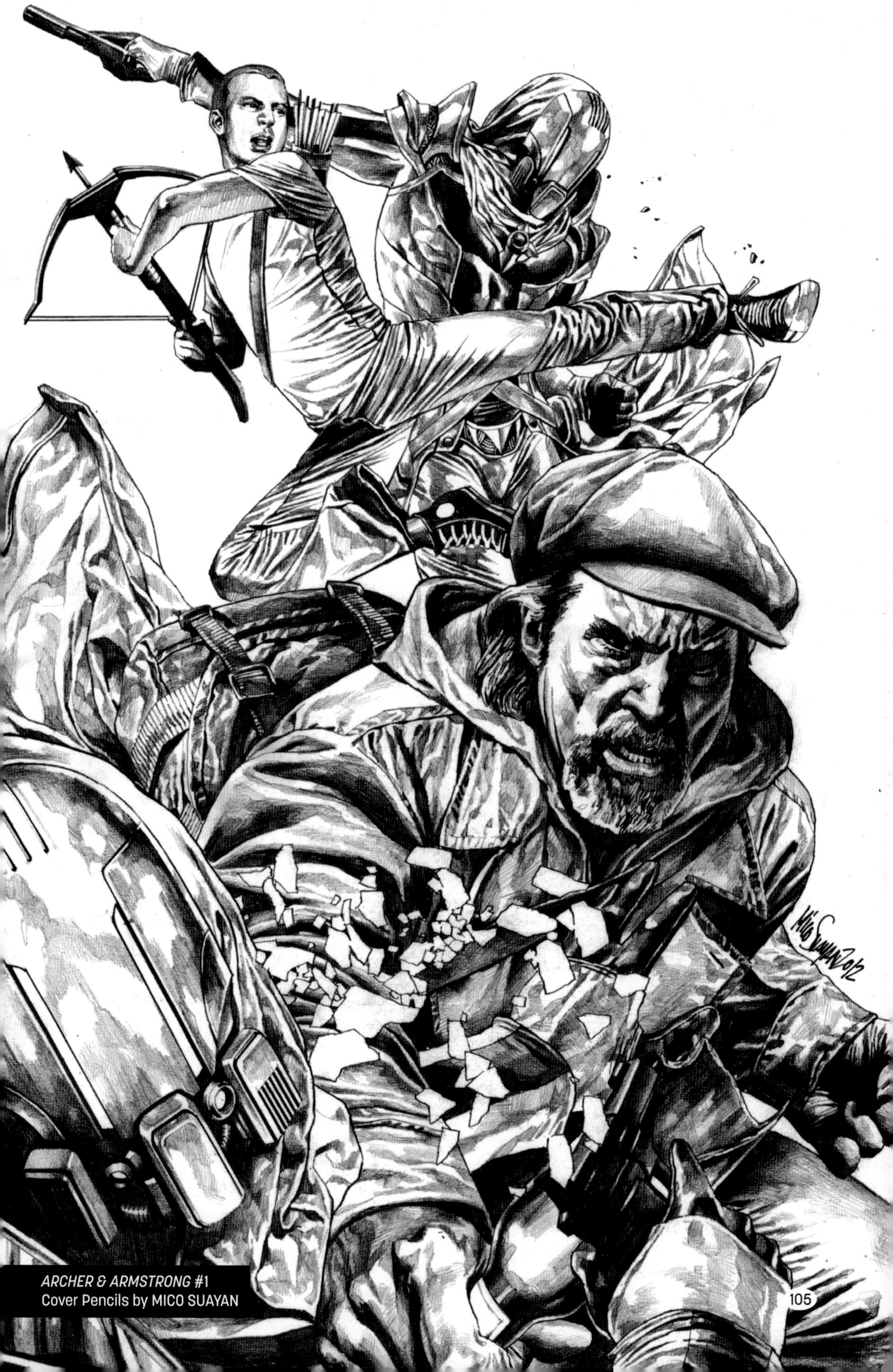

ARCHER & ARMSTRONG #1
Cover Pencils by MICO SUAYAN

Archer & Armstrong #1, page 4
Pencils/Inks by CLAYTON HENRY

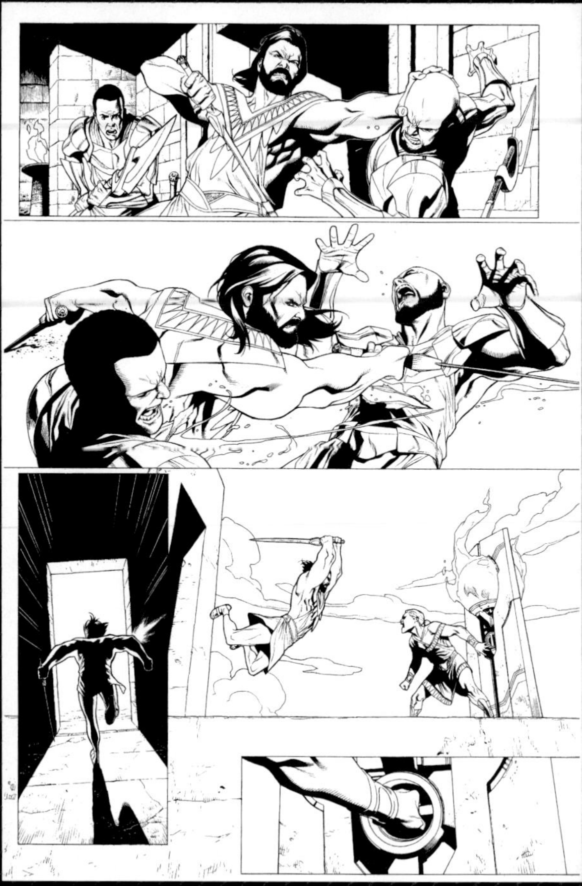

Archer & Armstrong #1, page 15
Pencils/Inks by CLAYTON HENRY

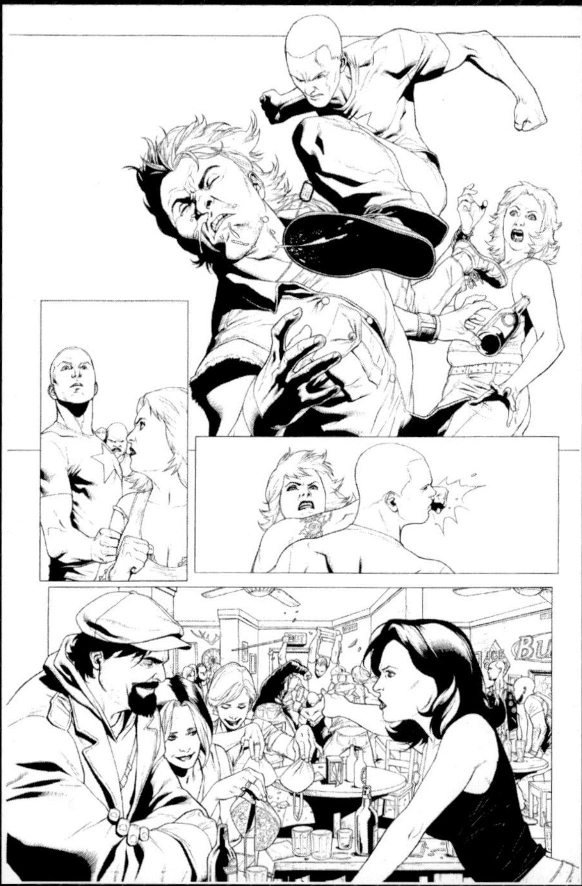

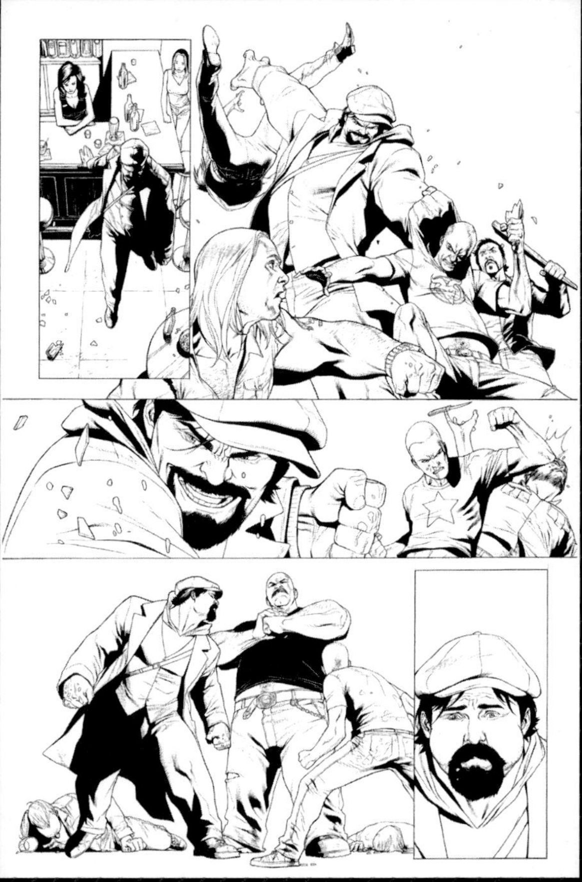

Archer & Armstrong #1, page 16
Pencils/Inks by CLAYTON HENRY

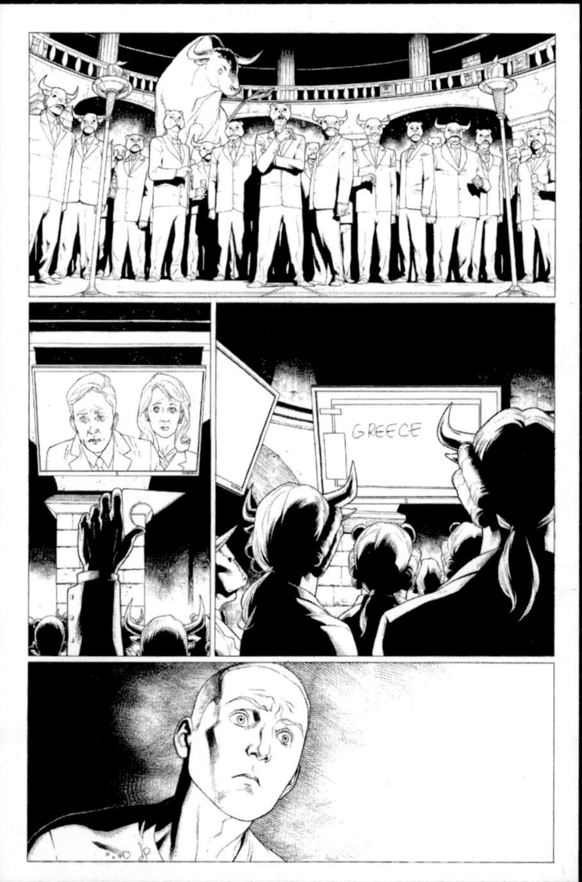
GREECE

Archer & Armstrong #1, page 23
Pencils/Inks by CLAYTON HENRY

Archer & Armstrong #2, page 5
Pencils/Inks by CLAYTON HENRY

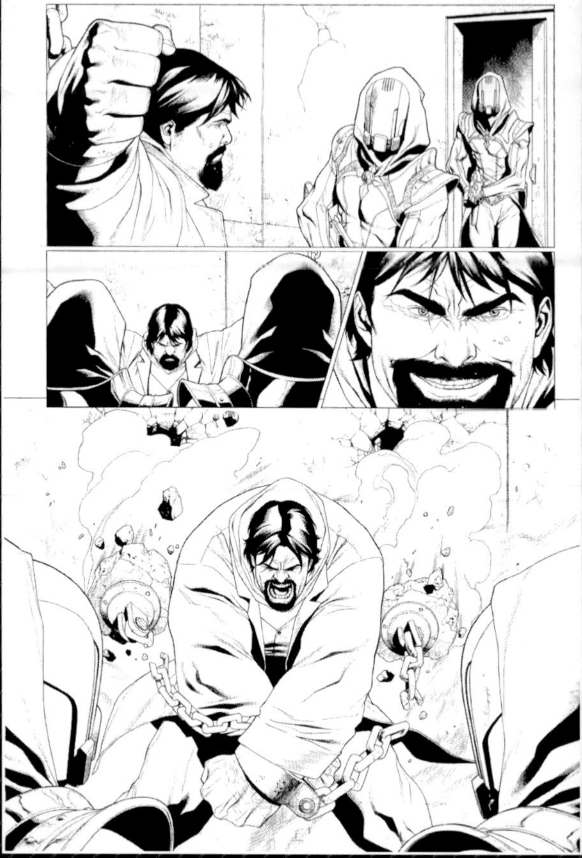

Archer & Armstrong #2, page 6
Pencils/Inks by CLAYTON HENRY

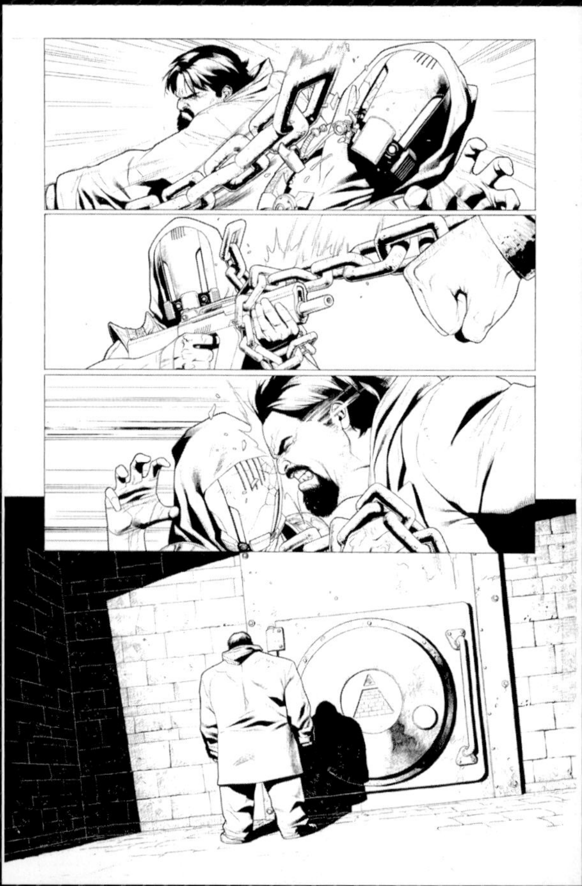

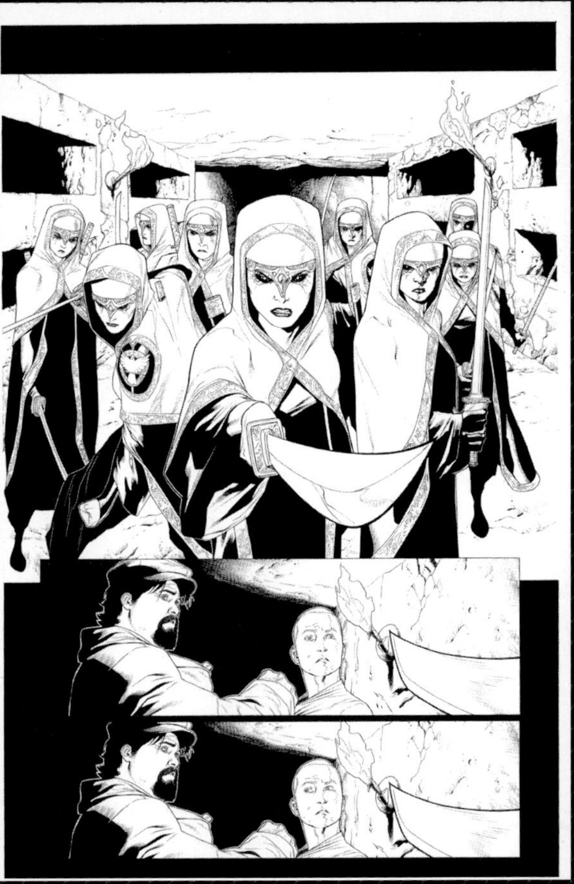

Archer & Armstrong #2, page 22
Pencils/Inks by CLAYTON HENRY

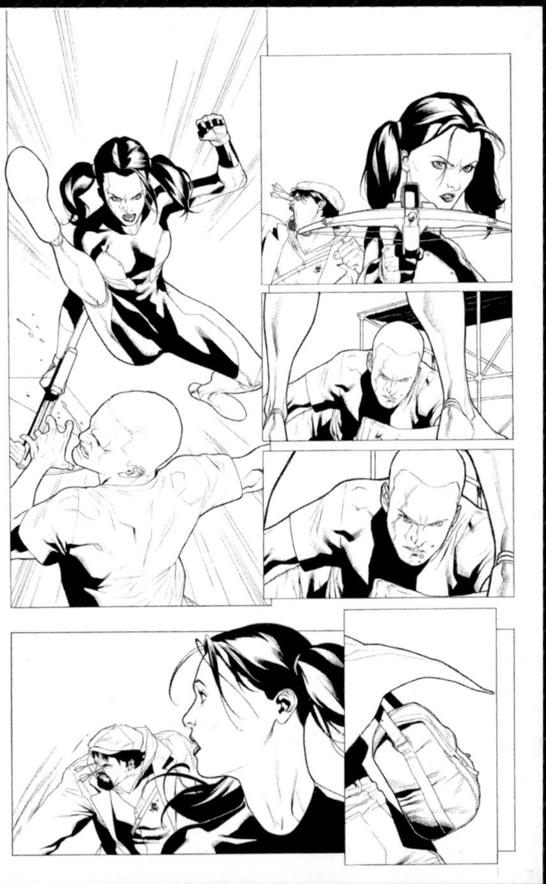

Archer & Armstrong #3, page 15
Pencils/Inks by CLAYTON HENRY

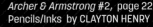

VALIANT MASTERS

A NEW LINE OF DELUXE HARDCOVERS COLLECTING THE ORIGINAL ADVENTURES OF VALIANT'S GREATEST HEROES FOR THE FIRST TIME ANYWHERE! FEATURING CLASSIC WORK BY SOME OF COMICS' MOST ACCLAIMED TALENTS.

VALIANT
KEVIN VANHOOK | DON PERLIN
BLOOD OF THE MACHINE
BLOODSHOT
VALIANT MASTERS
"Bloodshot reigns supreme as one of the best characters ever created."
- Ain't It Cool News

VALIANT MASTERS: BLOODSHOT VOL. 1: BLOOD OF THE MACHINE

Written by KEVIN VANHOOK
Art by DON PERLIN
Cover by BARRY WINDSOR-SMITH

- Collecting **BLOODSHOT #1-8 (1993)** and an all-new, in-continuity story from the original **BLOODSHOT** creative team of **Kevin VanHook**, **Don Perlin**, and **Bob Wiacek** available only in this volume
- Featuring Bloodshot's first solo mission in the Valiant Universe and appearances by **Ninjak**, the **Eternal Warrior** and **Rai**

HARDCOVER
ISBN: 978-0-9796409-3-3

VALIANT
MARK A. MORETTI | JOE QUESADA | JIMMY PALMIOTTI
BLACK WATER
NINJAK
VALIANT MASTERS
"Groundbreaking art and epic characters... [Valiant] set comics on its ears..."
- Ain't It Cool News

VALIANT MASTERS: NINJAK VOL. 1: BLACK WATER

Written by MARK MORETTI
Art by JOE QUESADA & MARK MORETTI
Cover by JOE QUESADA

- Collecting **NINJAK #1-6 and #0-00 (1994)** with covers, interiors, and rarely seen process art by best-selling artist and creator **Joe Quesada**
- Featuring the complete origin of Valiant's original stealth operative and appearances by **X-O Manowar** and **Bloodshot**

HARDCOVER
ISBN: 978-0-9796409-7-1

VALIANT®

EXPLORE THE VALIANT UNIVERSE

VALIANT
ROBERT VENDITTI | CARY NORD | STEFANO GAUDIANO | MOOSE BAUMANN
BY THE SWORD
X-O MANOWAR
"A complete knockout."
- Ain't It Cool News

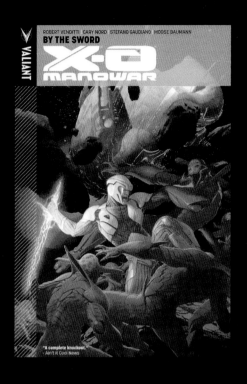

X-O MANOWAR VOL. 1:
BY THE SWORD

Written by ROBERT VENDITTI
Art by CARY NORD

Collecting **X-O MANOWAR #1-4**
TRADE PAPERBACK
ISBN: 978-0-9796409-4-0

VALIANT
JOSHUA DYSART | KHARI EVANS | LEWIS LAROSA | IAN HANNIN
OMEGA RISING
HARBINGER
"A book people need to know about."
- Comic Book Resources

HARBINGER VOL. 1:
OMEGA RISING

Written by JOSHUA DYSART
Art by KHARI EVANS & LEWIS LAROSA

Collecting **HARBINGER #1-5**
TRADE PAPERBACK
ISBN: 978-0-9796409-5-7

VALIANT
FRED VAN LENTE | CLAYTON HENRY | MATT MILLA
THE MICHELANGELO CODE
ARCHER & ARMSTRONG

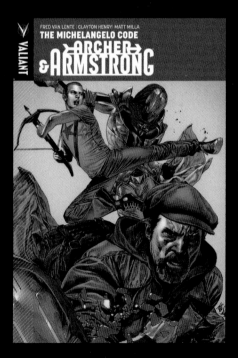

ARCHER & ARMSTRONG VOL. 1:
THE MICHELANGELO CODE

Written by FRED VAN LENTE
Art by CLAYTON HENRY

Collecting **ARCHER & ARMSTRONG #1-4**
TRADE PAPERBACK
ISBN: 978-0-9796409-8-8

VALIANT

ARCHER & ARMSTRONG

VOLUME TWO: **WRATH OF THE ETERNAL WARRIOR**

No one in the Valiant Universe is more dangerous or more experienced in the art of war than the undying Eternal Warrior. After thousands of years on the battlefield, he's a master of strategy and weaponry, an unrelenting force of nature capable of dismantling entire armies with little effort and less conscience. His brother Armstrong, on the other hand, likes to read poetry and drink beer. Maybe that's why they had such a bad falling out? But now - after years apart - the Eternal Warrior has a new mission: destroy young Obadiah Archer, Armstrong's best-est new buddy and teammate in the war against The Sect. And, like it or not, Valiant's history-smashing adventure duo are about to feel the brunt of the Eternal Warrior's fist and steel.

ARCHER & ARMSTRONG VOL. 2:
WRATH OF THE ETERNAL WARRIOR TPB

Collecting **ARCHER & ARMSTRONG #5-9** by New York Times best-selling author Fred Van Lente (*Amazing Spider-Man*) and critically acclaimed artist Emanuela Lupacchino (*X-Factor*), the second volume of the series that IGN calls "hilarious and action packed" slams into high gear with a savage manhunt straight through the heart of the Valiant Universe.

TRADE PAPERBACK
ISBN: 978-1-939346-04-9

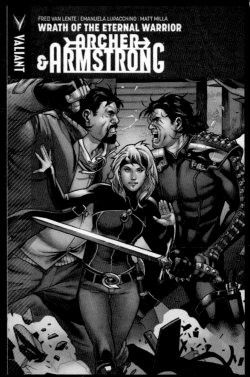

FRED VAN LENTE | EMANUELA LUPACCHINO | MATT MILLA
WRATH OF THE ETERNAL WARRIOR
ARCHER & ARMSTRONG

VALIANT